I0793336

IMAGES
of America
NEBRASKA CITY

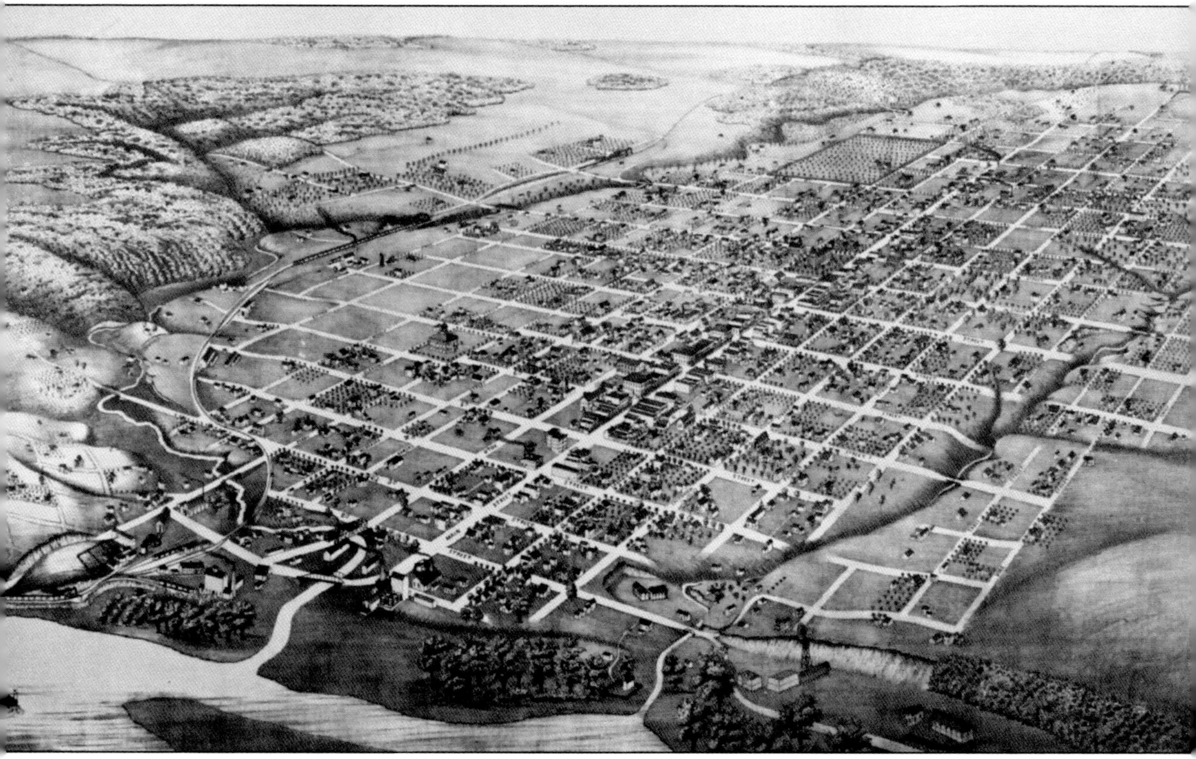

While the layout may be familiar, the early state and Native American street names were changed in 1888 to a numbering system. The road now known as Fourth Corso was previously called Ferry Street, as it was the location where ferries to and from Iowa were loaded and unloaded. (Courtesy of the Morton James Public Library.)

On the Cover: The Overland Theatre was a downtown attraction for nearly 40 years. The 850-seat venue celebrated its grand opening in December 1897. Pictured here are the cast and crew of the inaugural show, William Gillett's *Secret Service*. (Courtesy of Arbor Lodge.)

IMAGES
of America

Nebraska City

Tammy Partsch

ARCADIA
PUBLISHING

ISBN 978-1-4671-1449-3

Published by Arcadia Publishing
Charleston, South Carolina

Printed in the United States of America

Library of Congress Control Number: 2015940336

For all general information, please contact Arcadia Publishing:
Telephone 843-853-2070
Fax 843-853-0044
E-mail sales@arcadiapublishing.com
For customer service and orders:
Toll-Free 1-888-313-2665

Visit us on the Internet at www.arcadiapublishing.com

With all my heart, this book is dedicated to Dave and Luke

Contents

ACKNOWLEDGMENTS

One of my earliest memories involves spending time exploring the Otoe County Museum of Memories in Syracuse, Nebraska, while my mother volunteered making exhibits, giving tours, and cataloging donated items. The museum had a certain smell to it—a mix of antiques and sawdust. Even today, that smell puts me right back in those exhibits, a curious three-year-old at play. My love and respect for history grew from that time.

So many people and organizations helped me gather information for this book. I would like to thank Laura Steinman at Arbor Lodge; Amy Stouffer with the Arbor Day Foundation; Dorris Sackles; Jim Kuhn and the Nebraska City Historical Society; Bonnie Goodman with Main Street Historians; Gail Wurtele and Pat Friedli with the Wildwood Period House; the Morton James Public Library; Tim Pendrell and Amy Allgood at Nebraska City Tourism and Commerce; Bill Hayes with the Mayhew Cabin Museum; Erin Beethe with Kimmel Orchard; the Richard P. Kimmel and Laurine Kimmel Charitable Foundation; Dean Shissler with the Kregel Windmill Factory Museum; Tim Engel with the Grand Army of the Republic Memorial Hall; and Carol Randle and Tom Schreiner with the Nebraska City Museum of Firefighting. All of these people and organizations were so generous with their time and knowledge about all things Nebraska City, and I appreciate their help.

I would also like to thank the teachers and staff at Lourdes Central Catholic Schools for their patience with me as I researched this book while attempting to throw together lesson plans. I am grateful for the support of the administration that allows me to pursue my love of writing while teaching part-time.

My parents, Dean and Keitha Thomson, deserve a special thanks for their years of support. They have never laughed at my dreams, at least not to my face, and I love them both very much.

Finally, my thanks go to my favorite people on the entire planet, Dave and Luke Partsch. Dave, you continually do so much to better our hometown, and I respect and love you immensely. Luke, you bring joy to our home every day. Here it is in print again: I love you more.

INTRODUCTION

Nebraska City in the 21st century is known as a tourist destination, a town saturated with museums, a place to buy apples. From Arbor Lodge and Arbor Day Farm to downtown, from Northside Elementary School to the new CHI Health St. Mary's on South Eleventh Street, Nebraska City is a town alive with history that is moving into the future.

In April 1872, the name Nebraska City became firmly planted in history books with the celebration of the first Arbor Day. For nearly 20 years prior to that first celebration of nature, this Missouri River community bustled with never-ending activity that included stagecoaches, freighting, and manufacturing. The rest of the 1800s were not too shabby, either. Opera houses, unique retail stores, parks, and the latest in transportation were topics of conversation throughout the town. As the 20th century dawned, so did industry and orchards. Today, Nebraska City is known as a getaway town, ranked ninth on *Smithsonian* magazine's Top 20 Best Small Towns to Visit in 2014.

However, one can wonder, "What if?" What if half the town had not been destroyed by fire in 1860? What if the state capitol had been located here instead of Lincoln? What if the Union Pacific Railroad had chosen to build its headquarters in Nebraska City instead of Omaha?

On the other hand, what if J. Sterling Morton had decided not to move to Nebraska City in 1855? What if the Porters and the Kimmels had decided their orchards would not be worth recovering from the Armistice Day freeze of 1940? What if the Arbor Day Foundation had not invested millions in a state-of-the-art conference center and Tree Adventure in Nebraska City? Nebraska City could have gone the route of many small Midwestern towns and disappeared off the map. But, the legendary perseverance of the pioneers who tamed this land can be found in the townspeople living here today. They are the ones who prepare for record crowds every AppleJack weekend, the ones who send their children to our schools, who worship in our churches. For all the wonderful things about Nebraska City, and there are many, it is the people of Nebraska City who make it great.

In 1894, at an Arbor Day celebration at the Department of Agriculture in Washington DC, J. Sterling Morton, the founder of Arbor Day, spoke the following words: "So, every man, woman, and child who plants trees shall be able to say, on coming as I have come, toward the evening of life, in all sincerity and truth: 'If you seek my monument, look around you.' " Nebraska City can take these words to heart and know that our community has changed the world. It is truly a place where great ideas grow. Plant trees!

One

Blooming with History

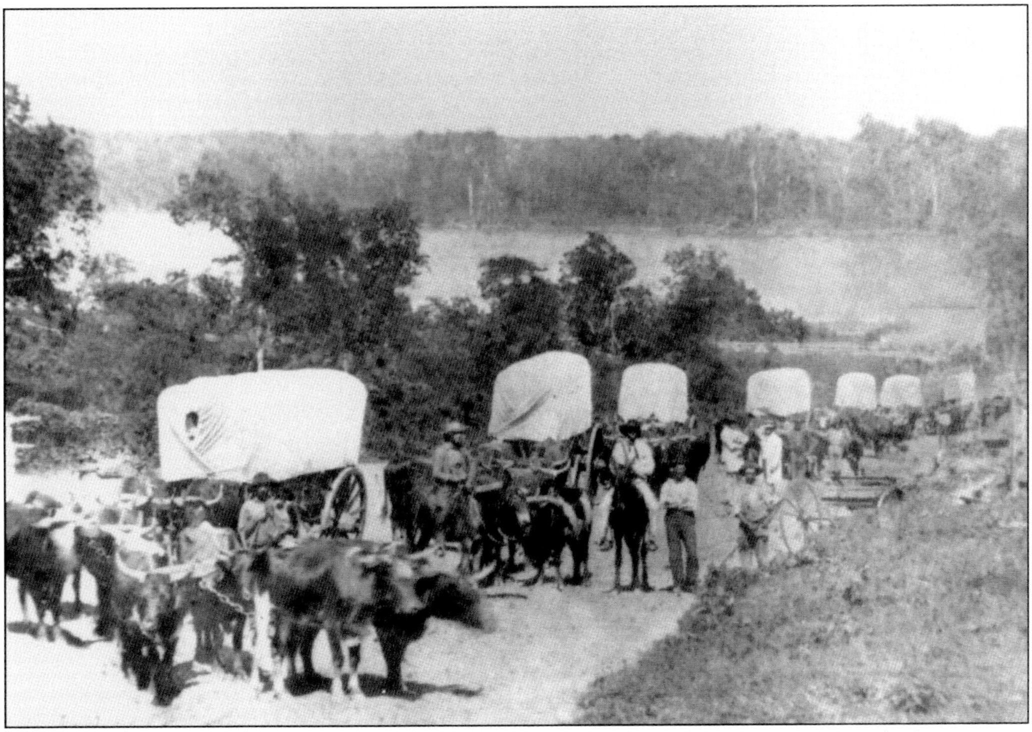

In 1804, Meriwether Lewis, William Clark, and the Corps of Discovery passed what is now Nebraska City on their journey up the Missouri River. Approximately 40 years later, the US Army wanted to build a new fort on the Great Plains, and they chose the same site. By 1859, when this wagon-train image was captured, Nebraska City had been platted and incorporated and was well on its way to becoming an industrial and transportation hub. (Courtesy of the Morton James Public Library.)

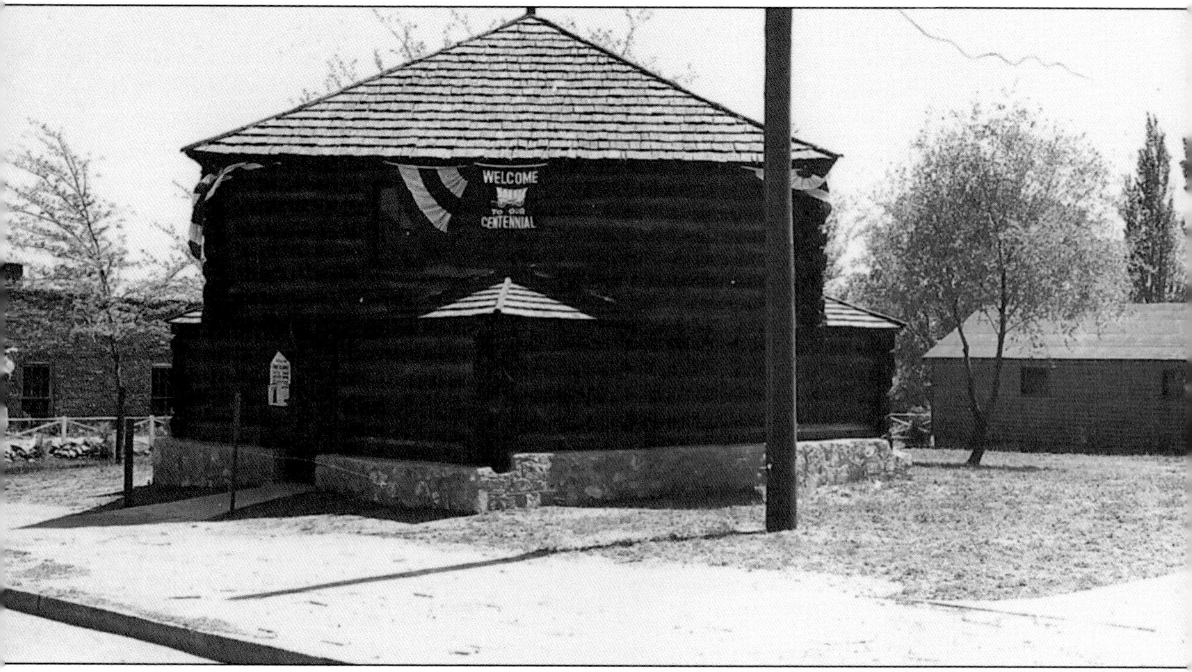

After a visit to the area in 1838, Col. Stephen Kearny recommended this site for a military outpost. Construction of Fort Kearny, as it became known, began in 1846. The buildings, including the blockhouse replicated here, were vacated a mere two years later when the Army decided to move the fort west to what is now Kearney, Nebraska. Platting of the actual city began on July 10, 1854, and Nebraska City was officially incorporated in March 1855. Wagon trains pulled by oxen and mules clogged the town's main thoroughfares. Those trains, called prairie schooners, carried settlers and supplies to California; New Mexico; Denver, Colorado; and Salt Lake City, Utah. From the 1850s through the 1860s, four thousand wagons left Nebraska City each year. (Courtesy of the Mayhew Cabin Museum.)

The Mayhew family settled in Nebraska City in the mid-1850s. In February 1859, John Henry Kagi, a brother of Barbara Kagi Mayhew, led a group of escaped slaves from Kansas through Nebraska City and then into Iowa. Kagi is believed to have been accompanied by famous abolitionist John Brown. For many years, John Brown's Cave was a tourist attraction, finally achieving recognition as an official stop on the Underground Railroad. (Courtesy of the Mayhew Cabin Museum.)

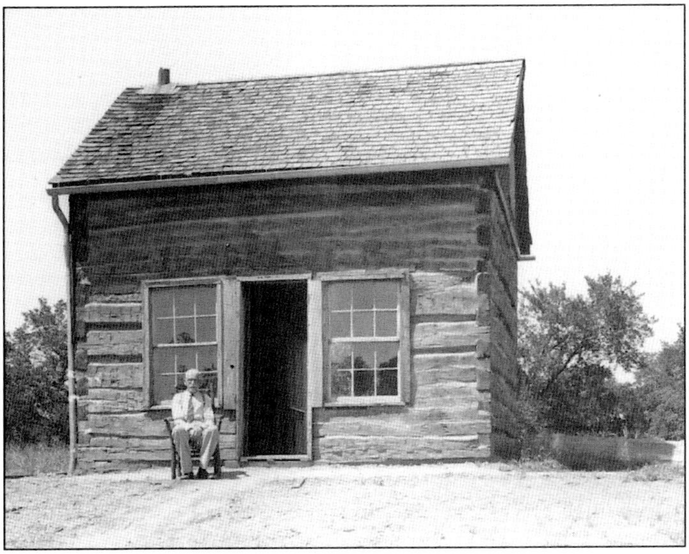

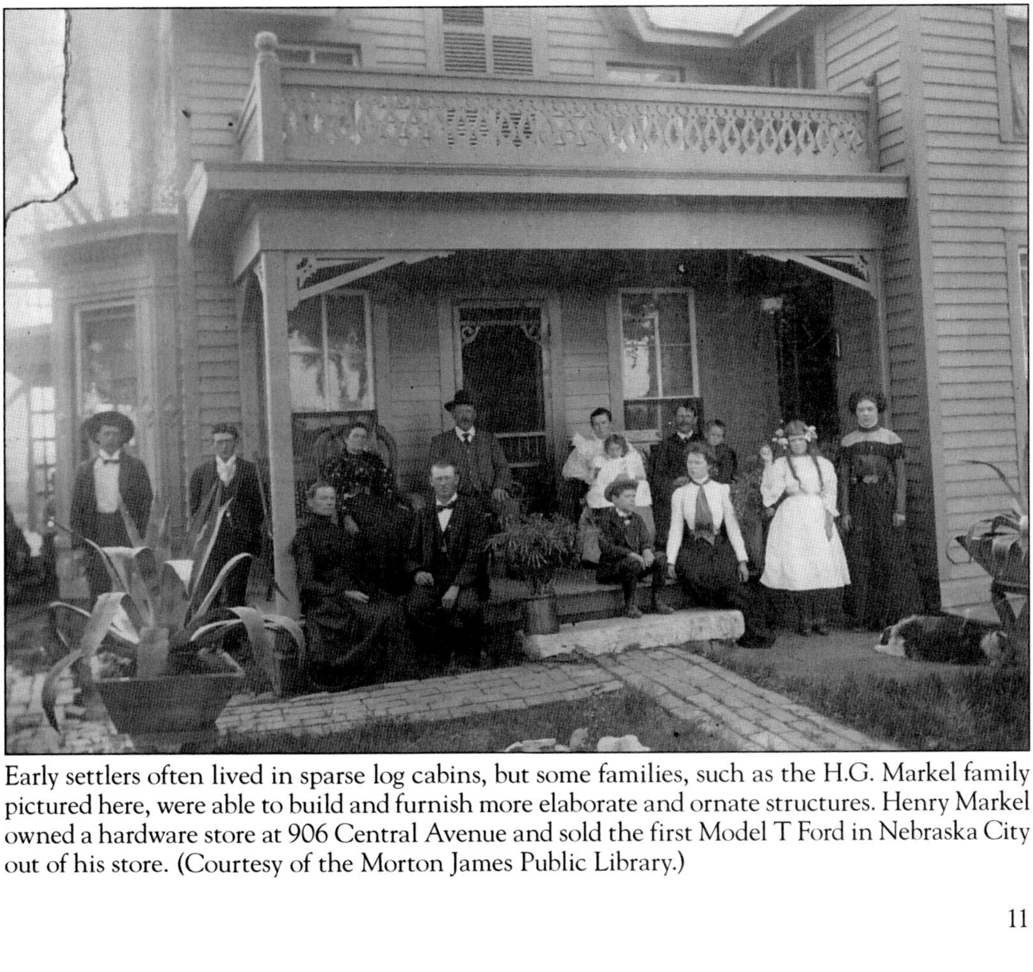

Early settlers often lived in sparse log cabins, but some families, such as the H.G. Markel family pictured here, were able to build and furnish more elaborate and ornate structures. Henry Markel owned a hardware store at 906 Central Avenue and sold the first Model T Ford in Nebraska City out of his store. (Courtesy of the Morton James Public Library.)

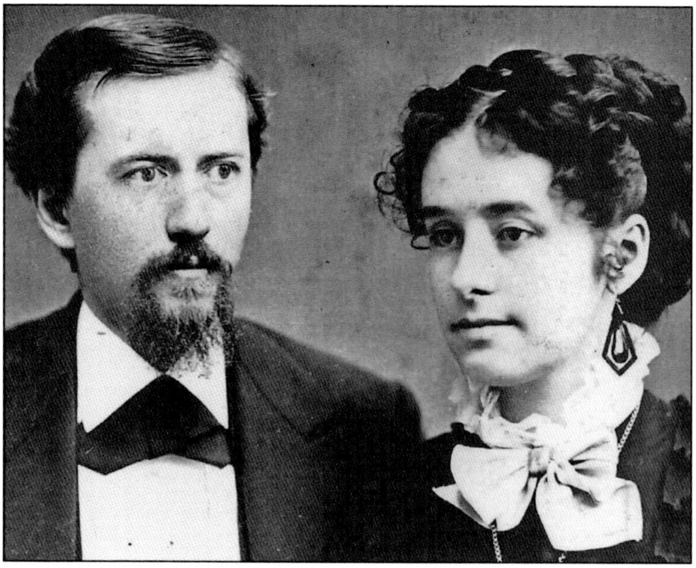

In 1855, J. Sterling Morton and his wife, Caroline, purchased 160 acres of treeless prairie west of Nebraska City. Morton, who was the new editor of the *News*, paid $1.25 an acre for the land. He established a working farm and orchard, writing in his later years that "there is beauty in a well-ordered orchard, which is a joy forever—it is a blessing to him who plants it." The property has grown apples continuously since Morton began planting. (Courtesy of Arbor Lodge.)

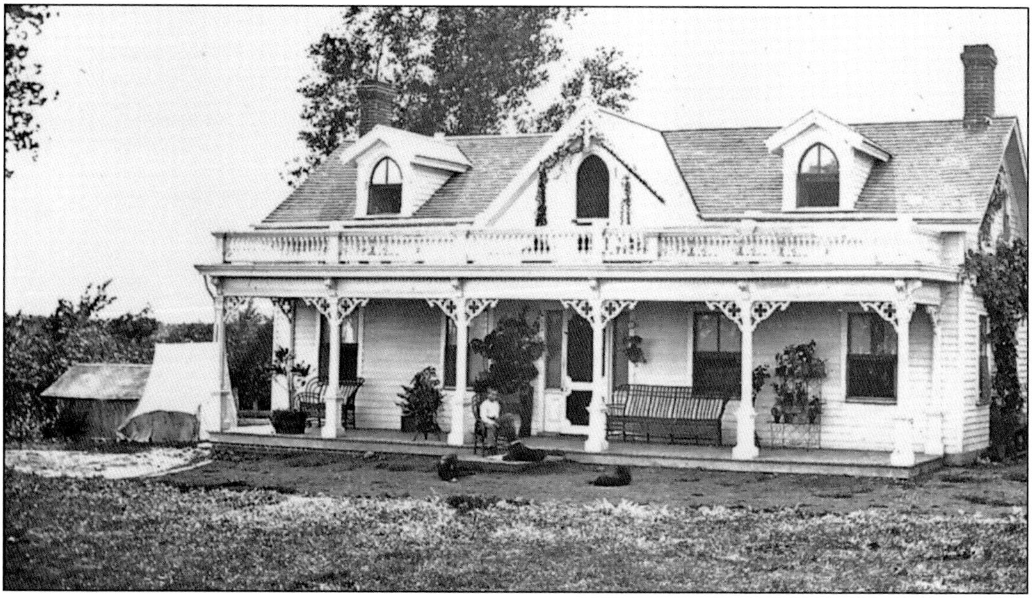

By 1860, the Mortons had built a four-room frame house and boasted more than 1,000 acres of property. They farmed corn, wheat, oats, potatoes, and hay and raised hogs and other animals. The Mortons had four sons: Joy, Paul, Mark, and Carl. Joy later founded the Morton Salt Company, while Paul became secretary of the Navy under Theodore Roosevelt. Mark worked on the Morton farms, and Carl was the principle founder and manager of Argo Starch Works in Nebraska City. (Courtesy of Arbor Lodge.)

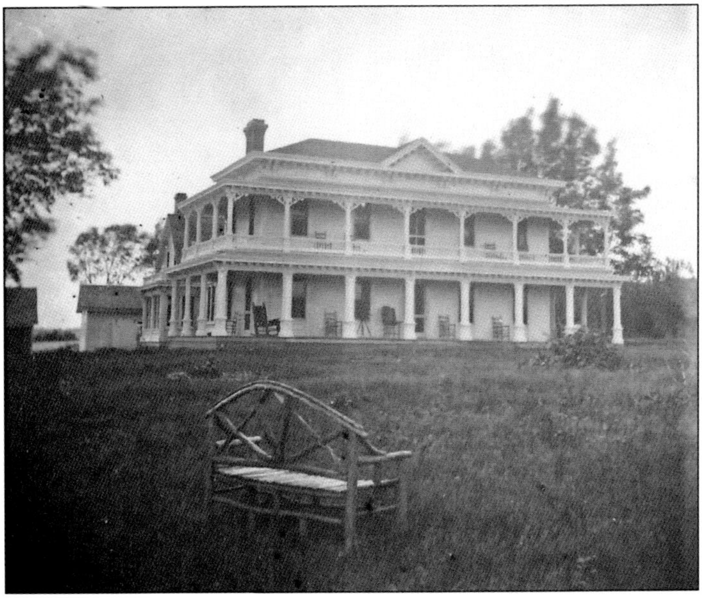

As the 1800s drew to a close, the Mortons continued to establish themselves in the community, investing in many industrial endeavors, including an opera house, creamery, cereal mill, printing establishment, grain elevators, and stockyards. A complete remodel of their home in the 1870s, including the addition of wraparound porches, transformed the house into a Victorian-era mansion. By 1875, Morton was calling his property Arbor Lodge. (Courtesy of Arbor Lodge.)

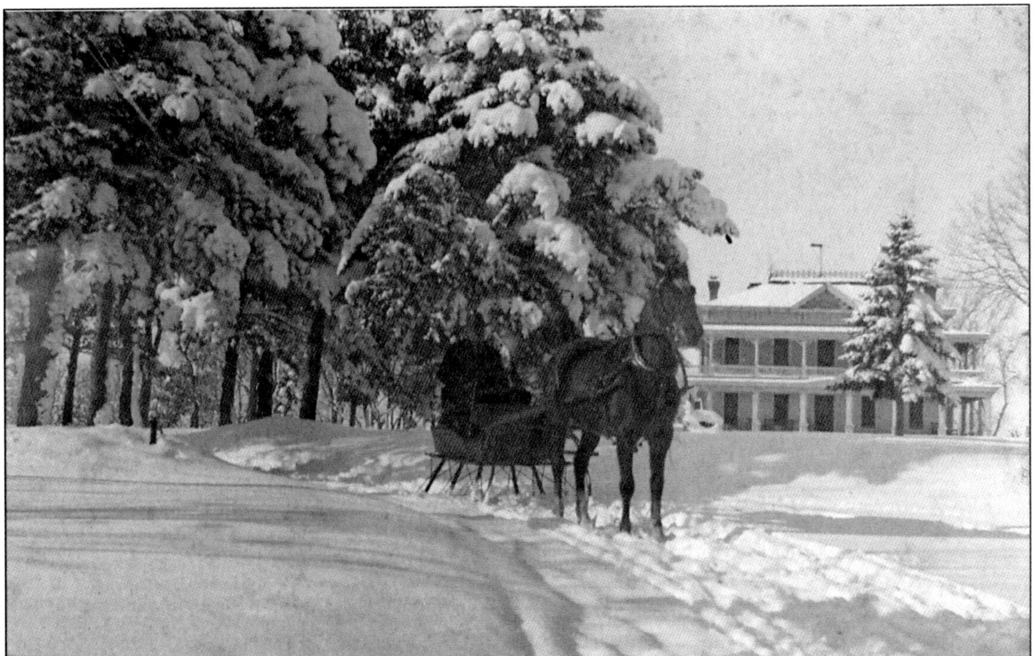

J. Sterling Morton was, by all standards, a prosperous man. He worked as a lawyer, politician, farmer, author, and editor. His hard work brought him wealth, which he used to improve his property and home. He filled his dwelling with fine furnishings and amassed a collection of carriages. The estate of J. Sterling Morton, now a museum, has many of those carriages on display. (Courtesy of Arbor Lodge.)

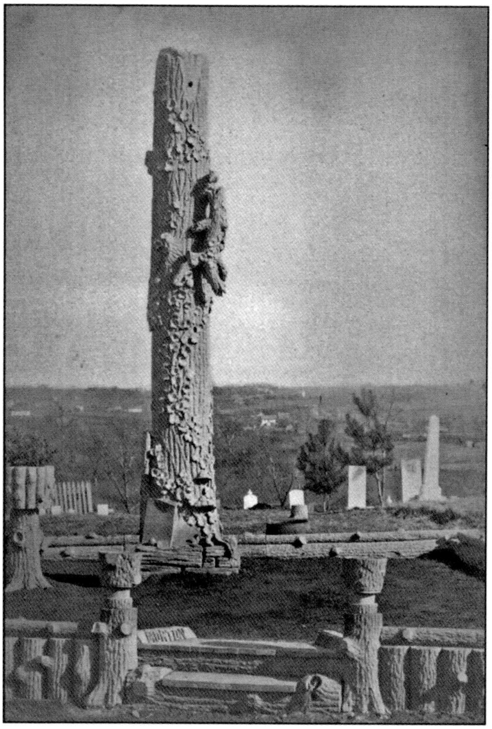

Caroline Morton died in 1881 and was buried in the Morton plot in Wyuka Cemetery in Nebraska City. J. Sterling Morton died in 1902. While he began his career as a newspaperman, Morton also dabbled in politics, serving as secretary of the Nebraska Territory from 1858 to 1861, acting governor in 1858 and 1859, and president of the State Board of Agriculture in 1873. Morton unsuccessfully ran for governor of Nebraska in 1880, 1882, 1884, and 1892. Pres. Grover Cleveland appointed Morton as the US secretary of agriculture from 1893 to 1897. (Courtesy of Arbor Lodge.)

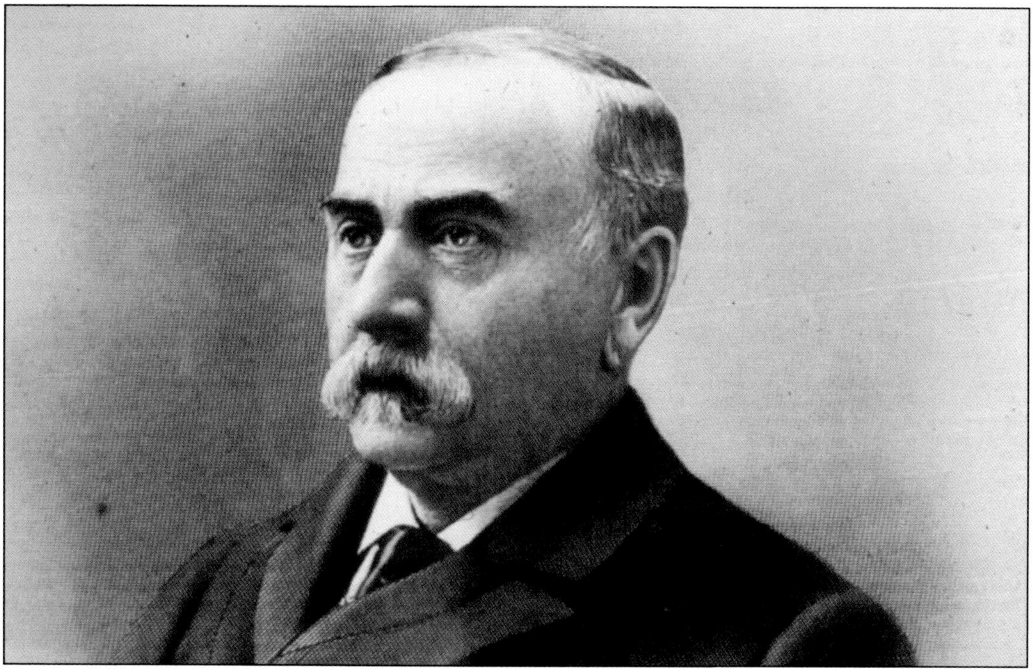

J. Sterling Morton is remembered as the "Father of Arbor Day." On the first Arbor Day in 1872, more than one million trees were planted in Nebraska. In 1885, Arbor Day was declared a legal holiday, and Morton's date of birth, April 22, was chosen to be the day to plant trees; however, in Nebraska, it is now celebrated on the last Friday of April each year. (Courtesy of the Arbor Day Foundation.)

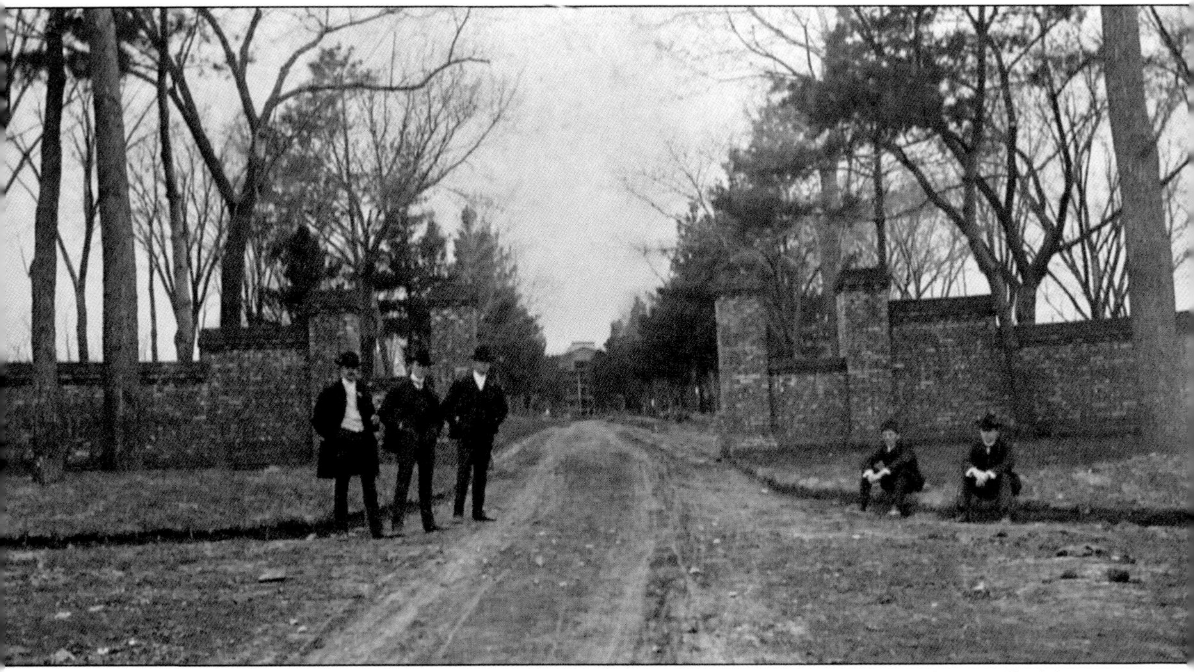

In 1903–1904, Joy Morton ordered the last major renovation to Arbor Lodge. The plans called for additional rooms to the home, increasing the total of rooms from 18 to 52. A long brick driveway was added, its entrance flanked by two large brick walls. (Courtesy of Arbor Lodge.)

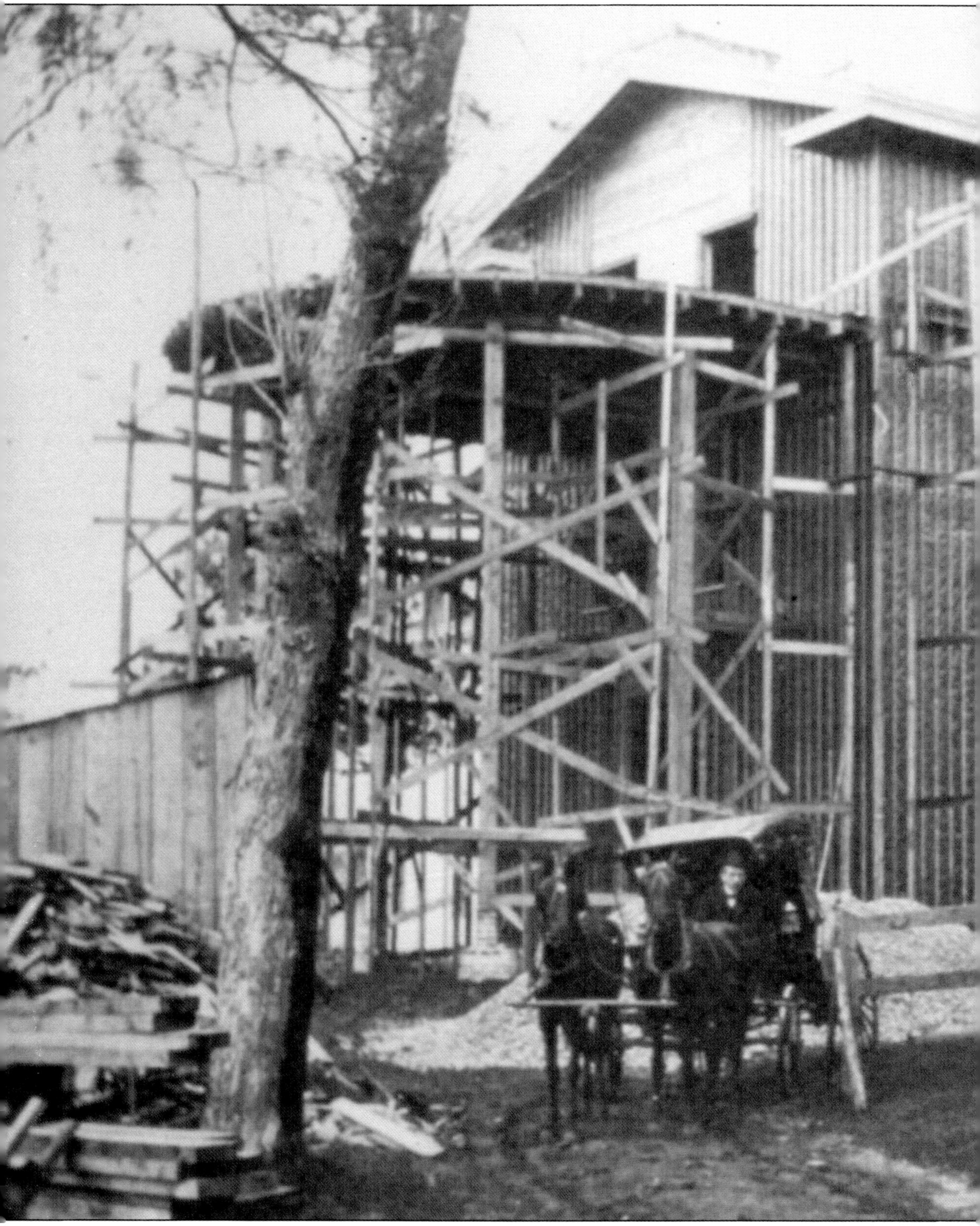

The reconstruction of Arbor Lodge in 1903 and 1904 styled the exterior of the house as a Neo-Colonial. The three-story addition to the front of the house called for curved porticos and

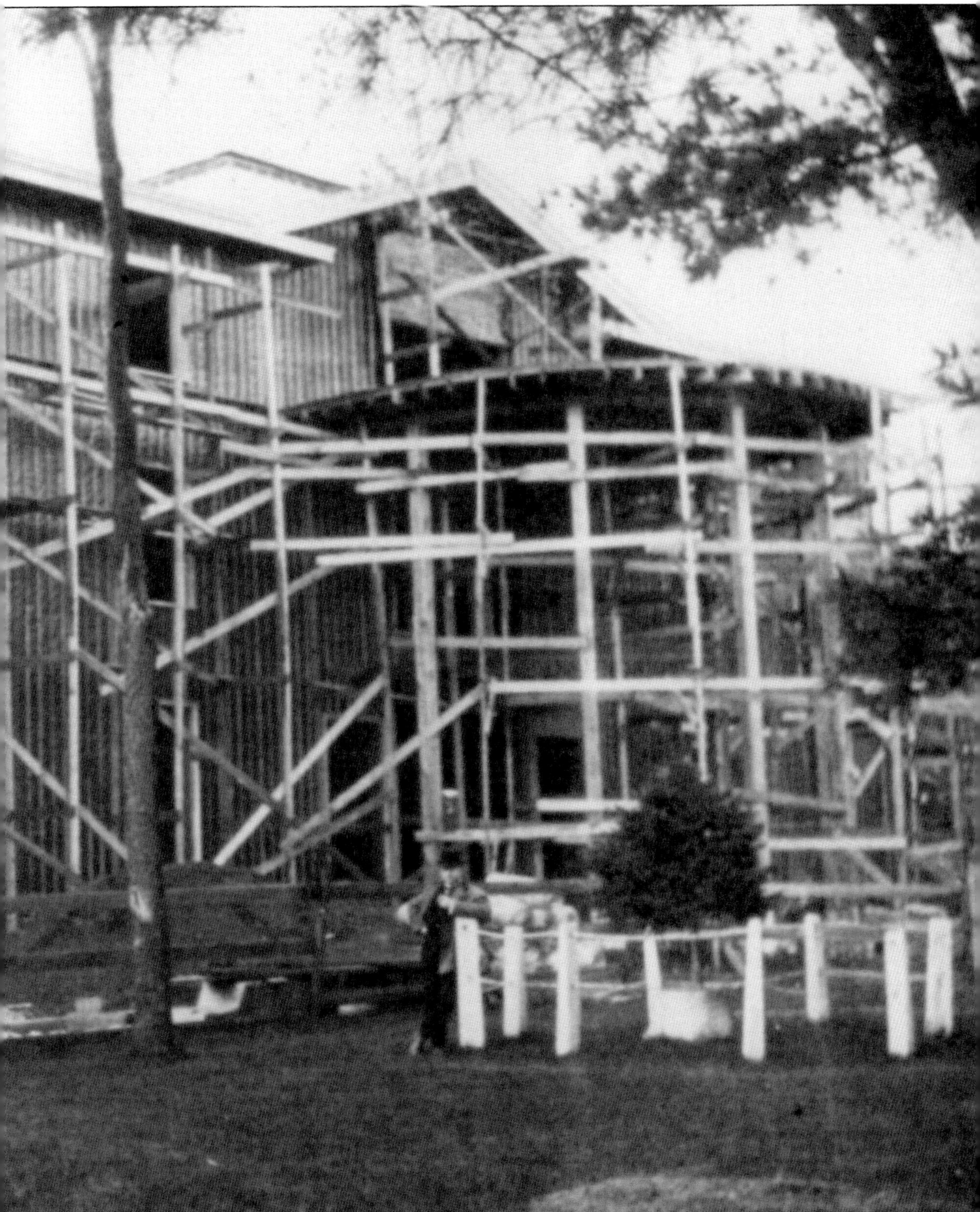

columns. Stucco was added to the exterior of the structure, and a bowling alley was installed in the basement. (Courtesy of the Arbor Day Foundation.)

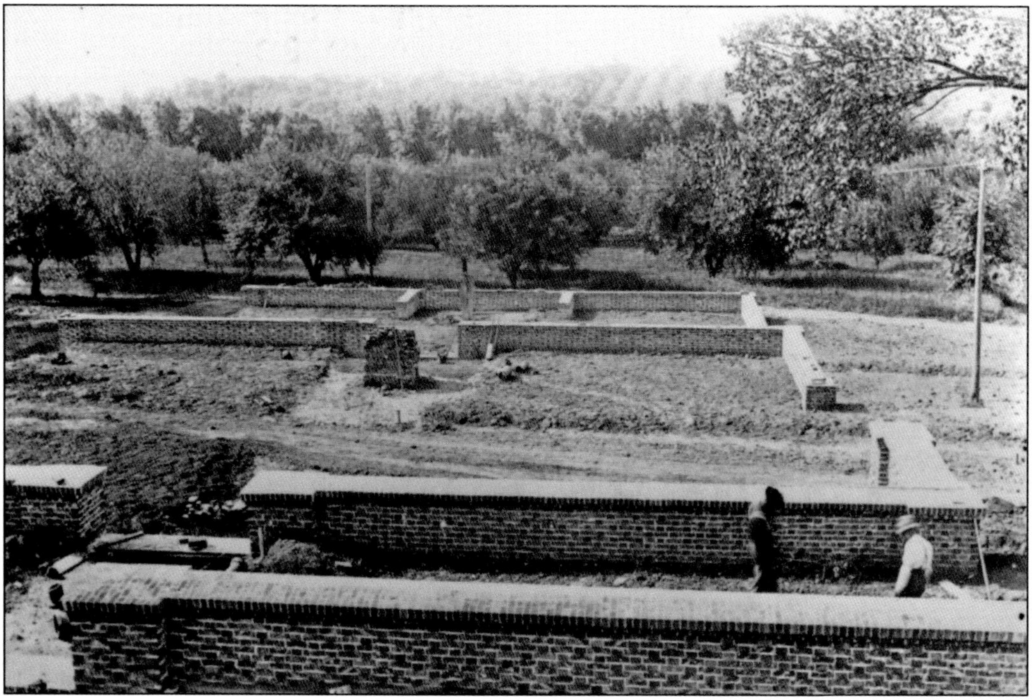

Chester Dwyer was hired by Joy Morton in 1904 to create a formal garden adjacent to the mansion. His plans included Italian-inspired terraces and varied plantings. These images show the construction of the formal garden. (Both courtesy of Arbor Lodge.)

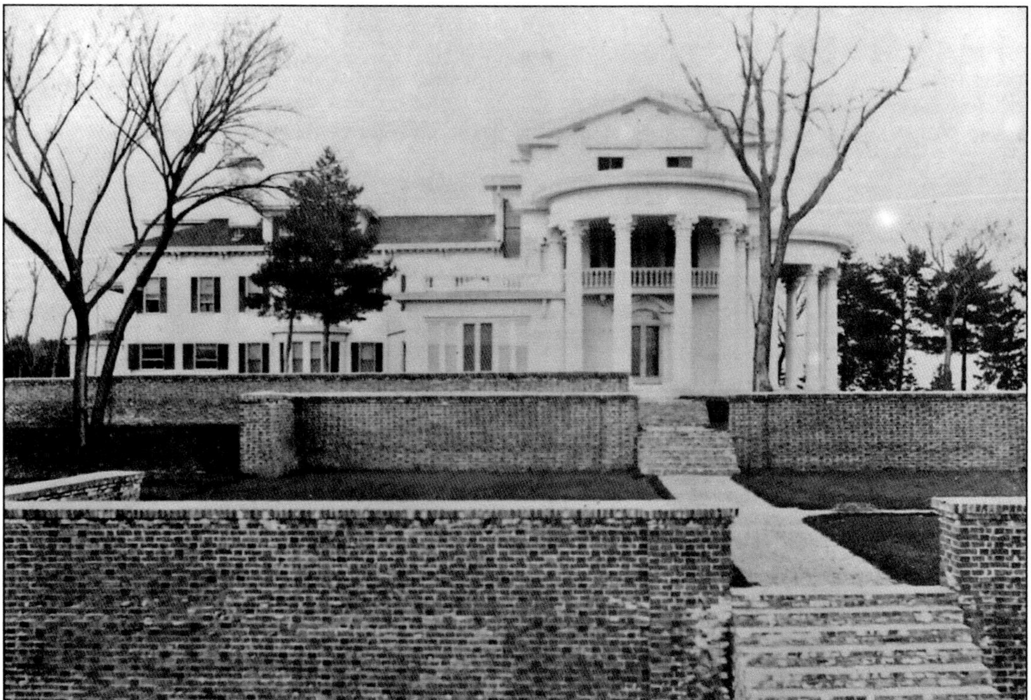

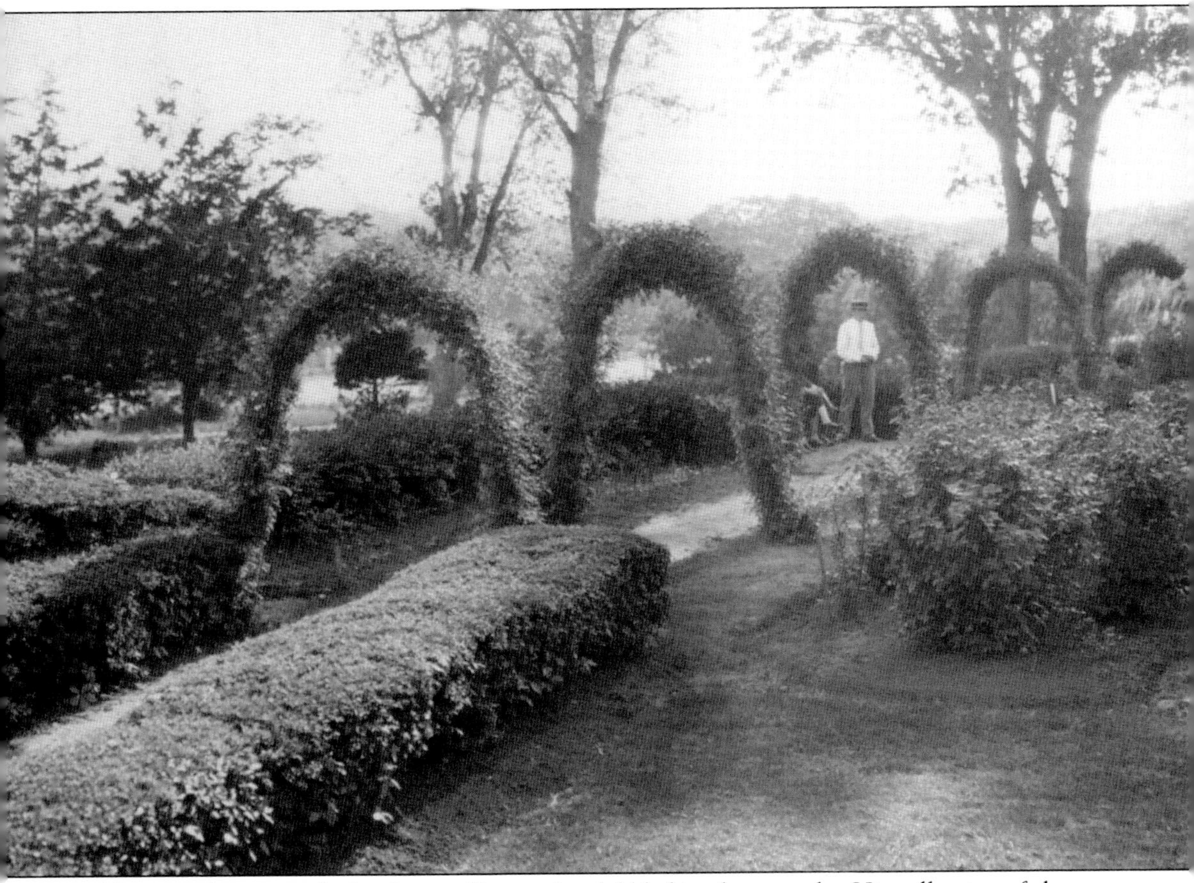

In addition to designing the landscape, Dwyer also dabbled in photography. His collection of glass plate negatives was donated to Arbor Lodge more than 100 years after he captured the images. (Courtesy of Arbor Lodge.)

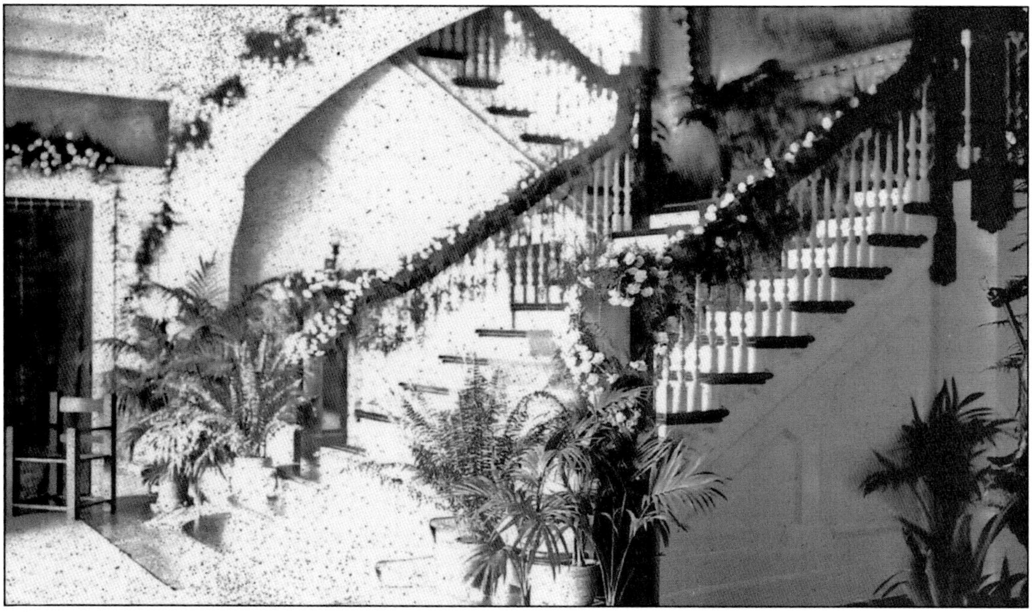

The 1903–1904 renovations to Arbor Lodge included the addition of a main hall featuring a grand staircase. In this photograph from October 1904, the hall is decorated for the wedding of Jean Morton, Joy Morton's daughter, to Joseph Cudahy. (Courtesy of Arbor Lodge.)

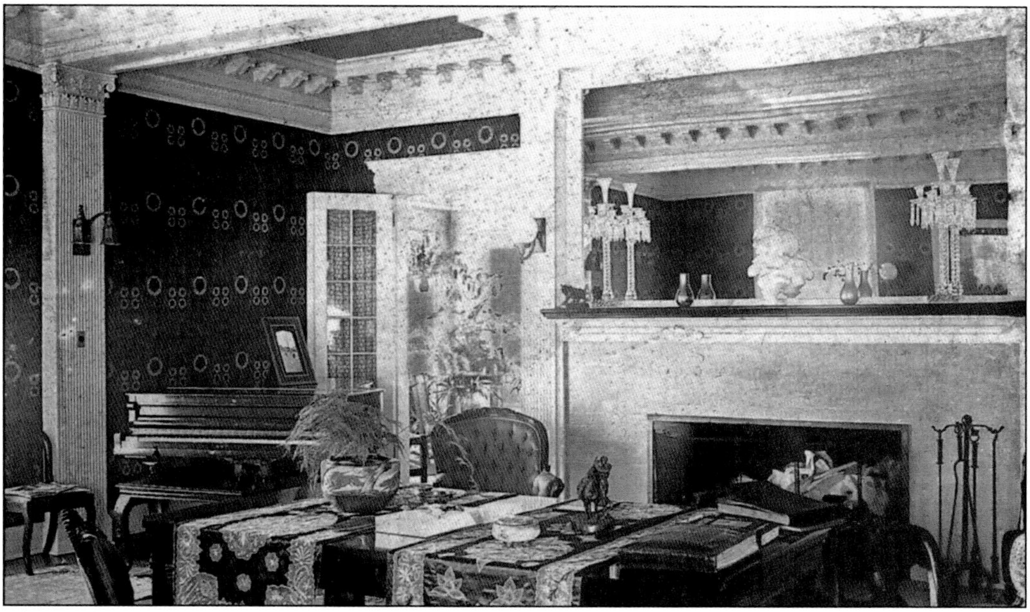

The walls of the parlor inside Arbor Lodge were covered in French silk tapestry and adhered with braids and nails. A Corinthian ceiling topped the room. In October 1905, a special monument was dedicated to J. Sterling Morton. Guests at the dedication included former US president Grover Cleveland and former US vice president Adlai Stevenson. Politicians, family, and friends of J. Sterling Morton gathered in the parlor the night prior to the monument unveiling to exchange stories about their friend. (Courtesy of Arbor Lodge.)

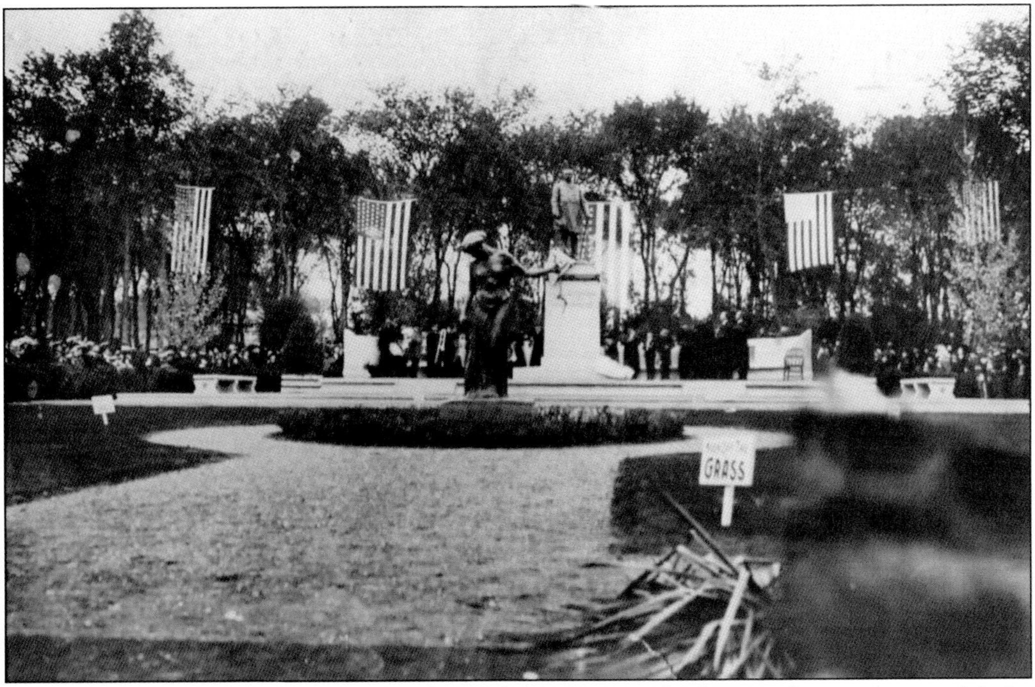

Morton's bronze sculpture was created by Rudolph Evans, who became known later in life for designing the bronze monument of Thomas Jefferson in the Jefferson Memorial in Washington, DC. At the unveiling of the Morton monument, Adlai Stevenson spoke to the large crowd about Morton, saying, "Under his guiding hand, a new day was added to the calendar . . . millions of trees now beautify and adorn this magnificent state. . . . Henceforth, upon its annual recurrence, ordinary avocations are to be suspended, and this day wholly set apart to pursuits which tend to beautify the home, make glorious the landscape, and gladden the hearts of all the people." (Both courtesy of Arbor Lodge.)

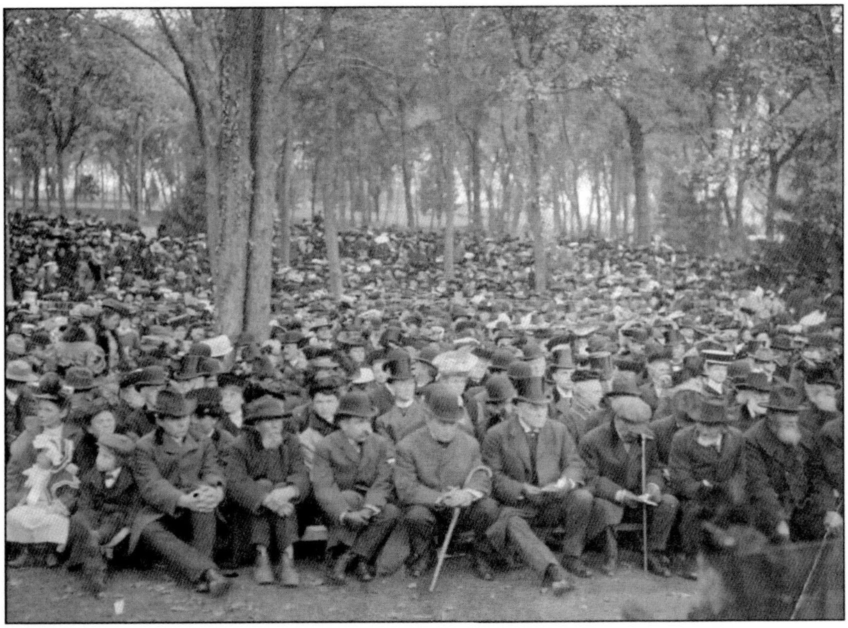

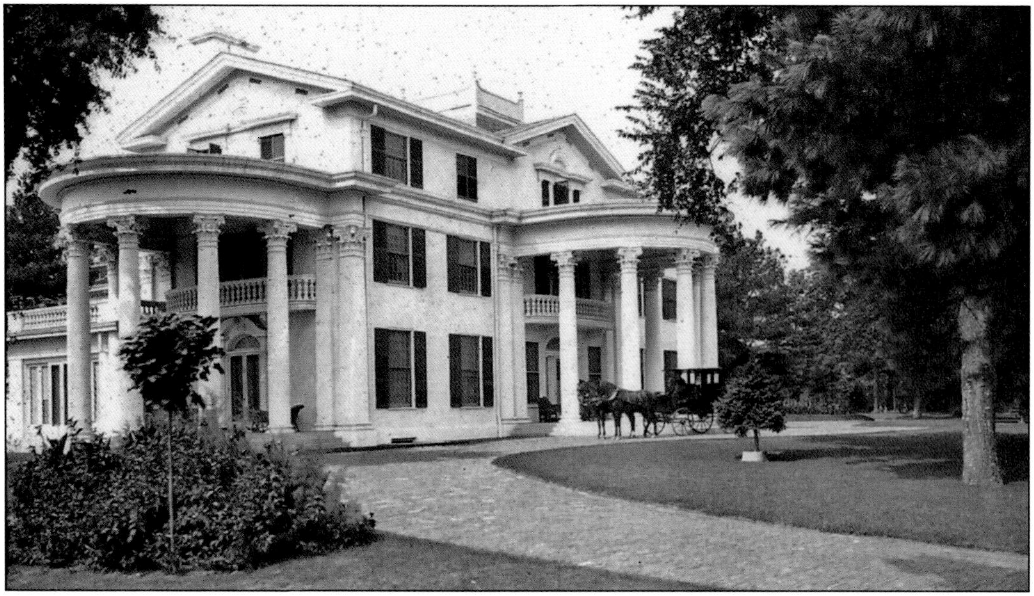

Joy Morton and his family used Arbor Lodge as a summer home in the early 1900s. Morton, who made his home in Chicago, would load his family, their bags, and even special pieces of furniture on a train every year and make the journey to Nebraska City, staying a few months before returning to Chicago. A staff of 20 would be employed to get the mansion ready for the family's visit. (Courtesy of Arbor Lodge.)

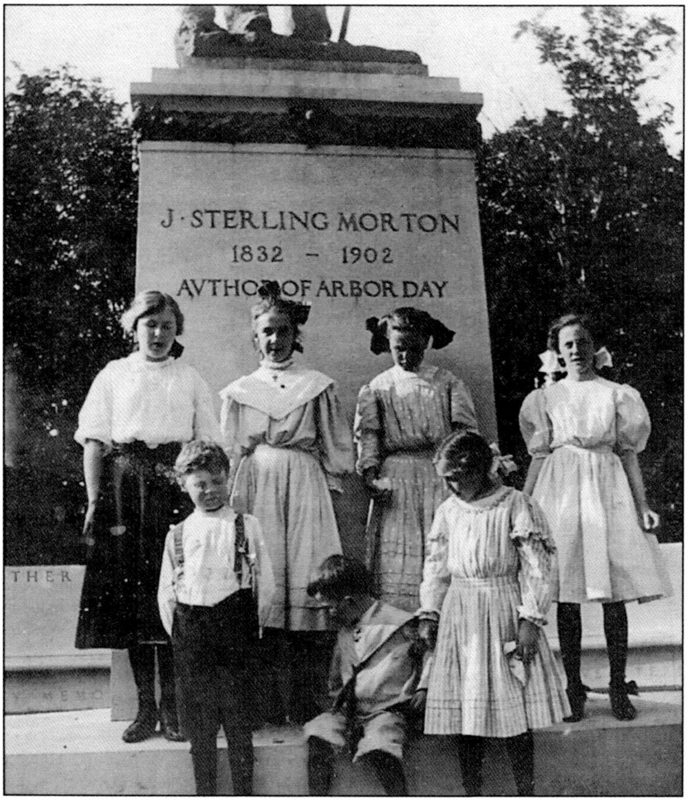

J. Sterling Morton's monument is located at the east end of his property in an area called Morton Park. It remains a popular spot for visitors. (Courtesy of Brett and Robyn Gay.)

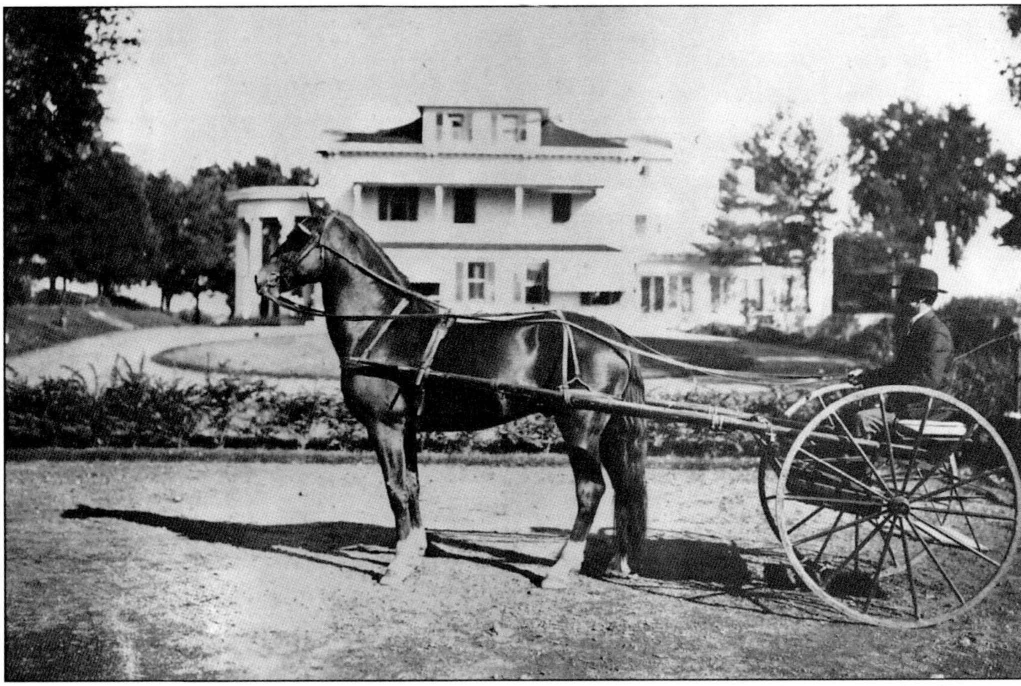

Joy Morton is known to have loved horses and used them as a source of power on the farm and his commercial orchard, Morton Orchard. (Courtesy of Arbor Lodge.)

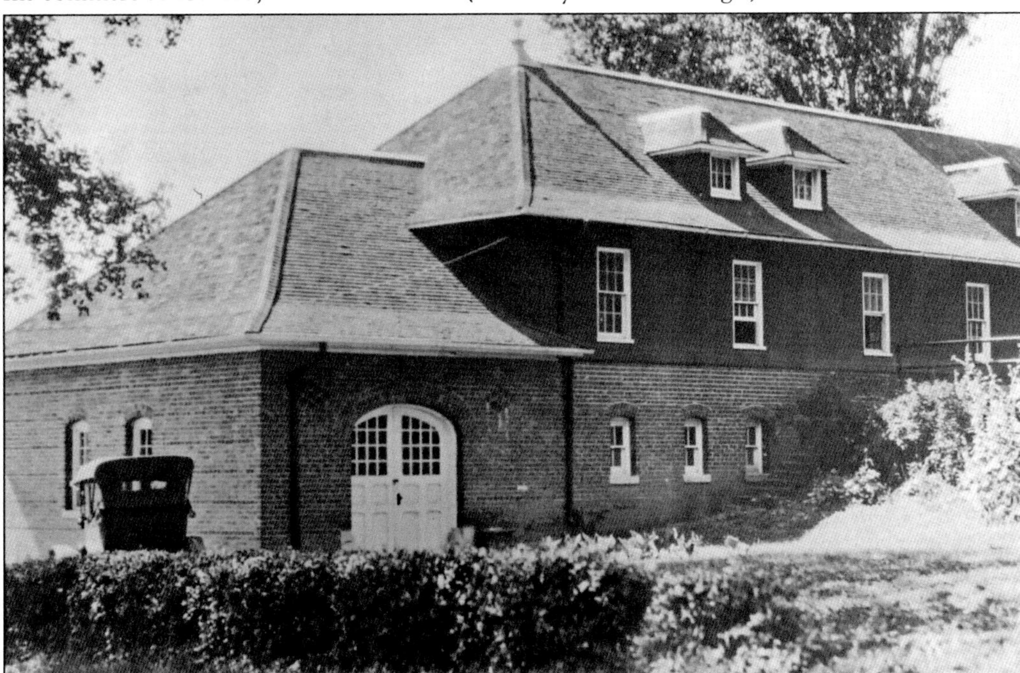

The carriage house behind Arbor Lodge was erected around 1900. It housed the family's collection of carriages, including the overland stagecoach purchased by J. Sterling Morton in 1894. Morton used the stagecoach to transfer guests from the train depot south of downtown Nebraska City to his property on the west side of town. (Courtesy of Arbor Lodge.)

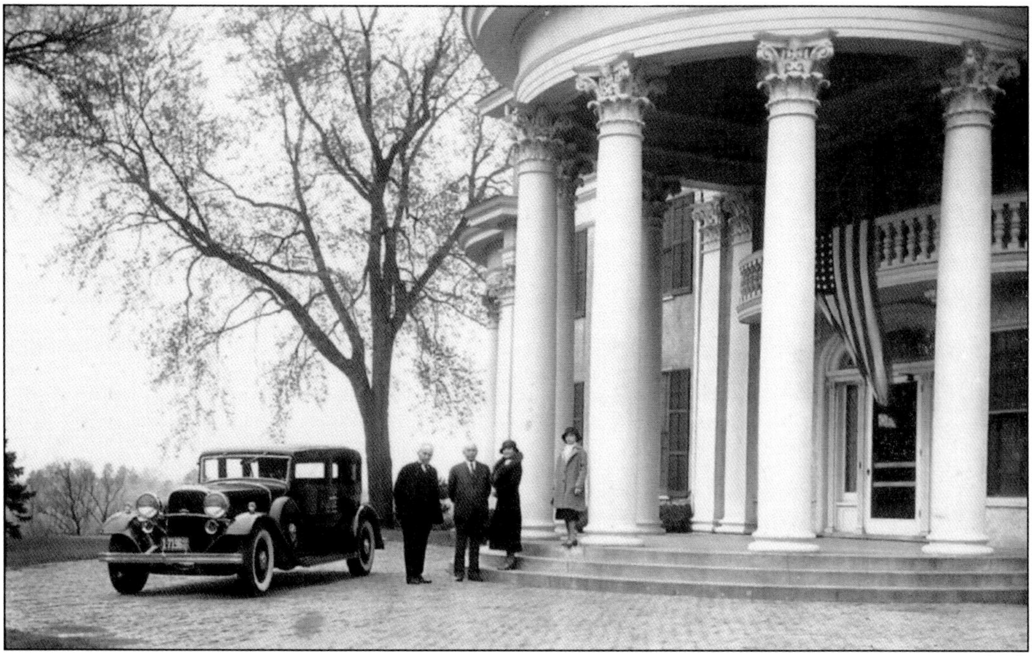

Joy Morton, pictured above (second from left), gave Arbor Lodge and the surrounding acres to the State of Nebraska in 1923. His goal was to have Arbor Lodge maintained as a historical museum and park. Today, Arbor Lodge and its grounds are a favorite destination for many, welcoming thousands of visitors each year. (Both courtesy of Arbor Lodge.)

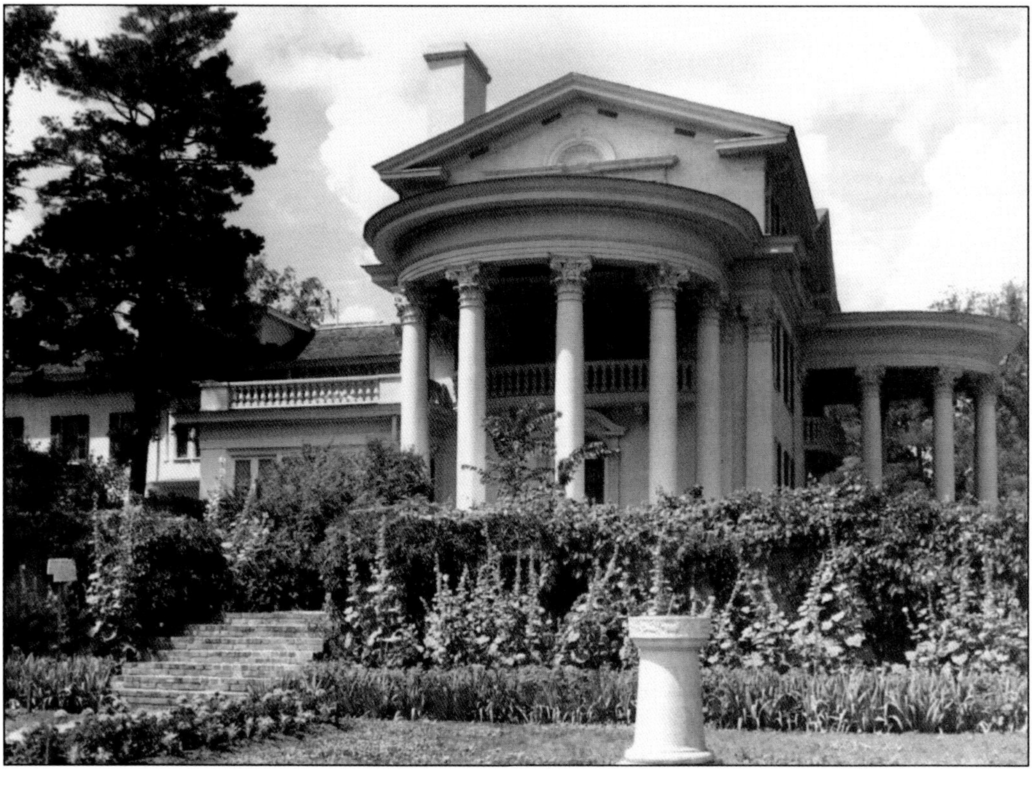

Two

TRANSPORTATION

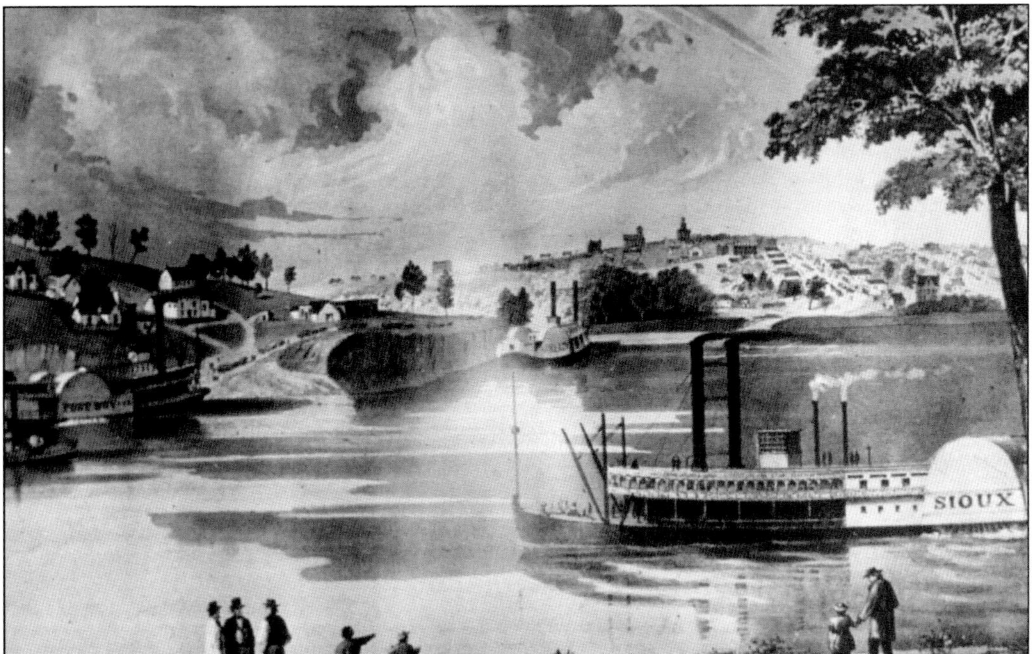

Nebraska City's proximity to the Missouri River made it a natural jump-off point for travelers heading west during the second half of the 1800s. Beginning in the late 1850s, steamboats crowded both sides of the river. More than 75 steamboats landed at Nebraska City during June 1859, with 200 recorded for that entire summer. This photograph is of a mural painted on the first floor of the Otoe County Courthouse in Nebraska City depicting the town in those early years. (Courtesy of the Arbor Day Foundation.)

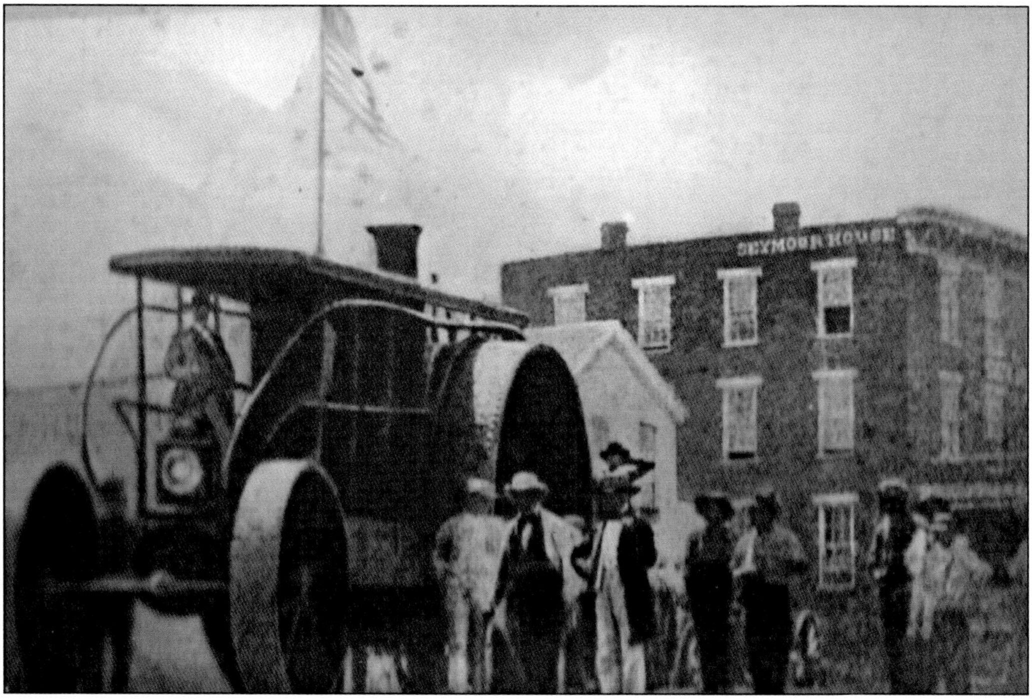

In July 1862, a unique contraption weighing 20 tons was unloaded at the Nebraska City docks. Dubbed the Prairie Motor, the one-of-a-kind machine was designed to transport goods and people from Nebraska City to Denver using only steam-generated power. The smaller front wheels stood six feet tall and were designed to ride over the rough prairie sod. Unfortunately, the "steamwagon," as it was informally called, only made it a few miles outside of town before breaking down. While citizens of Nebraska City remained positive it would get fixed, even voting to spend $2,500 to shore up the road and bridges, the steamwagon spent the next several decades rusting in a ditch off of what is now called Steamwagon Road. Its parts were eventually stripped for scrap metal. (Courtesy of Arbor Lodge.)

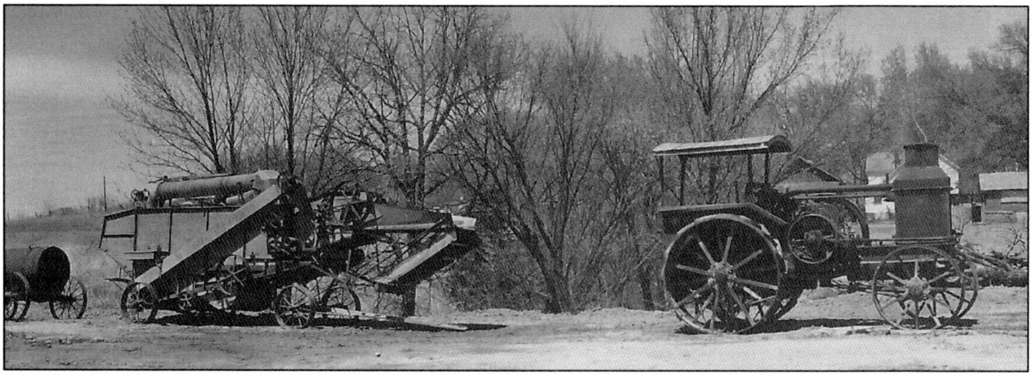

Even though steam power would quickly become a popular choice for transportation and work, as evidenced by the steam thresher outfit pictured here, many individuals and businesses remained committed to animal-drawn wagons. In 1858, the freighting firm Russell, Majors, and Waddell opened in Nebraska City. That year, it oversaw the transportation of 3.2 million pounds of goods to points west, all powered by ox, horse, or mule. Russell, Majors, and Waddell witnessed major growth in shipping over the next decade, reaching a high point of 4.4 million pounds of goods transported in 1865. (Courtesy of Sally Pierce.)

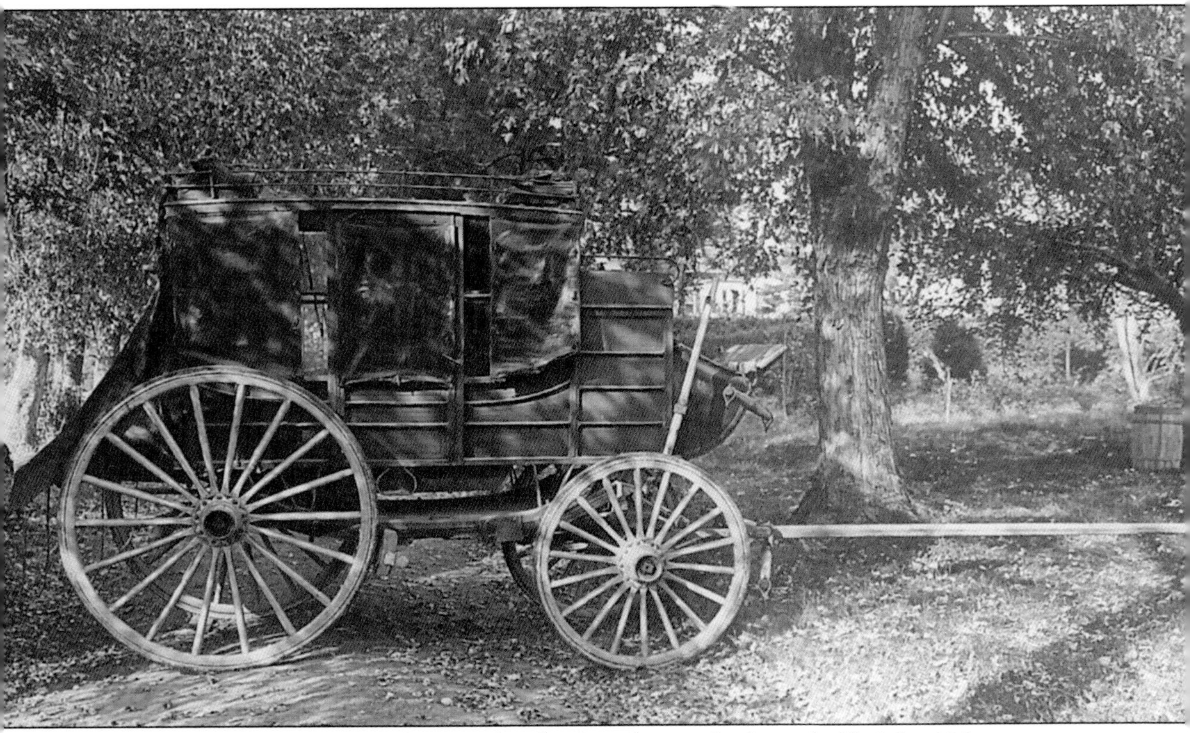

Stagecoaches were a common sight in Nebraska City during the latter half of the 19th century. In 1870, a passenger could ride a stagecoach from Nebraska City to Lincoln for $6 one way. This stagecoach, owned by J. Sterling Morton, was used from 1867 to 1871 to transport passengers from Nebraska City to Lexington, Nebraska. It was once driven by Buffalo Bill Cody. (Courtesy of Nebraska City Tourism and Commerce.)

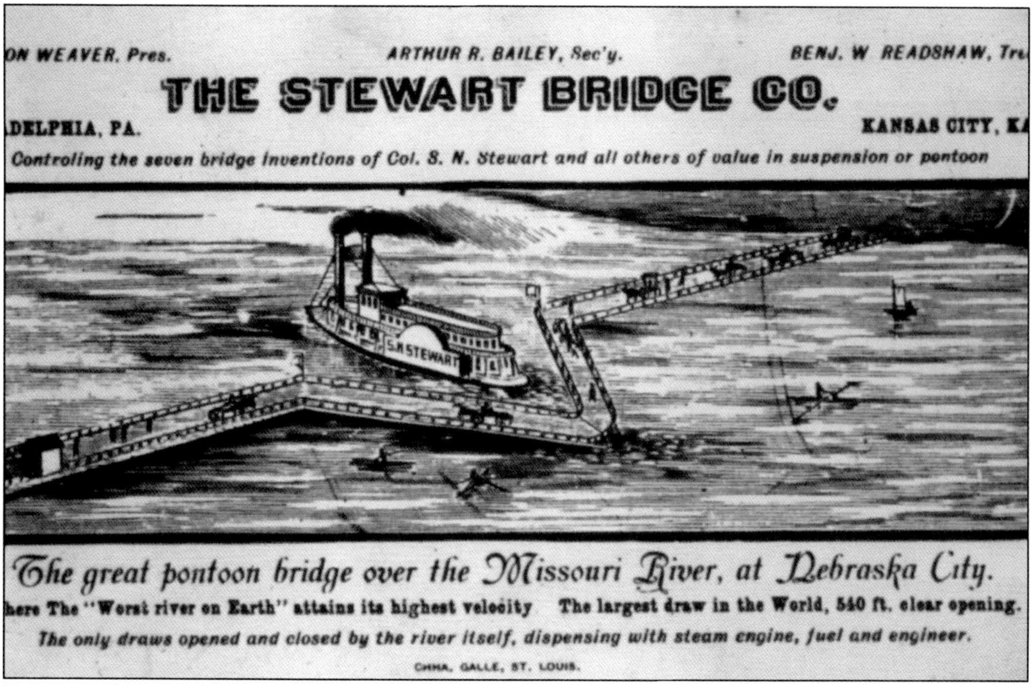

For more than 30 years, from 1853 to 1888, the only way to cross the Missouri River at Nebraska City was by ferry. By August 1888, two structures had been completed to allow for greater transportation across the river. First came a pontoon bridge with a V-shaped draw. The bridge was the brainchild of Col. S.N. Stewart of Philadelphia, Pennsylvania. He fronted half of the $20,000 cost with his own money, and Nebraska City residents supplied the rest. The draw of the 24-foot-wide bridge was constructed using a windlass, which needed only the strength of one man to operate it. When the pontoon-style bridge was completed, it was touted as the "longest, widest and best in the world." Wagons, horses, travelers, and even livestock took advantage of the unique crossing, bypassing the ferries that used to navigate the wide and unchanneled Missouri River. A horse and rider could cross the river for a 25¢ round-trip fare. Persons on foot were subjected to a 5¢ fare, and hogs could cross for 2¢ each. (Both courtesy of the Arbor Day Foundation.)

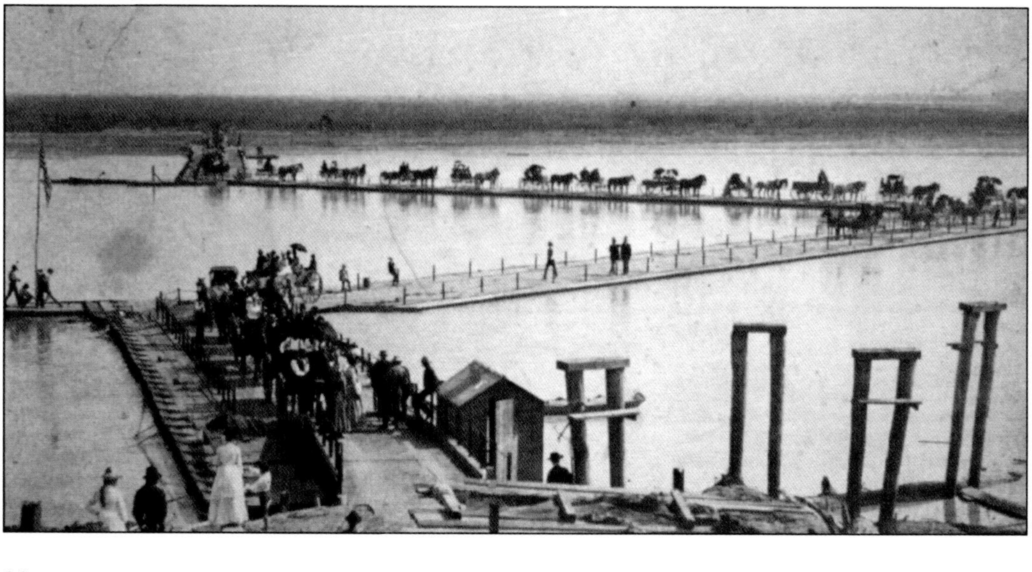

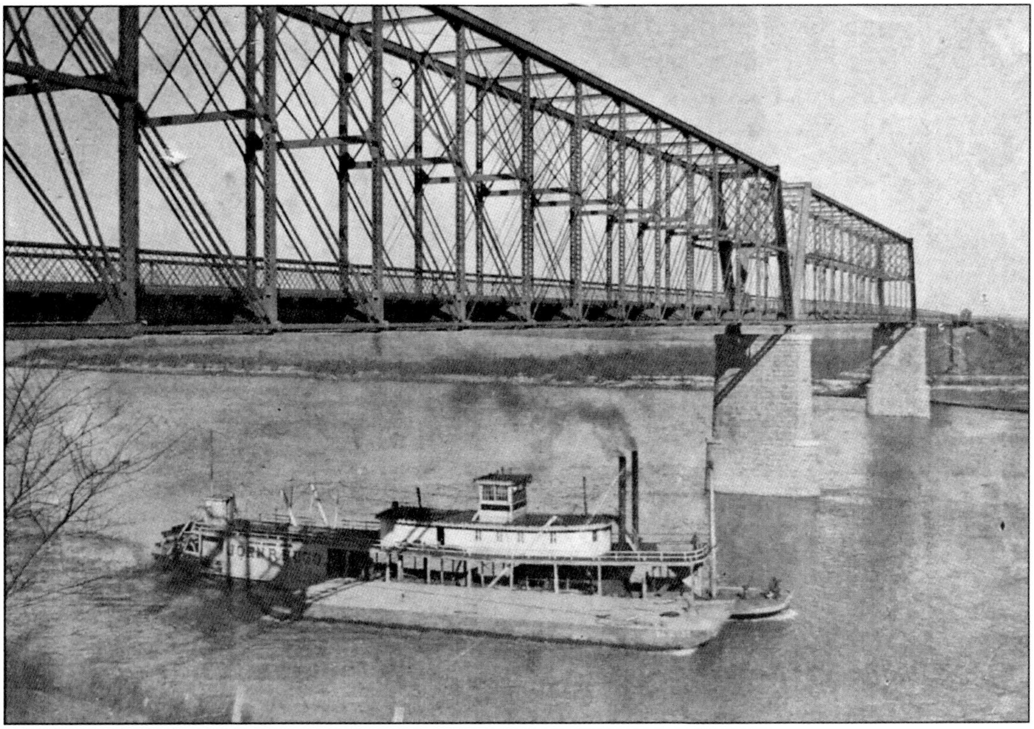

One week after the pontoon bridge was completed, the Burlington & Missouri River Railroad Bridge opened to traffic. The $1-million steel-construction bridge was built on stacked stone piers 85 feet high. The railroad bridge fared better than the pontoon crossing; in the spring of 1889, less than a year after it was completed, the pontoon bridge washed away in a heavy spring flood. It was never replaced. (Courtesy of the Nebraska City Museum of Firefighting.)

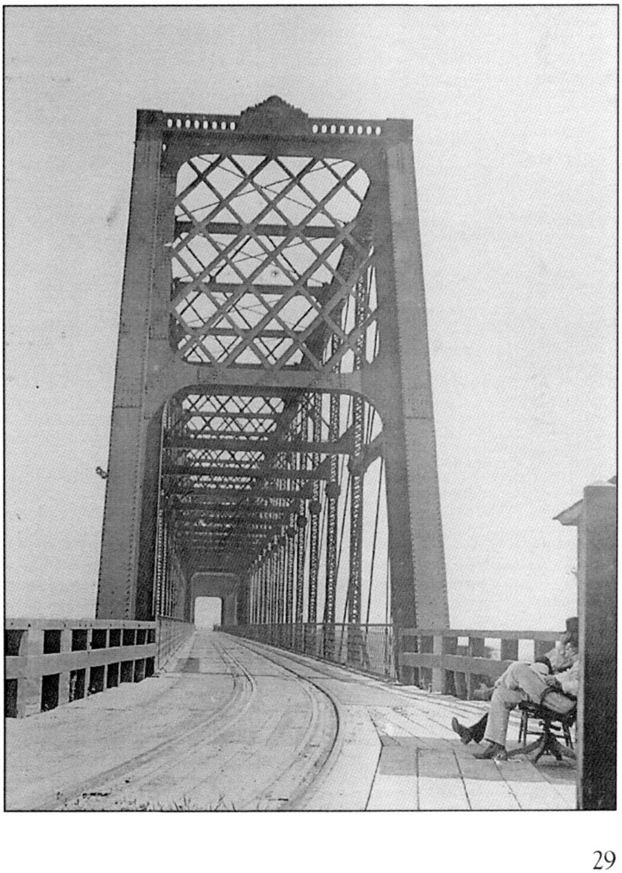

In 1891, the railroad bridge was planked for wagon traffic, and it remained the main source of river crossing until 1930. (Courtesy of Dorris Sackles.)

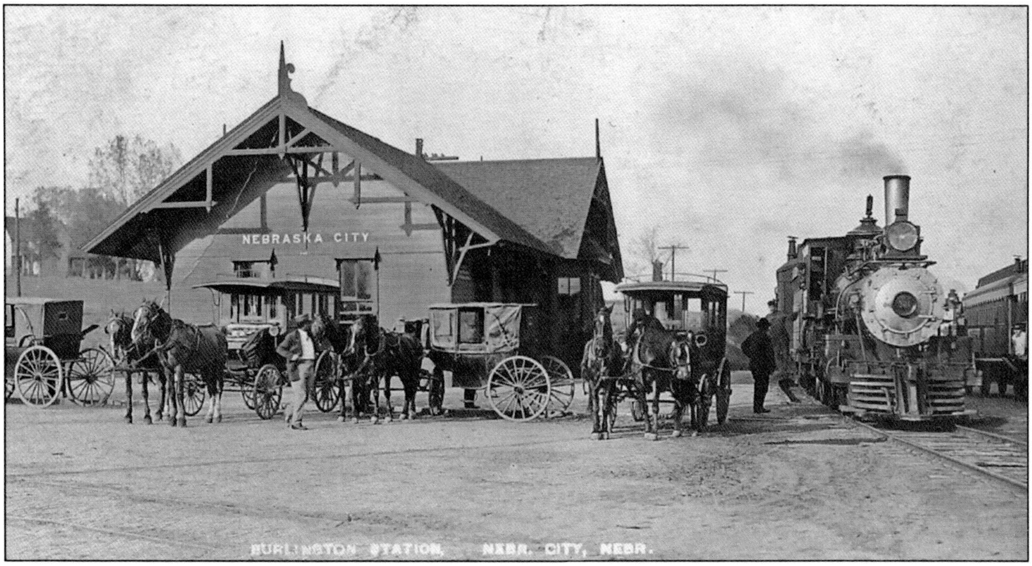

By the late 1880s, Nebraska City boasted two train depots frequented by both passenger and supply trains. One was located on South Sixth Street, and another, pictured here, was on Central Avenue between First and Second Streets. In this photograph, wagons and porters from various downtown hotels wait to gather passengers. (Courtesy of the Nebraska City Museum of Firefighting.)

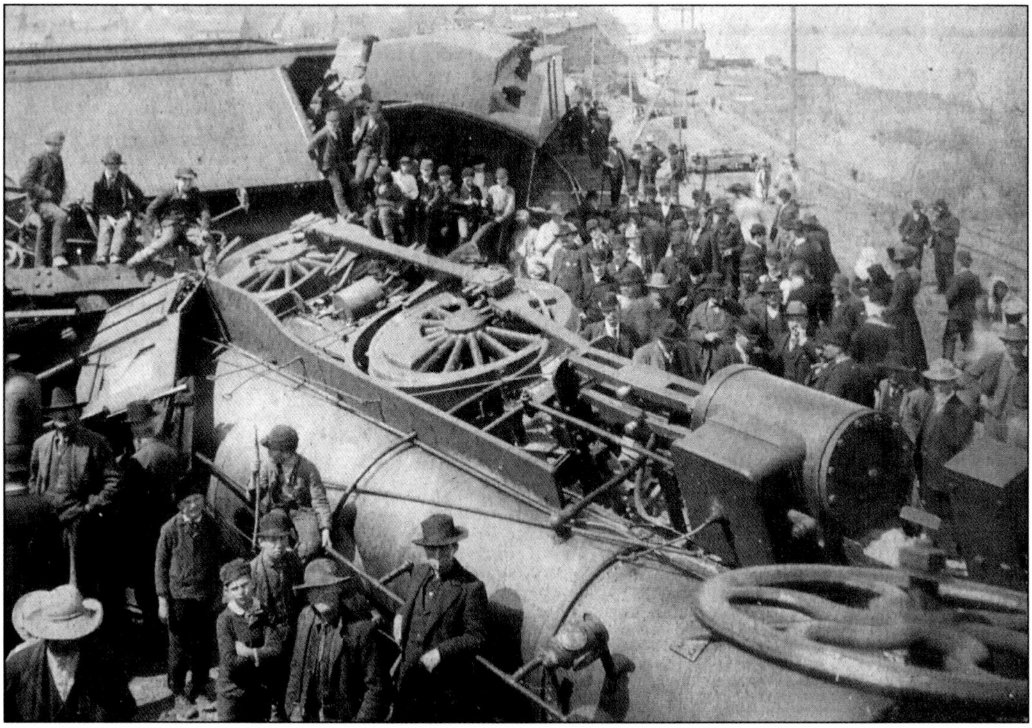

Crowds have gathered in the aftermath of a train crash on April 22, 1892. The Missouri Pacific Train derailed just north of the depot. (Courtesy of the Nebraska City Museum of Firefighting.)

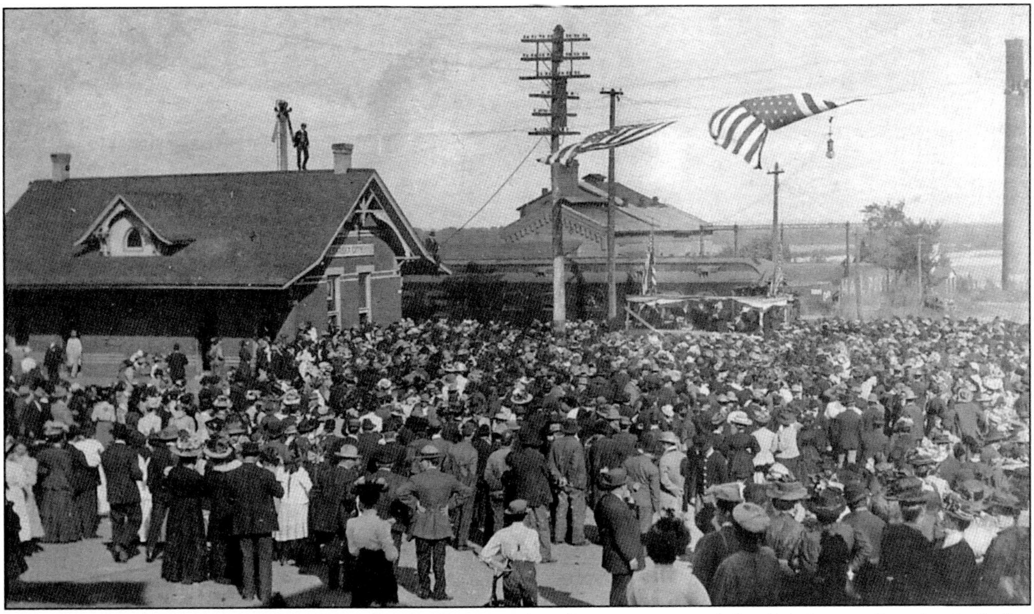

In 1908, William Howard Taft embarked on a whistle-stop tour of the Midwest that included a stop in Nebraska City. The Republican Taft was campaigning against Nebraska's William Jennings Bryan, a Democrat who was making a third attempt to secure the presidency. Even though a large crowd gathered to hear Taft speak, Bryan carried Nebraska on Election Day. Taft did, however, win the national election by a landslide. (Courtesy of Dorris Sackles.)

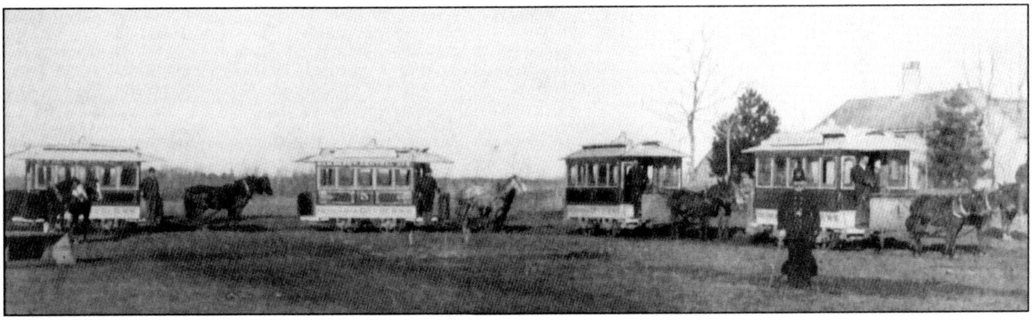

In 1889, Nebraska City invested in public transportation with the introduction of horse- and mule-drawn streetcars. The cars were centered on tracks that ran through downtown on Central Avenue and along South Sixth Street to the train depot. In this photograph, the streetcars are shown on one of their first days in operation. When not in use, the streetcars were stored in a barn near Twentieth Street and Second Avenue. (Courtesy of the Nebraska City Historical Society.)

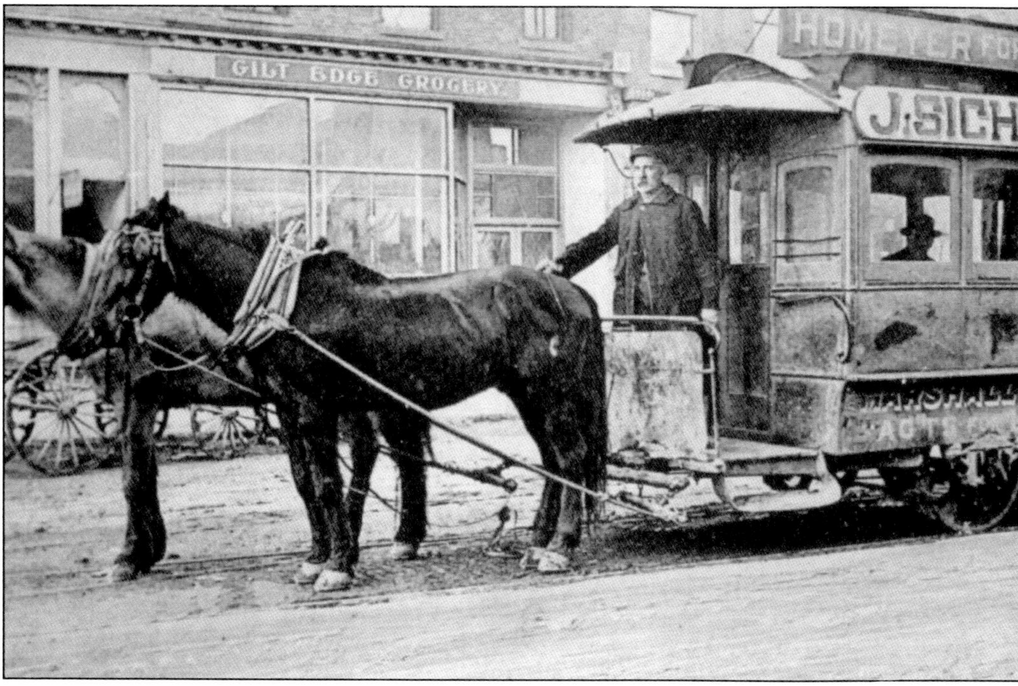

Passengers could ride a streetcar for only 5¢ per trip. Much like modern public transportation, the cars provided space for advertising. The streetcars ceased operations in 1910. (Above, courtesy of the Arbor Day Foundation; below, the Nebraska City Historical Society.)

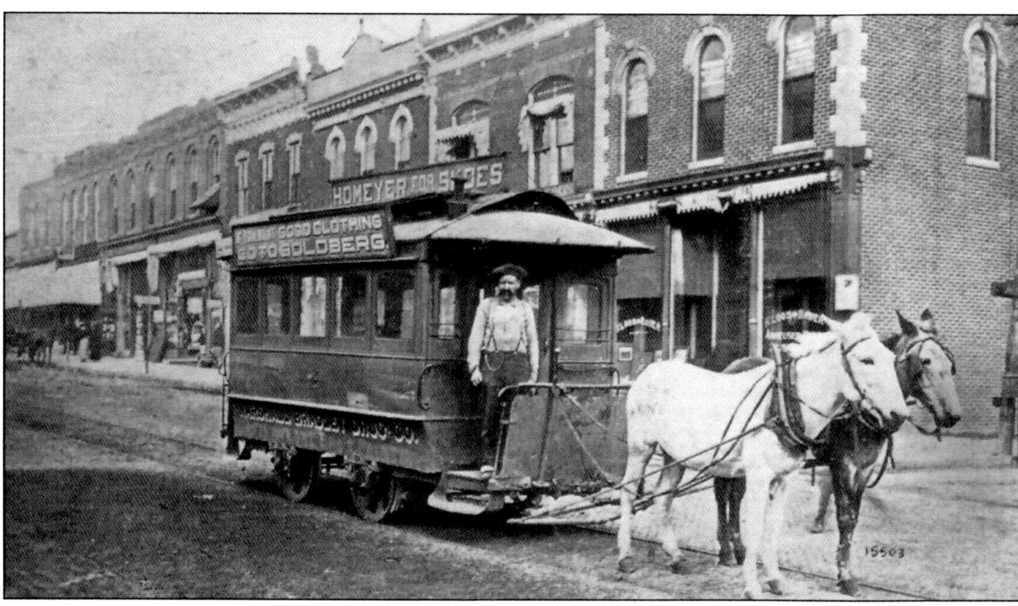

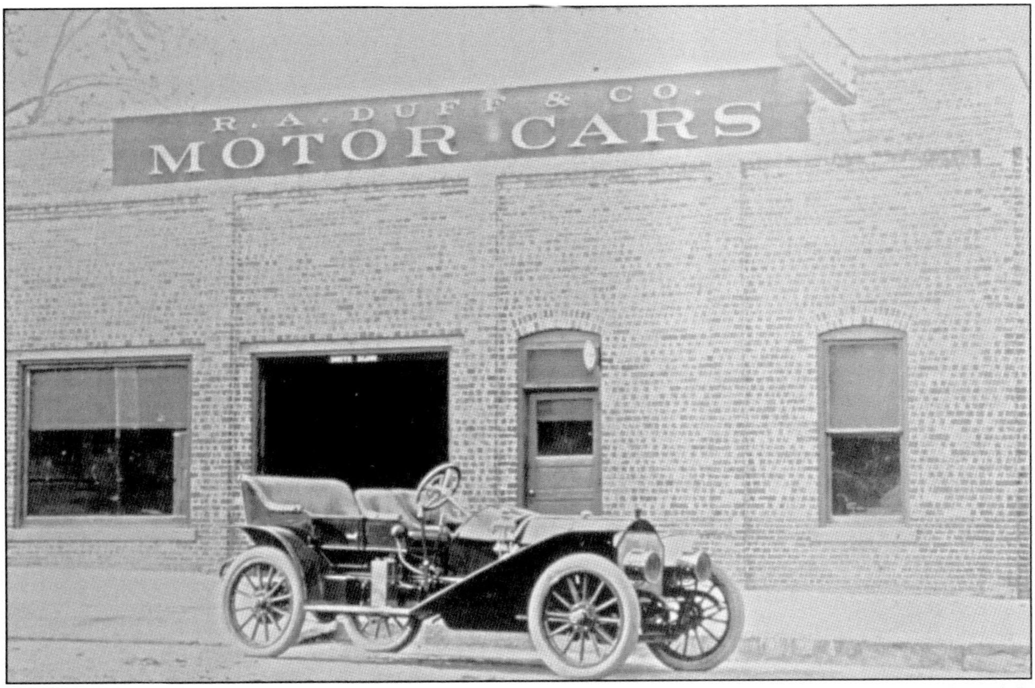

The first automobile arrived in Nebraska City in 1901 and belonged to William Hayward. Ralph Duff, owner of Duff's Garage on Fifth Street and Central Avenue, operated the town's first sales and service garage for automobiles. (Courtesy of the Arbor Day Foundation.)

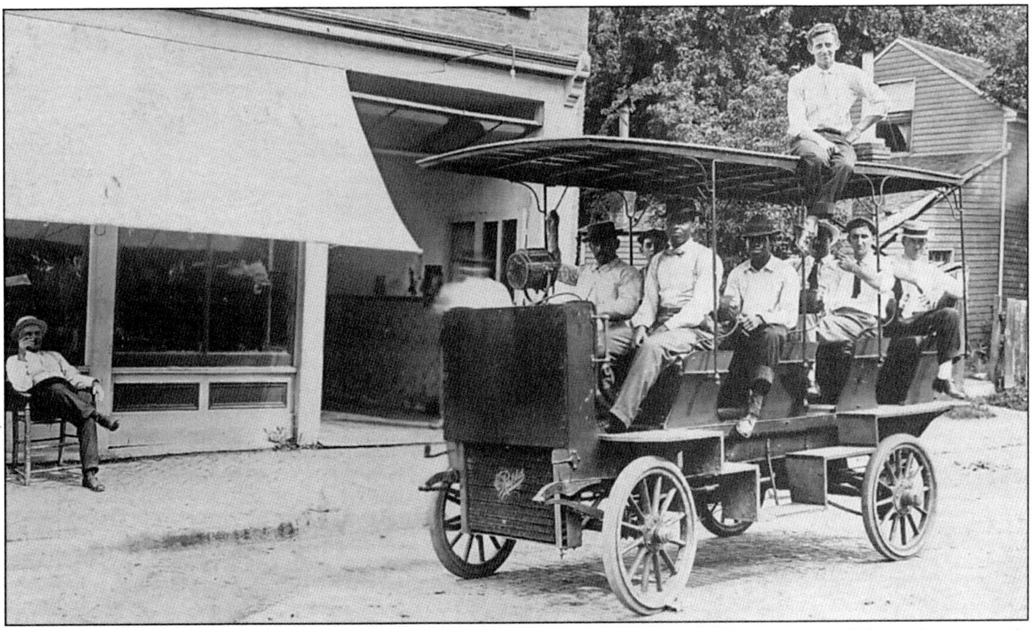

In the early 1900s, Nebraska City was already known as a tourist destination. This photograph depicts a sightseeing automobile. (Courtesy of Nebraska City Tourism and Commerce.)

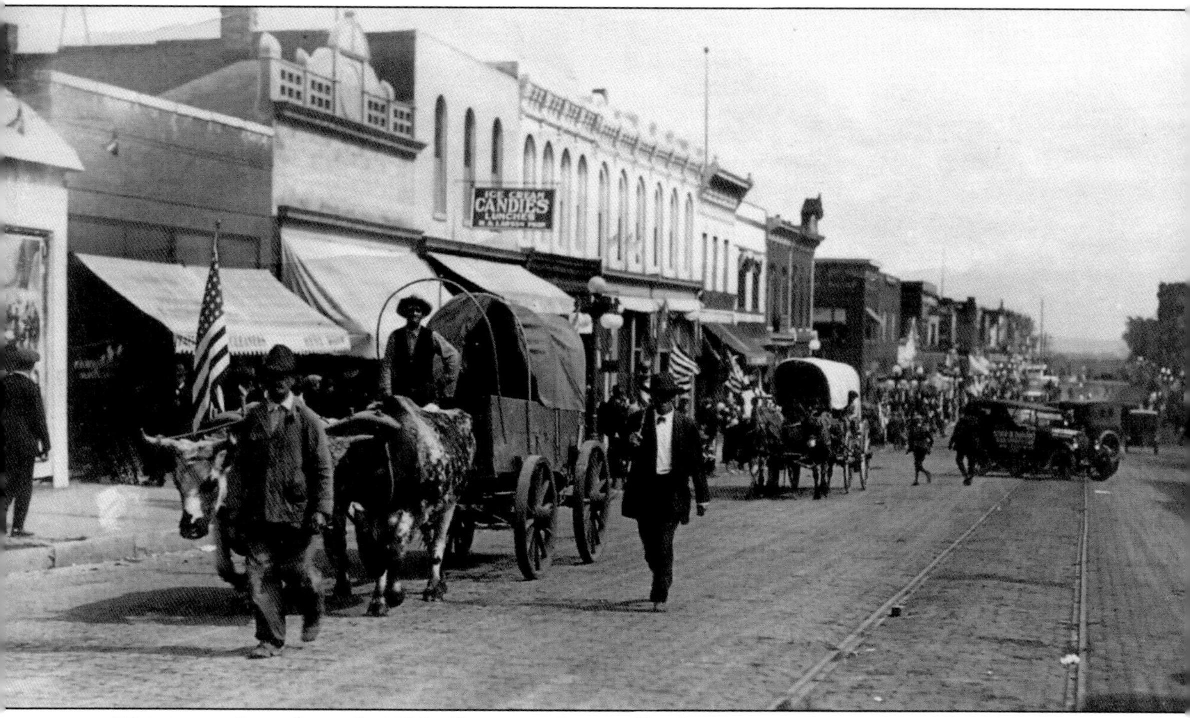

This image from the early 1900s illustrates the rapidly changing transportation options for Nebraska City residents. For a time, oxen and wagons shared the roadway with automobiles. (Courtesy of the Nebraska City Historical Society.)

Three

Downtown

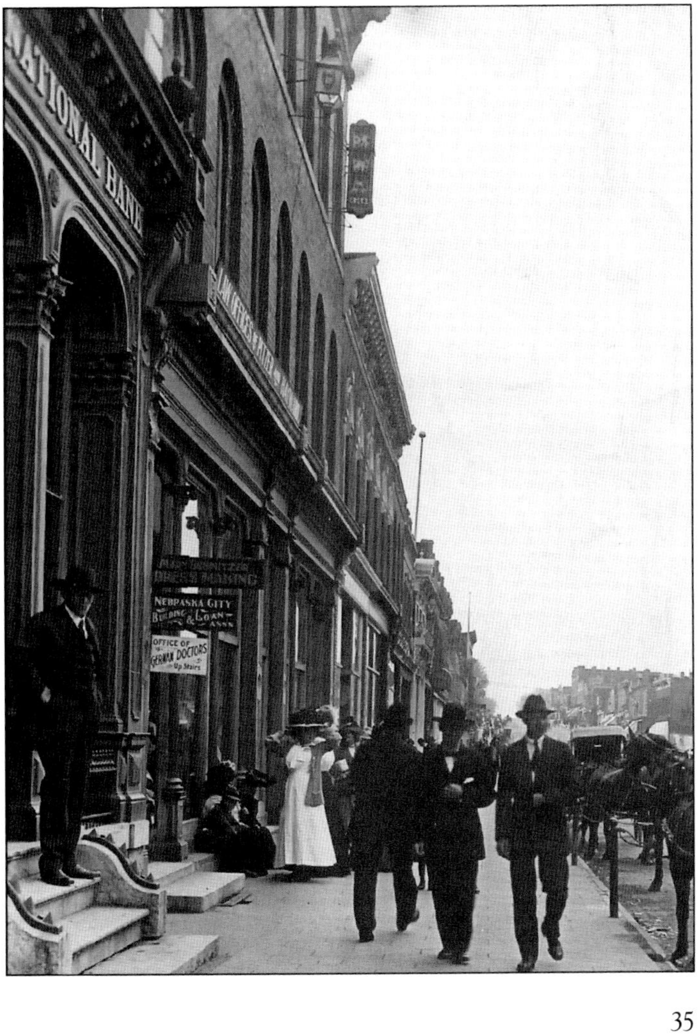

From its beginnings in the 1850s as the address of Fort Kearny, the main street of Nebraska City has been the core of the community. Called Main Street for many years, the road now known as Central Avenue has been home to banks, jewelry stores, salons, saloons, retailers, grocery stores, medical offices, and hotels. Pictured here in the 1880s is a bustling, thriving downtown street scene. (Courtesy of the Nebraska City Historical Society.)

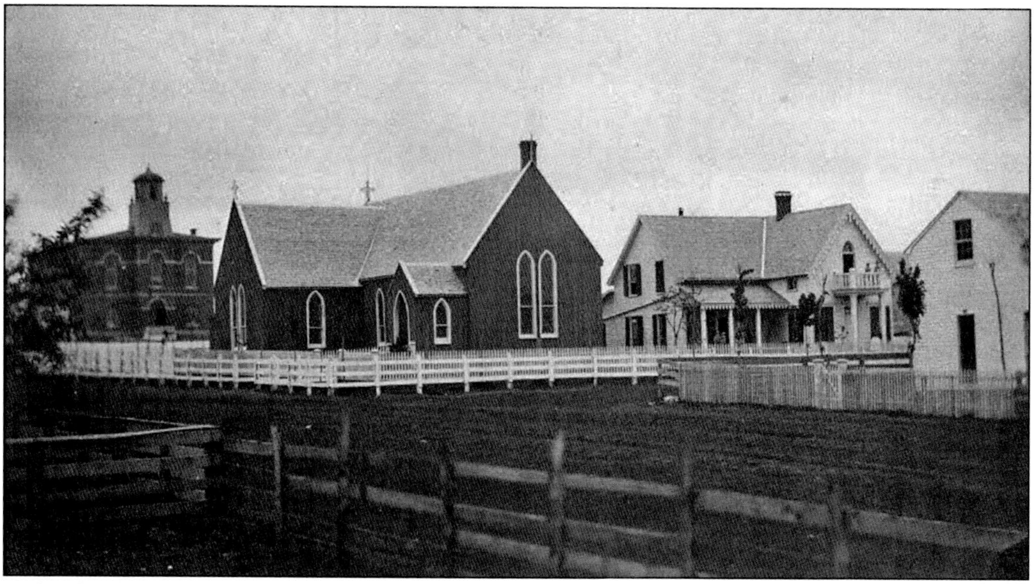

Before brick and paved roads, Nebraska City streets were muddy. The northwest corner of First Corso and Ninth Street, with St. Mary's Episcopal Church in the foreground, is pictured here. The Otoe County Courthouse is in the background. (Courtesy of the GAR Hall.)

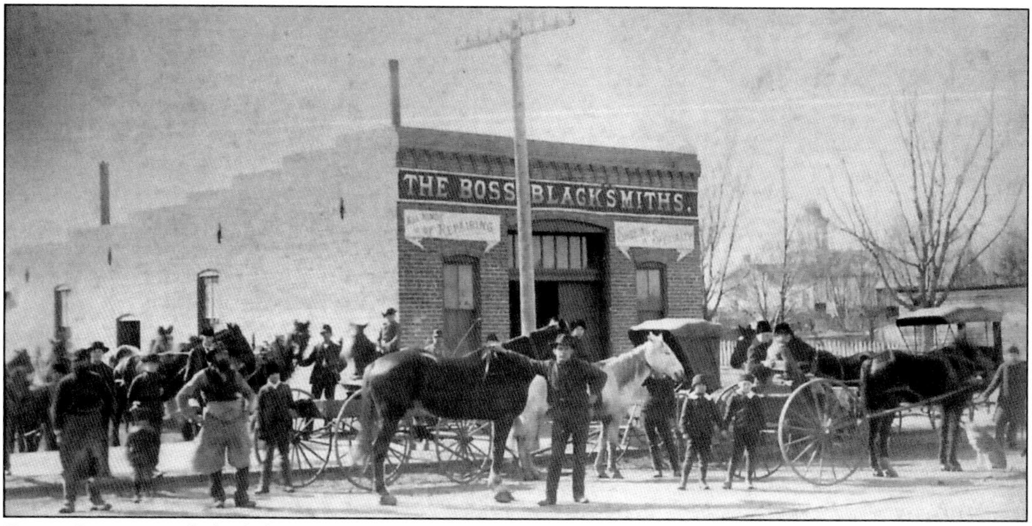

Since the automobile did not arrive in Nebraska City until after 1900, horses and carriages were the main form of transportation for the town's first 50 years. Pictured is the William Brower blacksmith shop. (Courtesy of the Nebraska City Historical Society.)

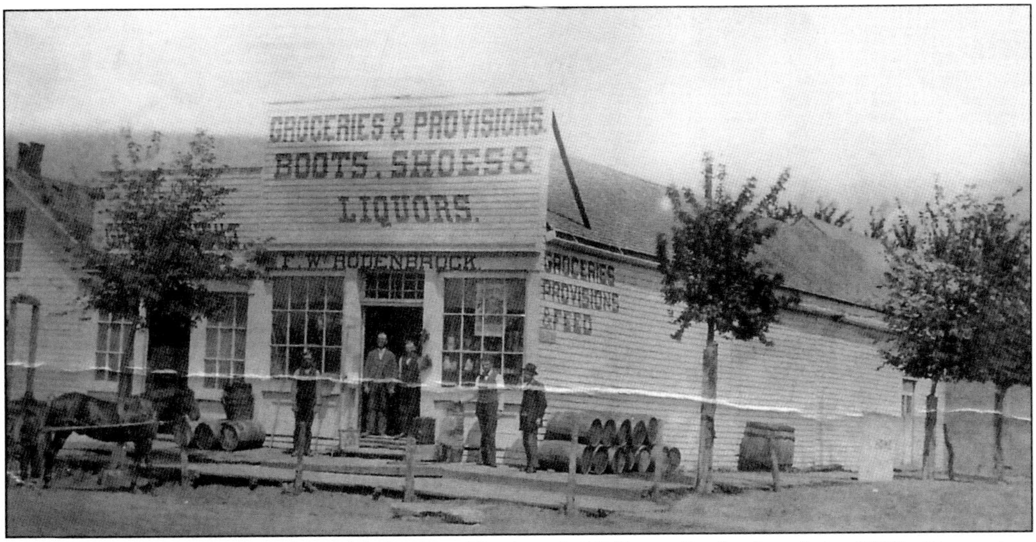

This store was owned and established by Frederick William Rodenbrock in 1873. Groceries, provisions, boots, shoes, and liquor were all important items to settlers traveling west as well as Nebraska City residents. In 1890, Rodenbrock built a new store at the northwest corner of Twelfth Street and Central Avenue. (Courtesy of the Nebraska City Historical Society.)

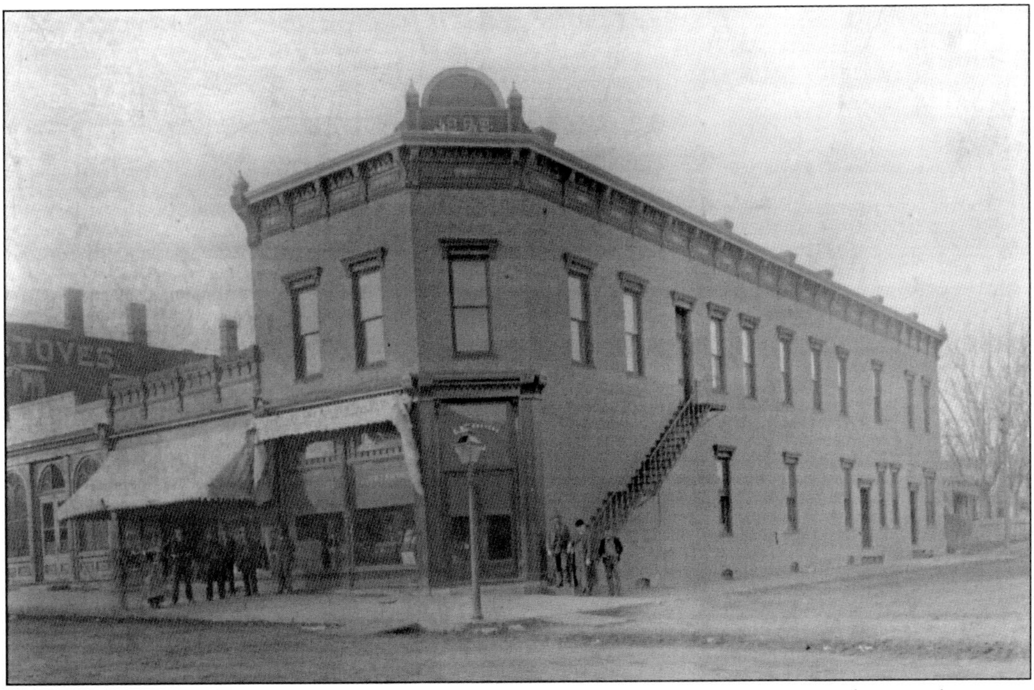

Built in 1889, the imposing structure on the northwest corner of Ninth Street and Central Avenue was home to Karstens Furniture and Undertaking. While that may seem like a strange pairing to people today, historically, undertakers made coffins, so it was a natural fit to include furniture crafting and sales to their business. (Courtesy of the Nebraska City Historical Society.)

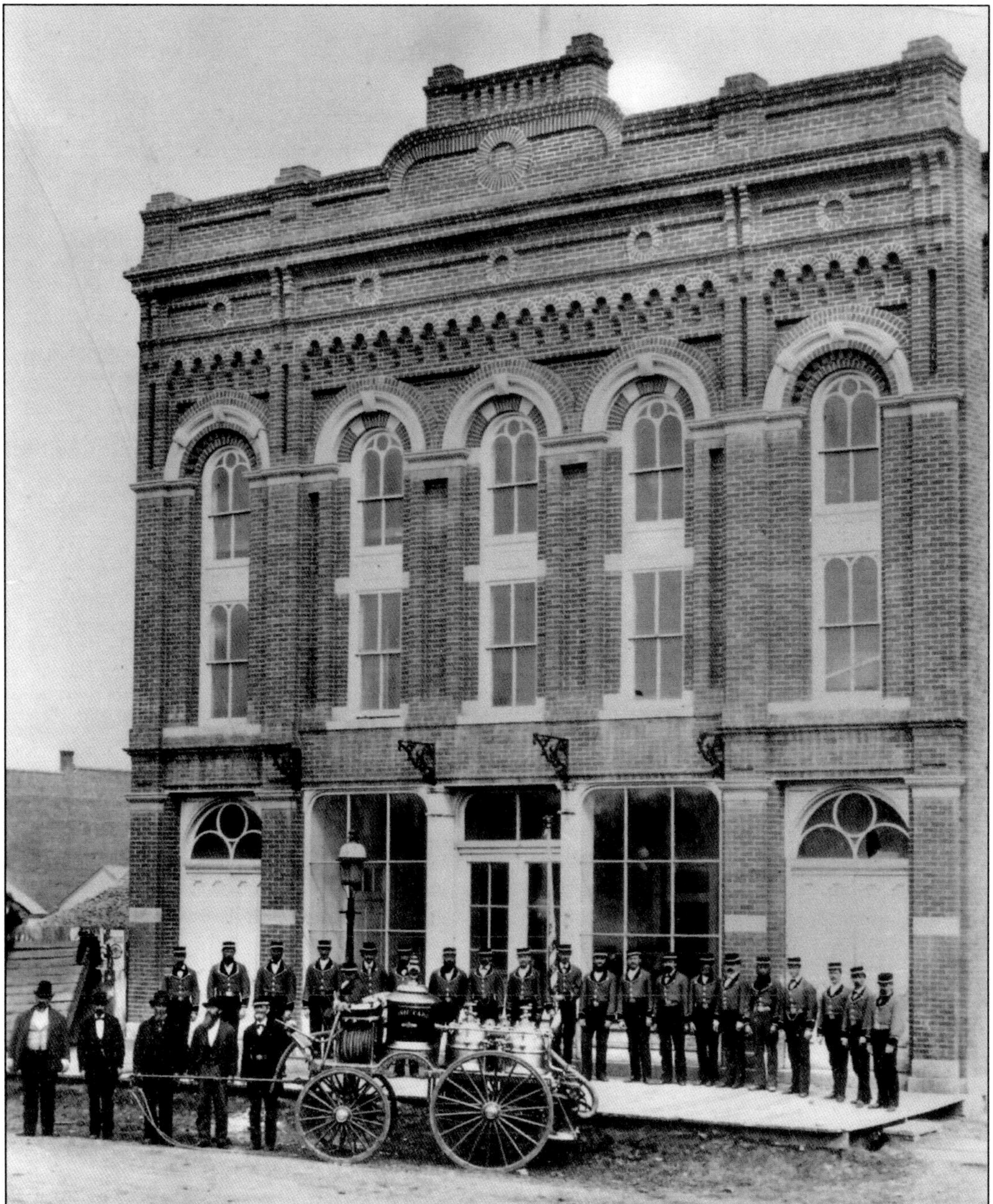

The German Opera House, located on First Corso between Sixth and Seventh Streets, opened in 1873. Seating 600 spectators, the building witnessed many performances in its time, including a sharpshooting demonstration by Buffalo Bill Cody. The opera house was sponsored by the German Turner Society. (Courtesy of the Nebraska City Historical Society.)

Located next to the opera house on the northwest corner of Sixth Street and First Corso was the Overland Theatre. A newspaper account of the opening night in December 1897 reported, "From the daintily carved screens that enclose the boxes to the broad relief frieze of balcony front and arching molds of the proscenium there is a refinement and harmony of detail and color that will delight the eye for all time." (Courtesy of Arbor Lodge.)

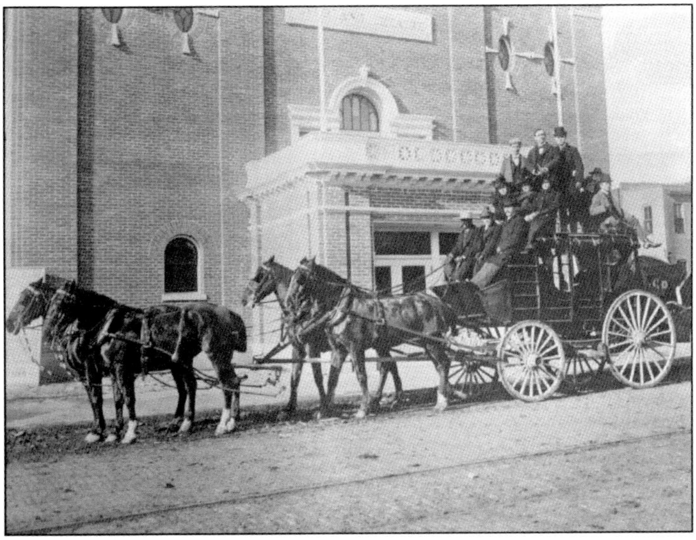

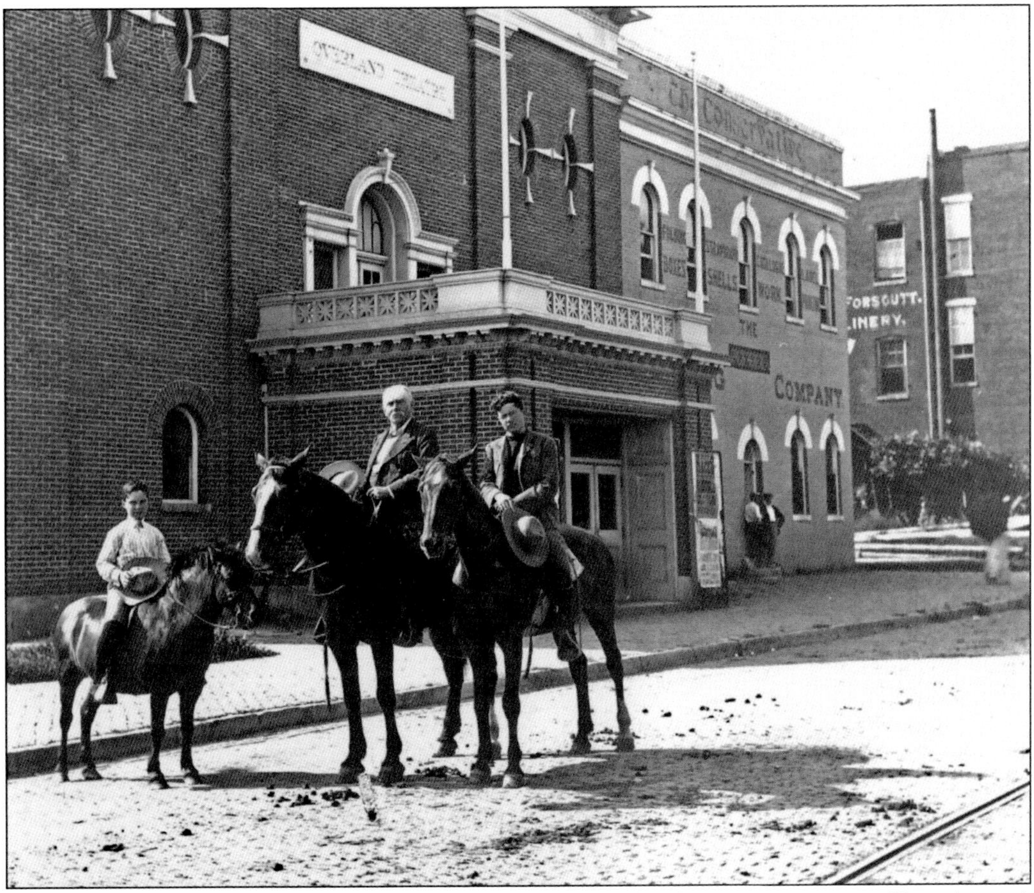

The Overland Theatre was funded by the J. Sterling Morton family. Morton is pictured here (center) with grandsons Wirt (left) and Sterling. The richly appointed Overland served as a playhouse, a burlesque theater, and finally a movie house. Abandoned in 1938, the building burned down in 1943. (Courtesy of Arbor Lodge.)

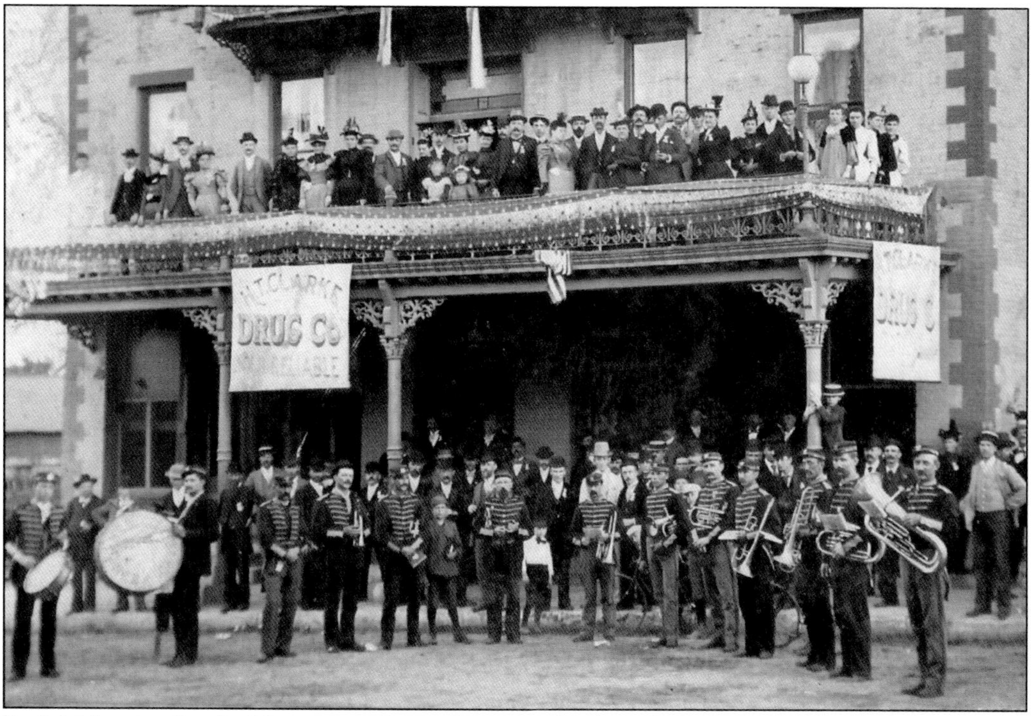

Early Nebraska City buildings varied in architectural style. While there were plenty of log cabins, there were also many brick and stone structures. Soon, builders started to experiment with different architectural styles such as Greek Revival, Italianate, Romanesque, Gothic, Neo-Colonial, and especially Victorian, as evidenced here by the Seymour House on Central Avenue between Fourth and Fifth Streets. (Courtesy of the Nebraska City Historical Society.)

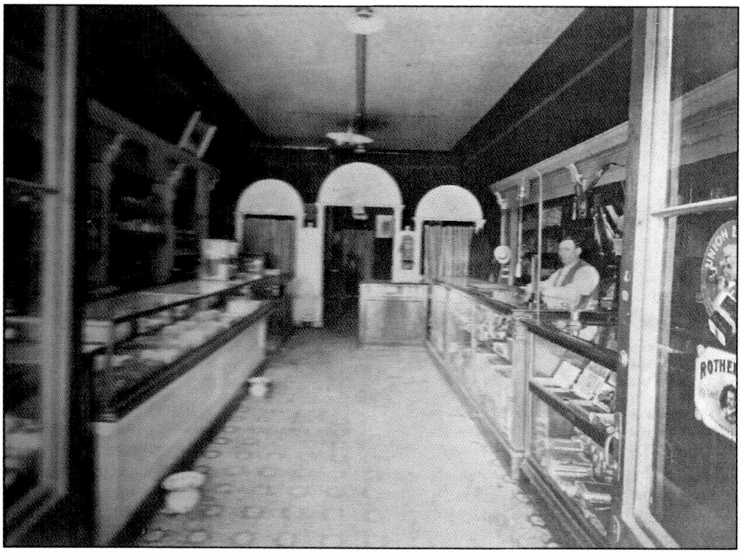

Nebraska City boasted several cigar factories in the 1800s, with the first one opening in 1867. The Charles Shaw Cigar Store was located downtown. (Courtesy of the Nebraska City Museum of Firefighting.)

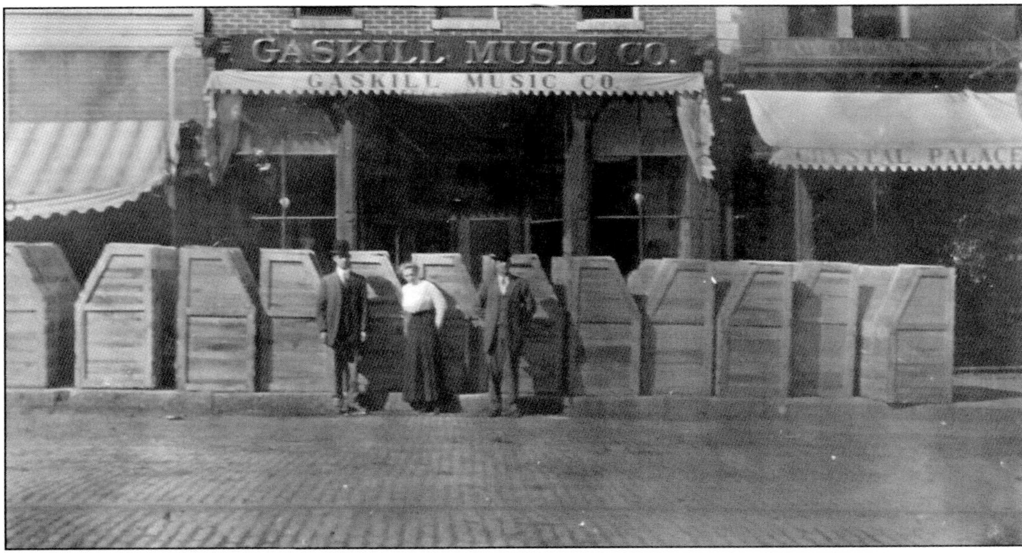

The early settlers of Nebraska City did not wish to live without some of the modern conveniences they knew from back east. Above, the Gaskill Music Company welcomes a shipment of pianos. The Gaskill Music Company not only stocked pianos, but also sold jewelry. (Both courtesy of the Nebraska City Historical Society.)

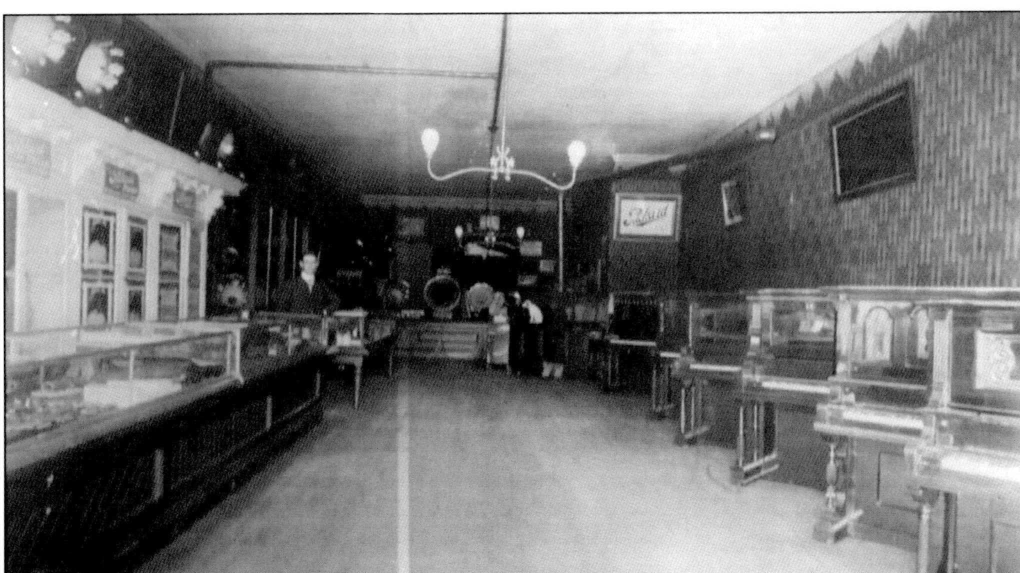

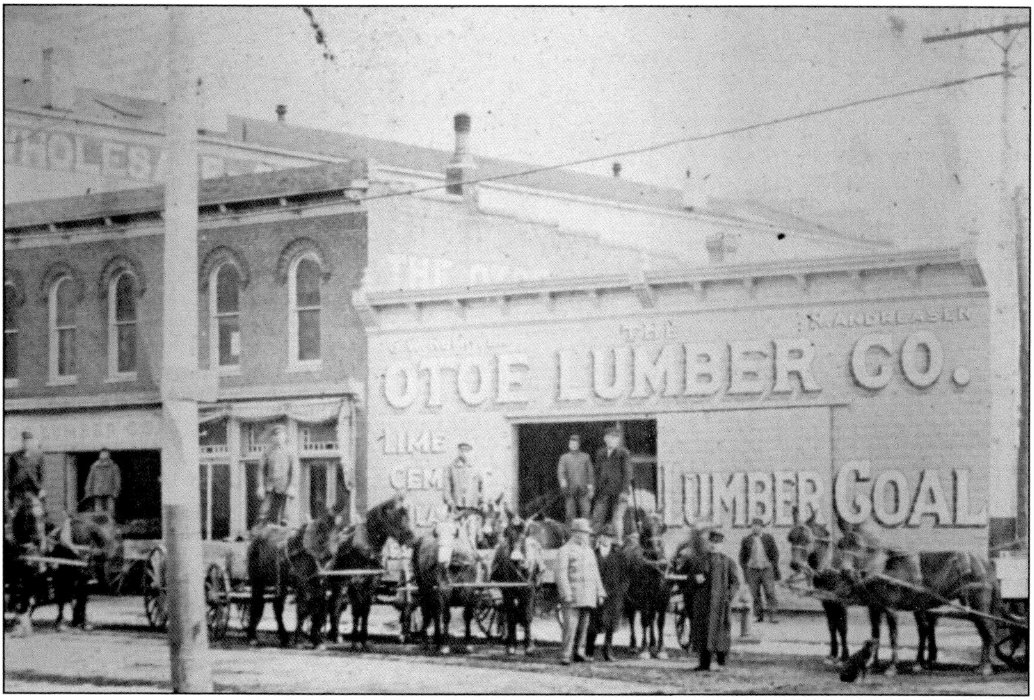

As the Nebraska Territory opened up, there were four distinct settlements with their own business and residential areas that emerged at this location. In 1858, those four towns—Nebraska City, Kearney City, South Nebraska City, and Prairie City—merged together to form one community: Nebraska City. Downtown businesses tried to meet every need of settlers in the area. Lumberyards such as the Otoe Lumber Company, pictured here at the northeast corner Sixth Street and First Corso, were common. (Courtesy of the Arbor Day Foundation.)

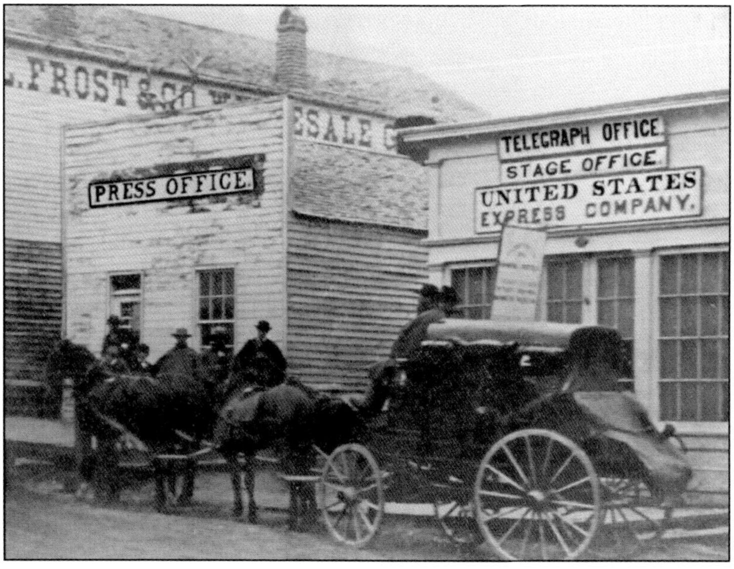

One of the first businesses in Nebraska City was the *News*, a newspaper that started in 1855. Three years later, the *Press* began publication. There were several other periodicals to come and go over the next few decades, including a German newspaper, but none lasted. In 1925, the *News* and the *Press* joined together become the *Nebraska City News Press*. (Courtesy of the Nebraska City Historical Society.)

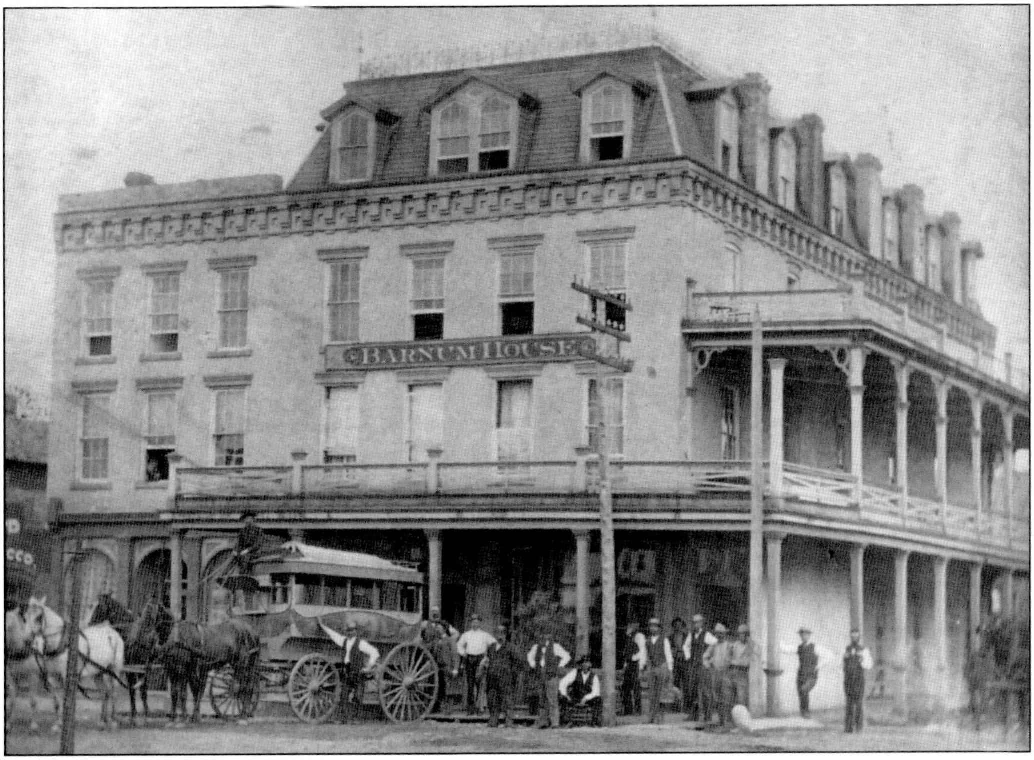

Downtown Nebraska City boasted numerous hotels during the early years, including the Morton House (later renamed the Seymour House and then the Frontier Hotel), the Marcus Hotel, and the Grand Hotel. The Barnum House (pictured), on the southeast corner of Eighth Street and Central Avenue, was a four-story brick hotel with 50 rooms. It was renamed the Watson Hotel and was severely damaged by a nighttime fire in 1911. It was condemned and torn down. (Courtesy of the Nebraska City Historical Society.)

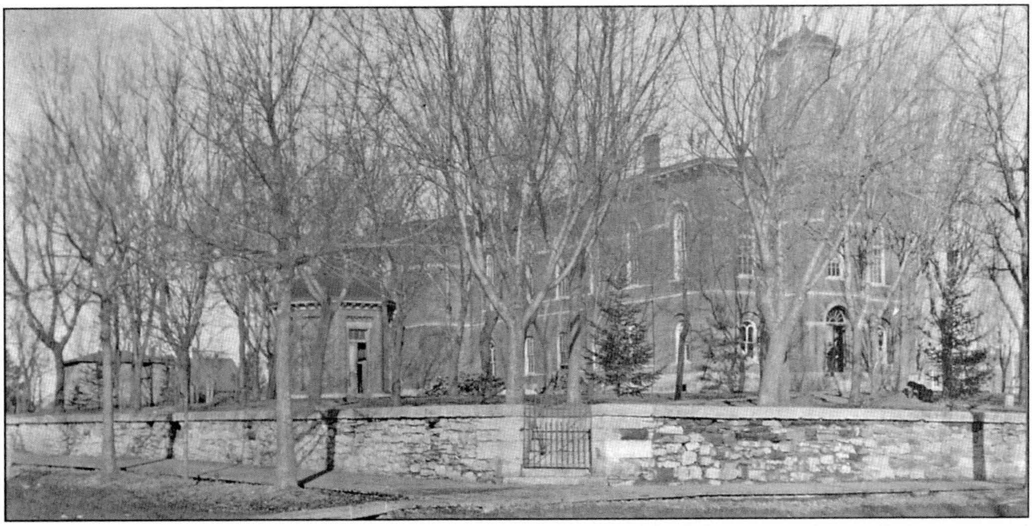

The Otoe County Courthouse was built on a whole city block between Central Avenue and First Corso and Tenth and Eleventh Streets. The large grassy lawn and grown trees beautified downtown. (Courtesy of the Nebraska City Museum of Firefighting.)

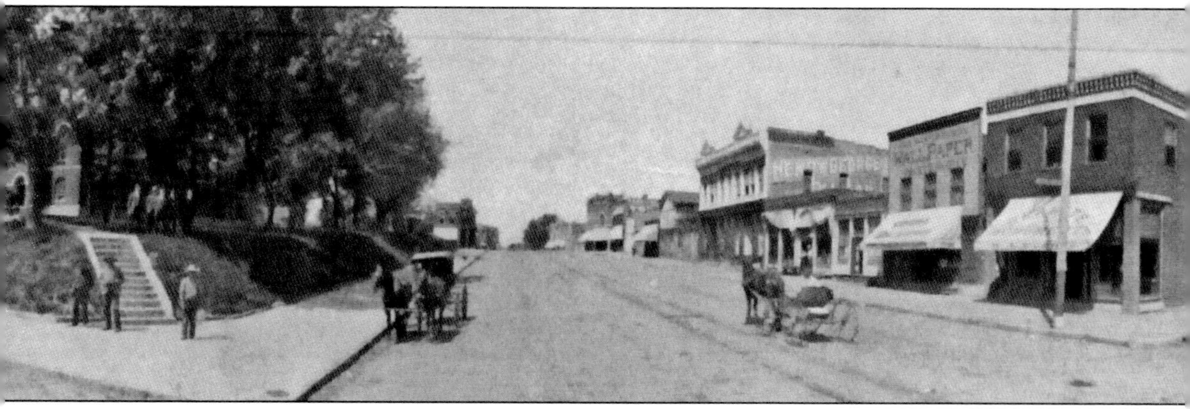

This panoramic photograph was captured in 1908. The photographer is standing in the street at the intersection of Central Avenue and Tenth Street with the Otoe County Courthouse at the

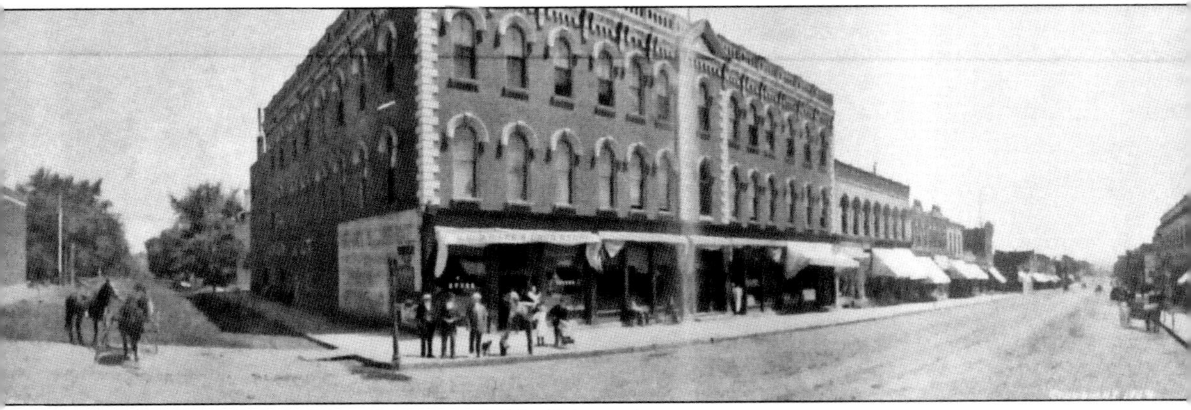

far left. (Courtesy of the Morton James Public Library.)

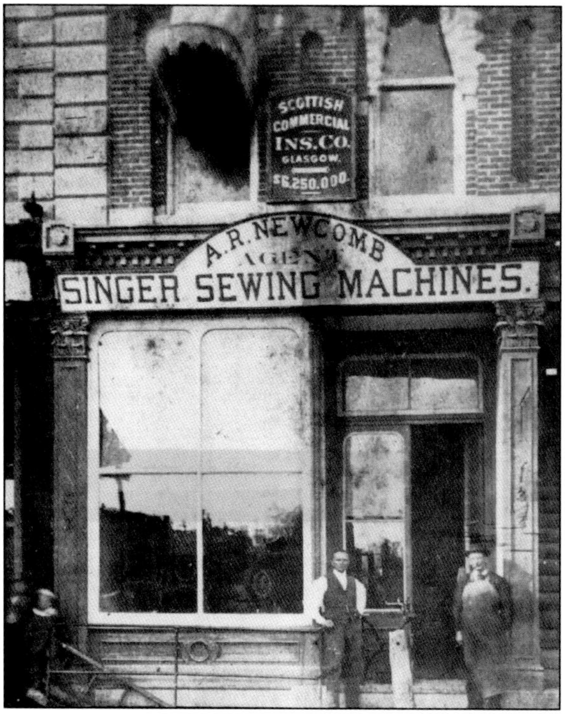

As Nebraska City grew and changed, the business landscape shifted as well. According to business directories from the late 1800s, Singer Sewing Machines relocated several times over the years, all up and down Central Avenue. (Courtesy of the Nebraska City Historical Society.)

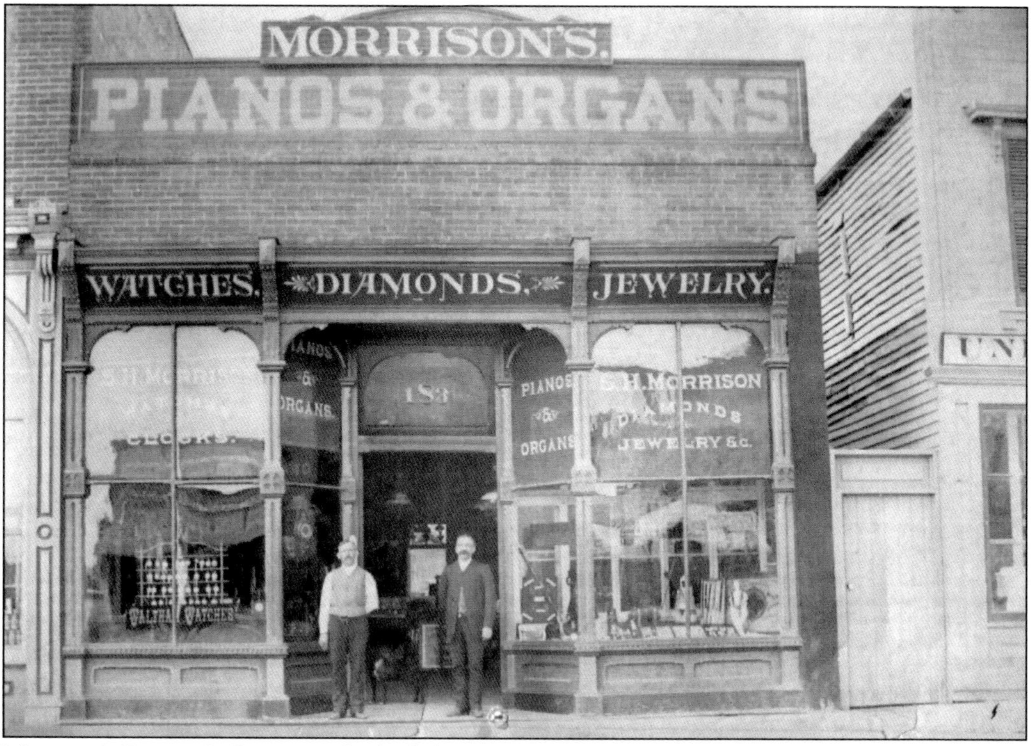

Morrison's Pianos & Organs embodied the entrepreneurial spirit of the Midwest. In addition to pianos and organs, it also sold watches, diamonds, jewelry, and clocks. (Courtesy of the Nebraska City Historical Society.)

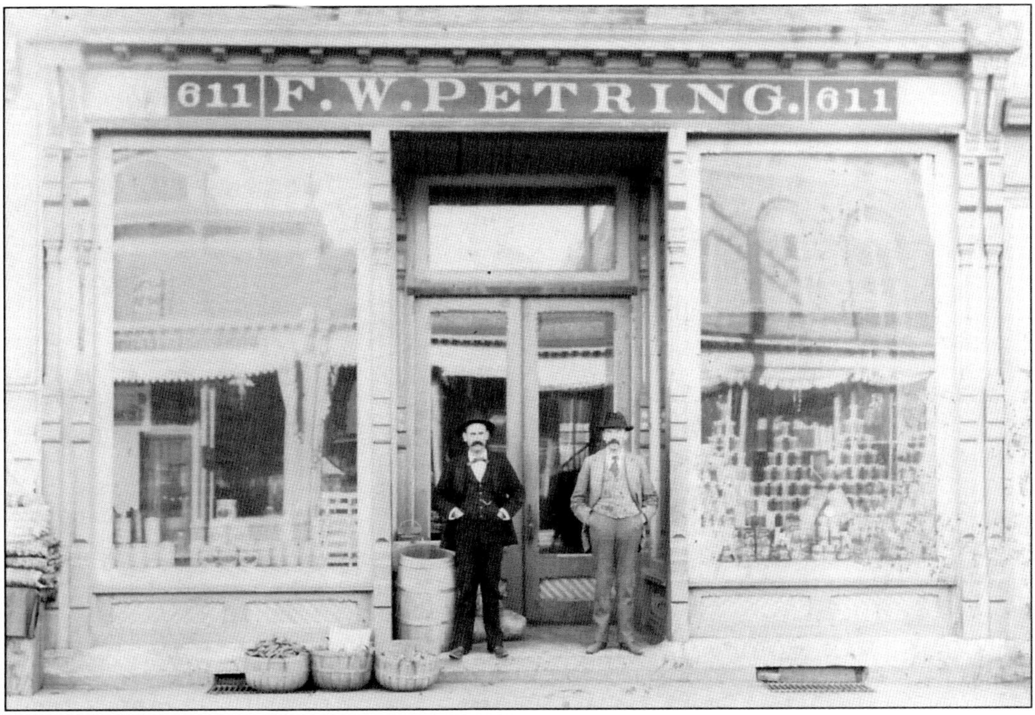

The Petrings were one the early families of Nebraska City. Throughout the years, they catered to the ever-changing population of the town by selling everything from produce (above) to auto parts (below). In 1860, Nebraska City was home to 1,922 residents. While some records say the population was up to 12,000 by 1890, others argue against that number, accusing town leaders of counting the graves in Wyuka Cemetery to pad numbers. By 1900, Nebraska City was one of the largest communities in the state, with a population of 7,380. It has averaged 7,000 residents since that time. (Both courtesy of the Nebraska City Historical Society.)

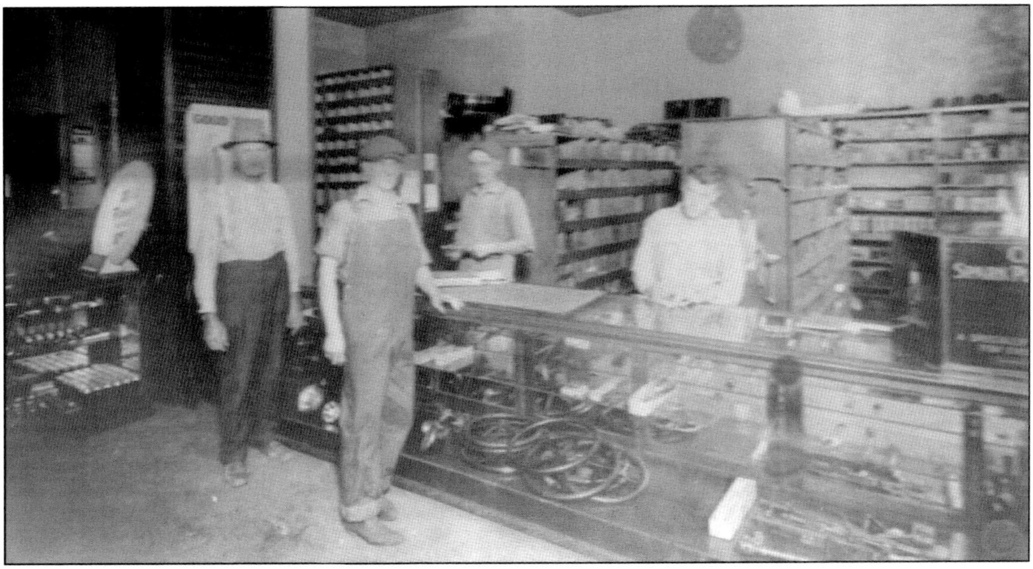

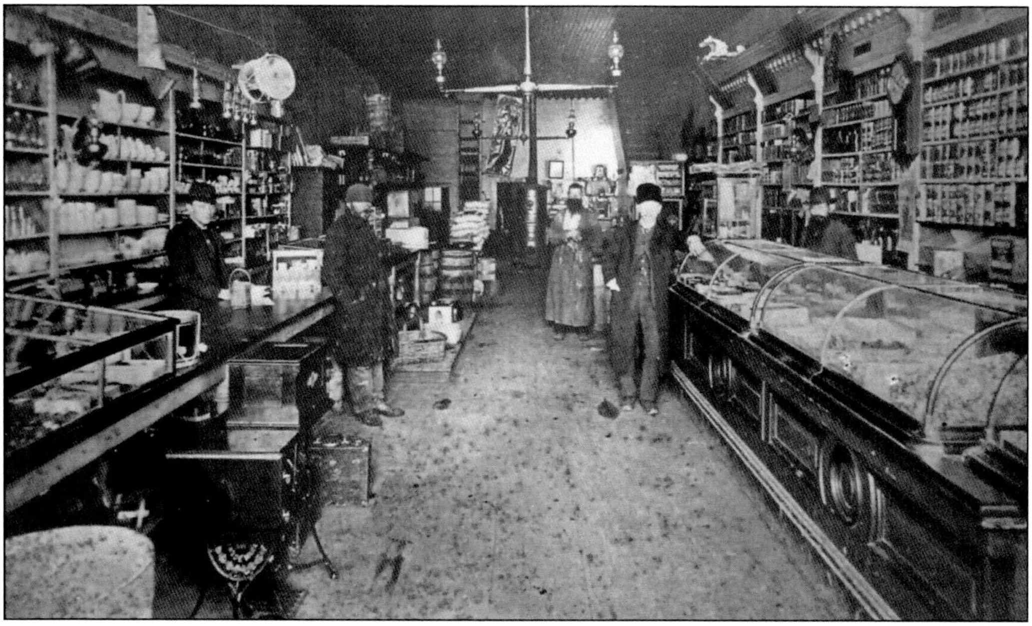

Many Nebraska City merchants volunteered their time to help the community. George Kees (far left) owned a general store and was a member of the Great Western Fire Company No. 1. (Courtesy of the Nebraska City Historical Society.)

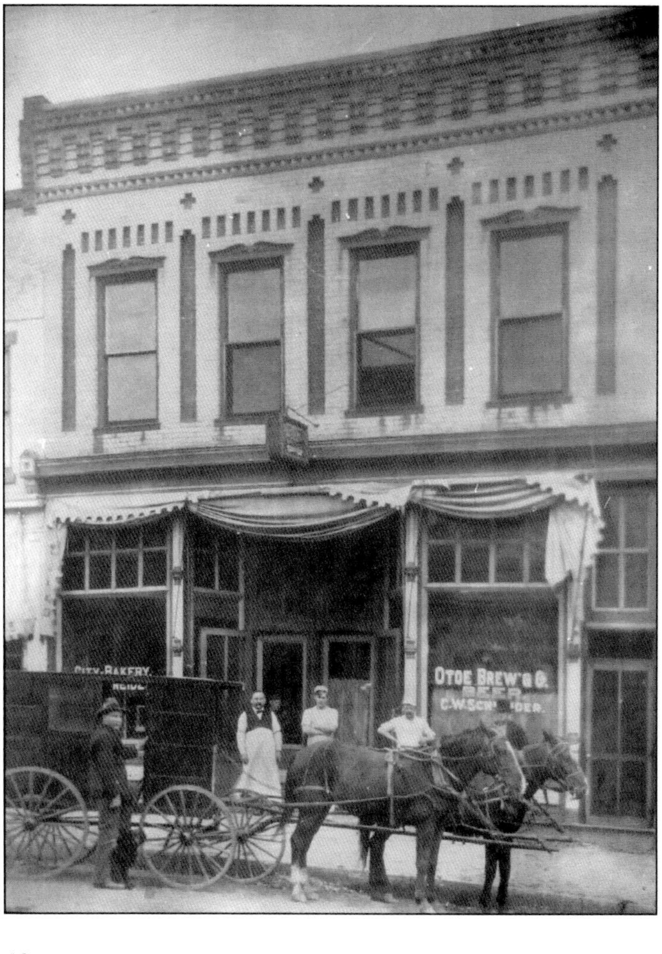

The Otoe County Bakery and the Otoe Brewing Company were next door to each other in downtown Nebraska City. While most businesses took the name of their proprietor, a few did pay homage to Indian tribes who once called the area home. (Courtesy of the Nebraska City Historical Society.)

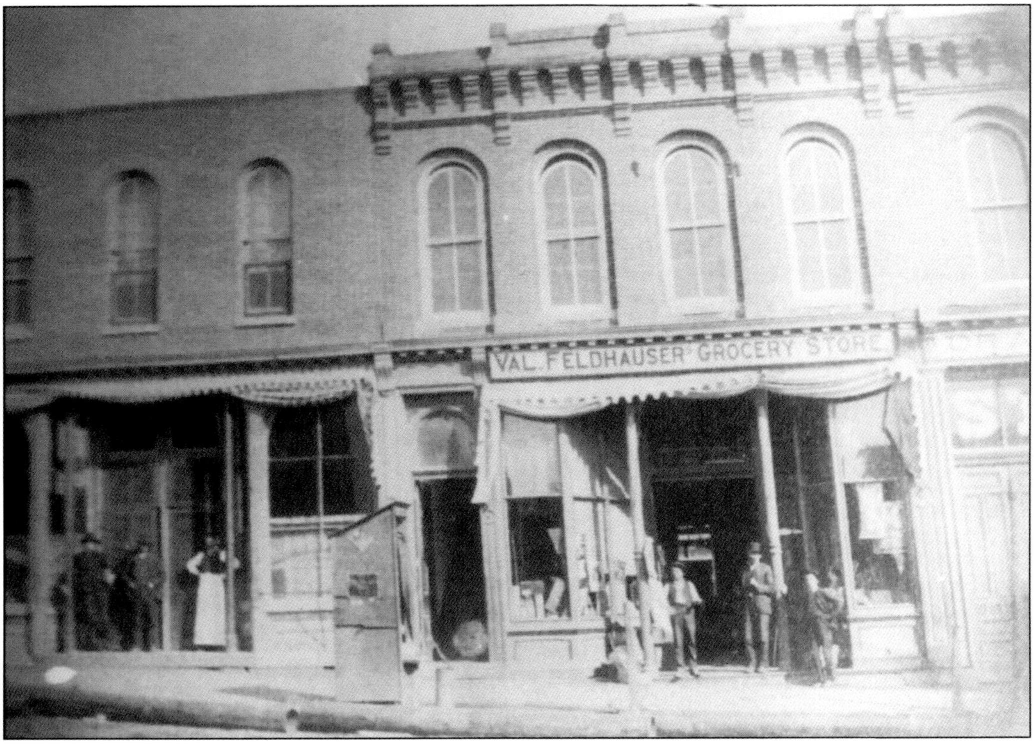

General stores and grocery stores were a necessity for early settlements. The Valentine Feldhauser grocery store (above) was located at 812 Central Avenue. Feldhauser volunteered on the Otoe Hook and Ladder Company. (Both courtesy of the Nebraska City Historical Society.)

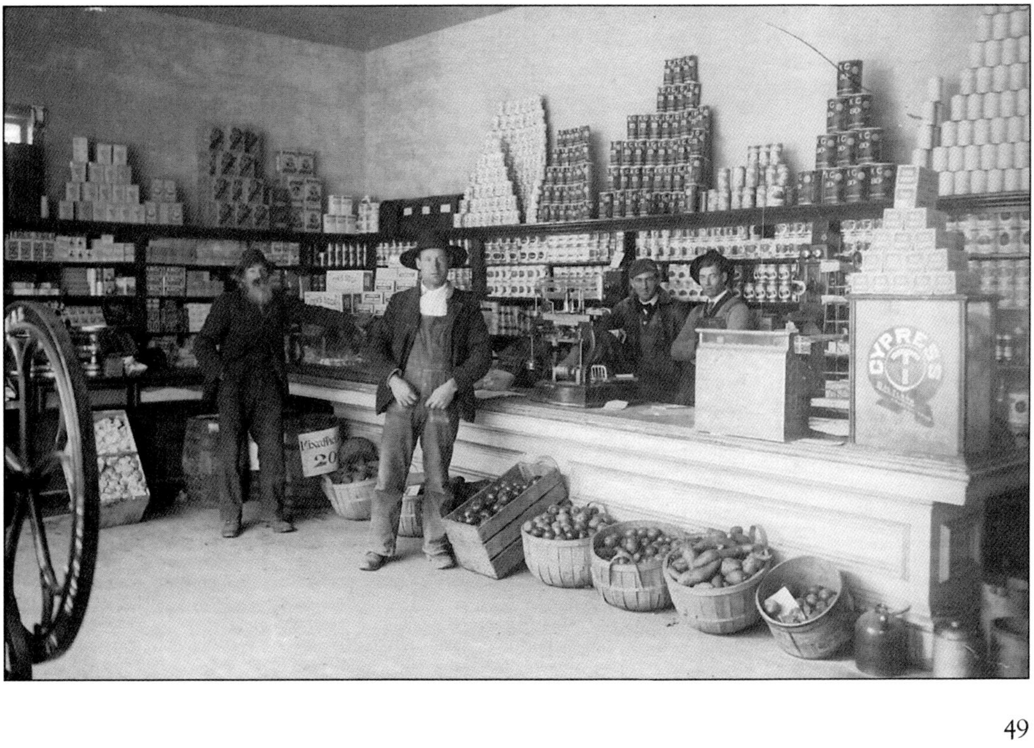

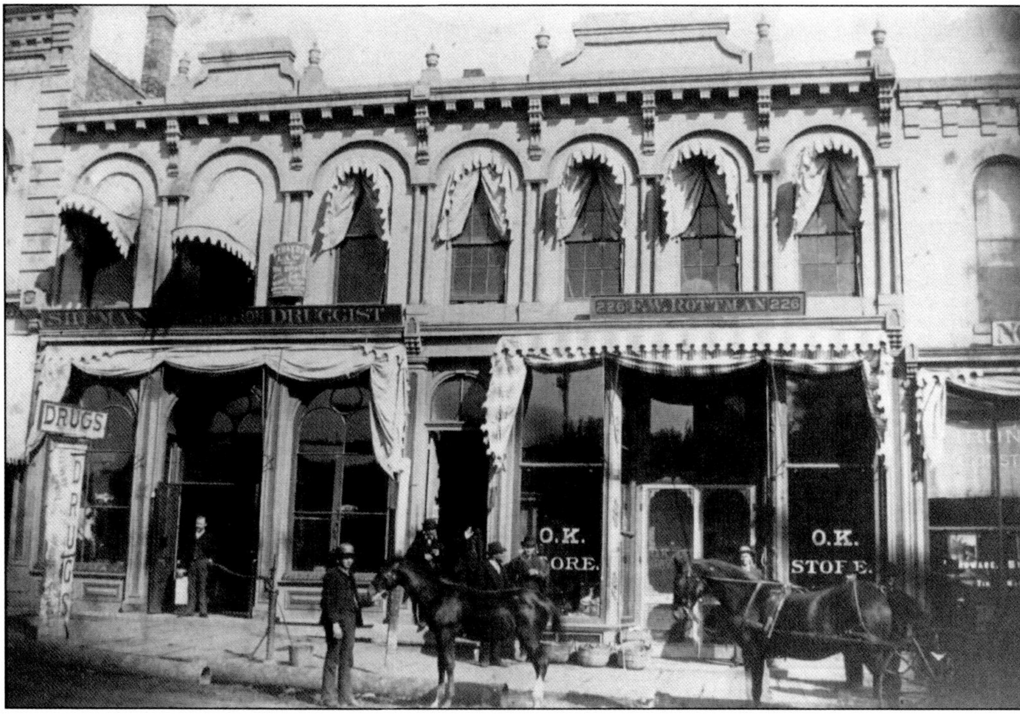

F.W. Rottman was a German immigrant and one of the early settlers of Nebraska City. His store sold groceries and general merchandise. Rottman was active in community affairs, serving as president of the Nebraska City Canning Company and director of the Otoe County Fair Association. While the store has an address of 226 Main Street, it was located on the north side of Central Avenue between Ninth and Tenth Streets. (Courtesy of the Nebraska City Historical Society.)

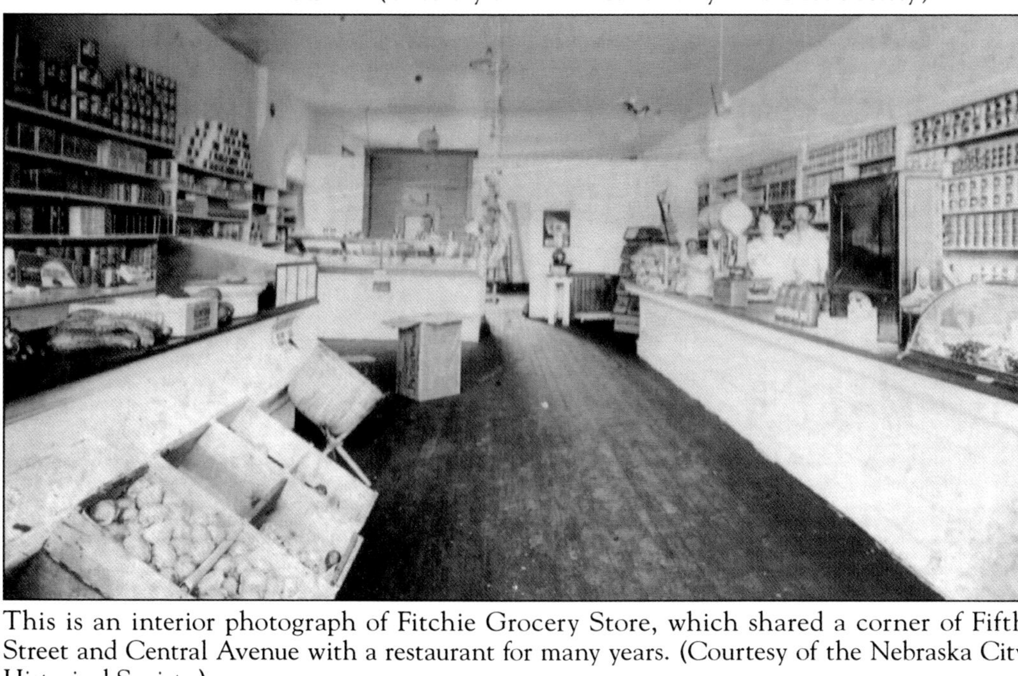

This is an interior photograph of Fitchie Grocery Store, which shared a corner of Fifth Street and Central Avenue with a restaurant for many years. (Courtesy of the Nebraska City Historical Society.)

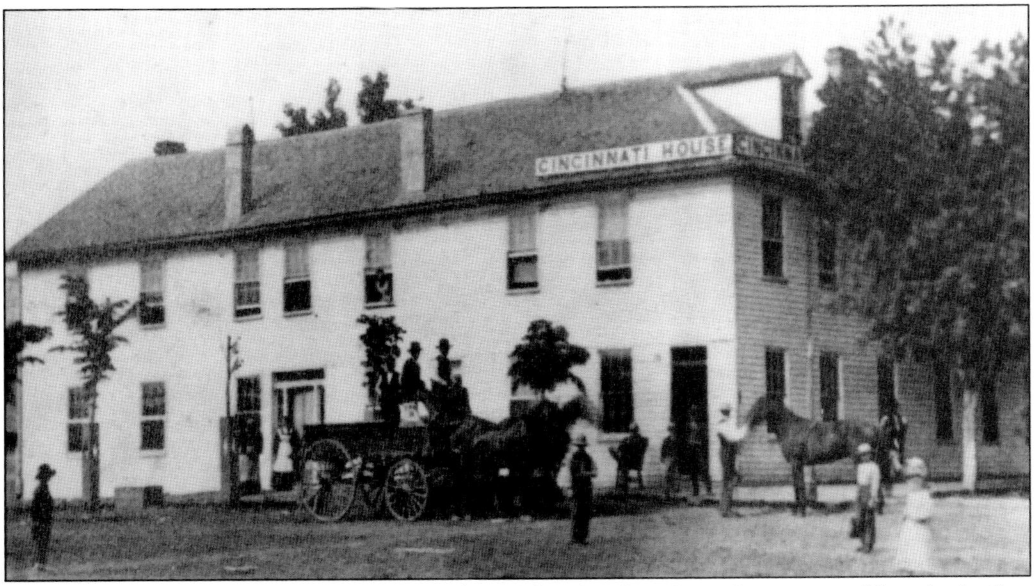

When John Hamlin and his family moved to Nebraska City from Cincinnati, Ohio, he built a windowless, floorless log cabin near Eighth Street and First Corso. As the years went by, Hamlin added on to the structure when he could. By 1866, it was a wood-framed hotel named the Cincinnati House. Part of the structure is still standing today and serves as a retail space. (Courtesy of the Nebraska City Historical Society.)

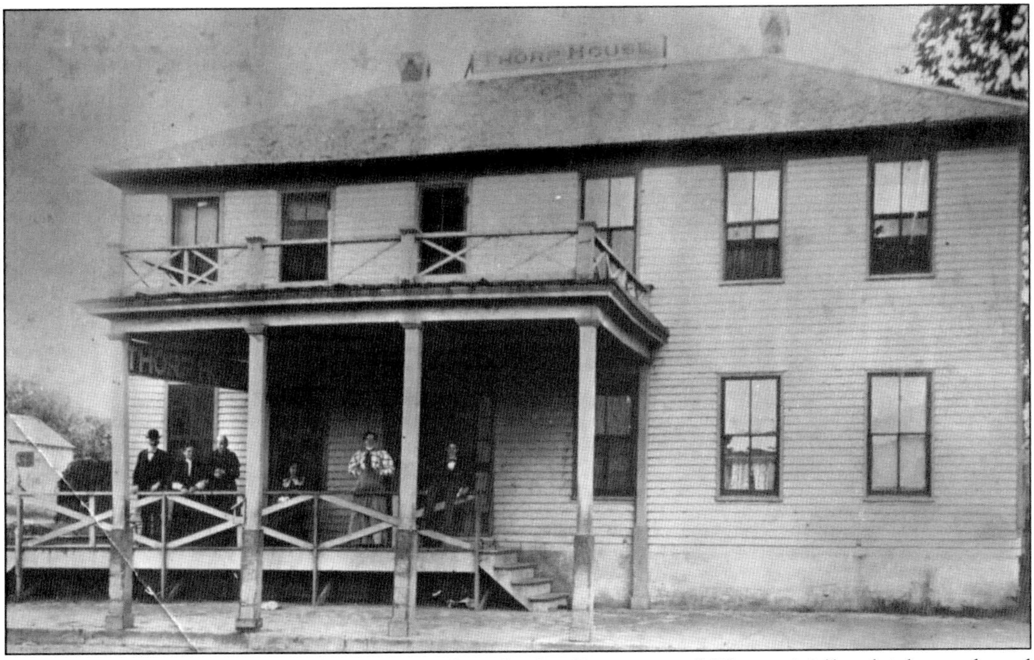

The name Thorp was mainly associated with the Pinney and Thorp Mill, which produced 5,000 barrels of flour per year. The mill burned in 1877. (Courtesy of the Nebraska City Historical Society.)

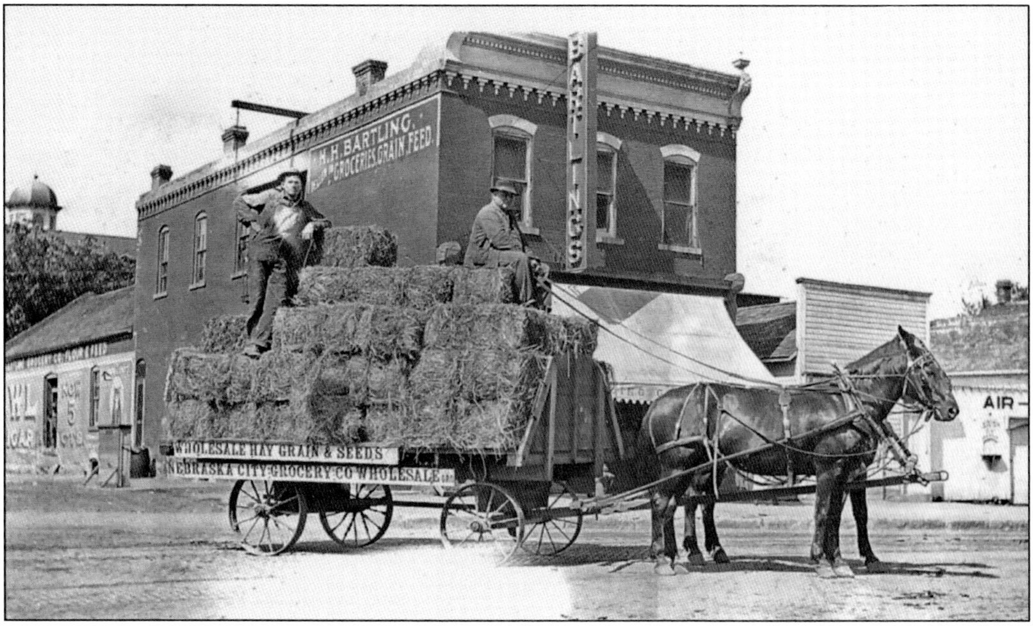

Herman Henry Bartling, a German immigrant, owned and operated a general store at Eleventh Street and Central Avenue for many years, beginning in 1875. Bartling served the community as mayor of Nebraska City and also served on the council of the Evangelical Lutheran Church. (Above, courtesy of Nebraska City Tourism and Commerce; below, the Nebraska City Historical Society.)

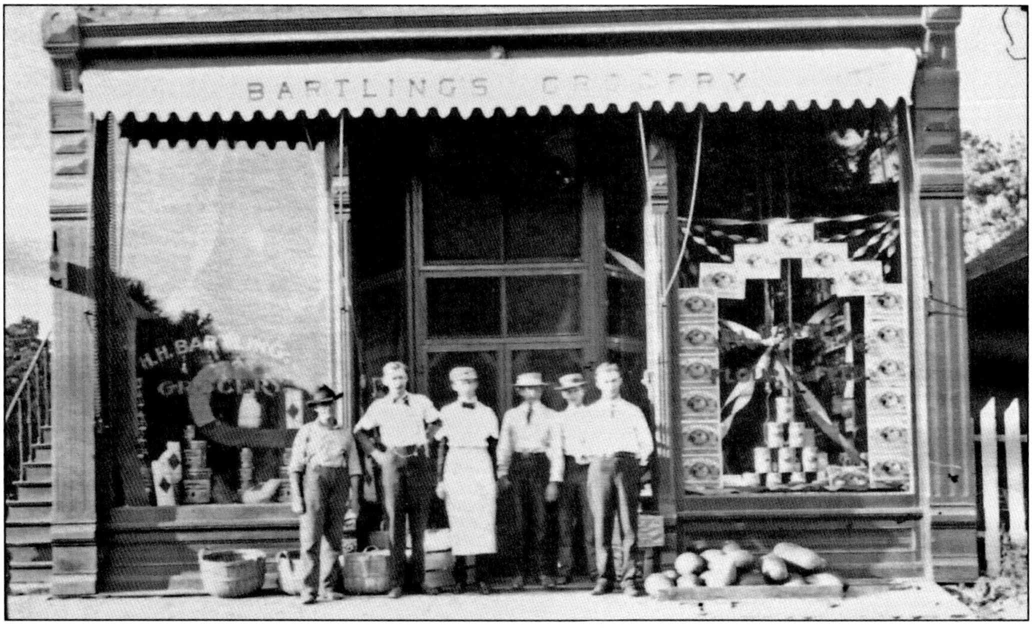

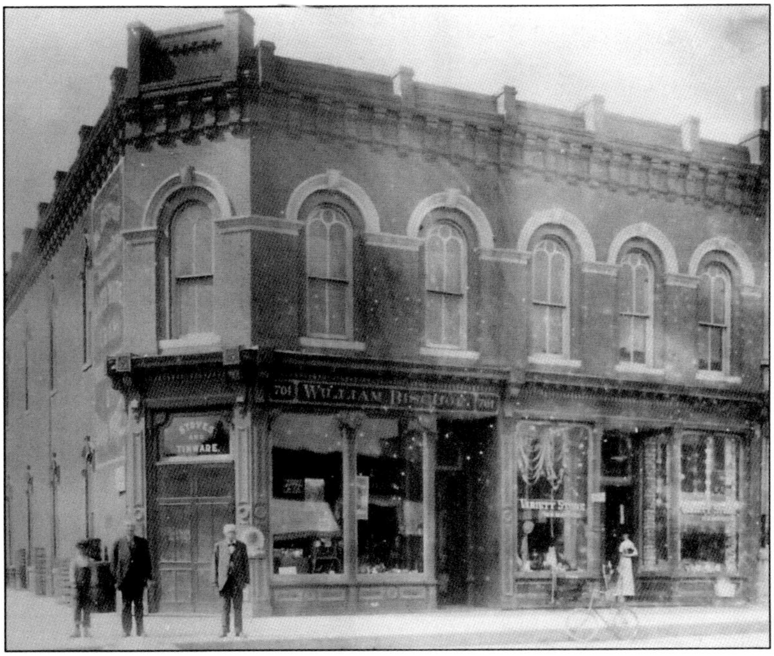

The structure on the southwest corner of Seventh Street and Central Avenue is easily recognizable to current residents and visitors. It was built as a hardware store in the late 1860s for William Bischof, who worked as a freighter when he first came to Nebraska City. Bischof's closed in 1978 after more than 100 years in business; the building is still used as a retail store today. (Courtesy of the Nebraska City Historical Society.)

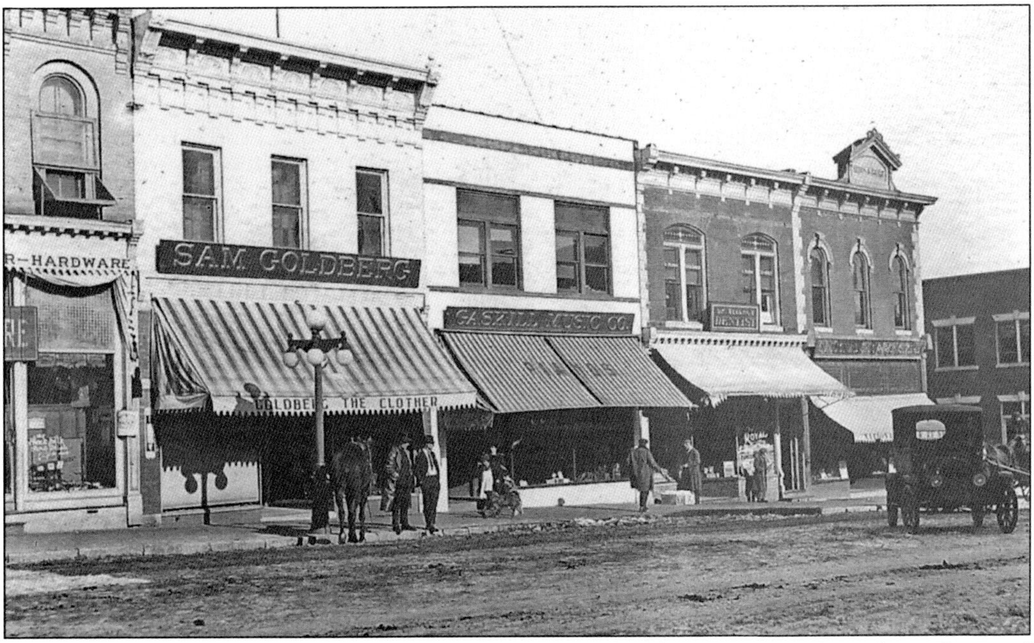

Shops in downtown Nebraska City catered to every need of the community's residents. Pictured here on the north side of Central Avenue between Eighth and Ninth Street is a hardware store, clothing store, music store, and a dentist. Apartments were located on the second floors. (Courtesy of Dorris Sackles.)

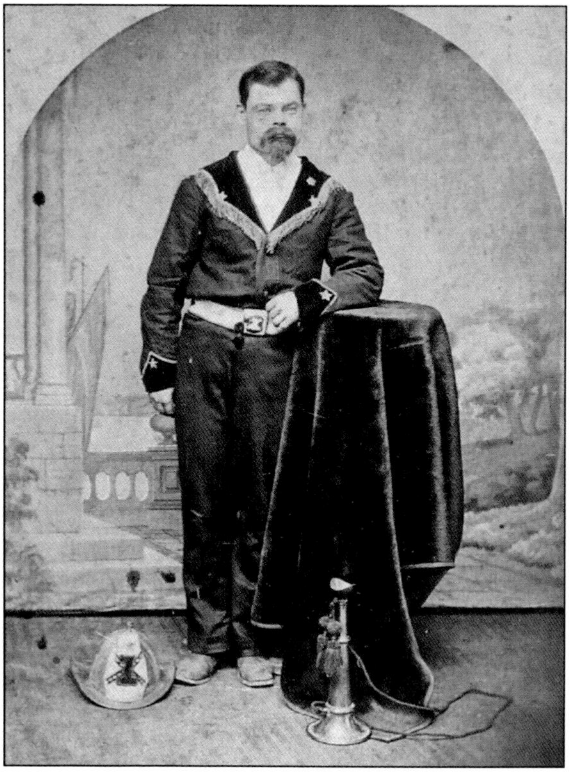

One early businessman was J.W. Faunce, pictured here in 1873 as a member of the Otoe Hook and Ladder Company. Faunce and McNamara was one of many general goods stores in downtown Nebraska City. (At left, courtesy of the Nebraska City Museum of Firefighting; below, the Nebraska City Historical Society.)

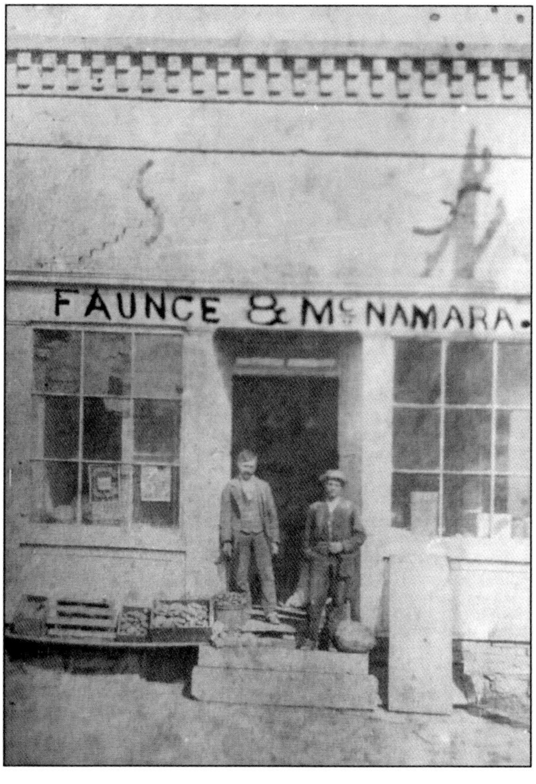

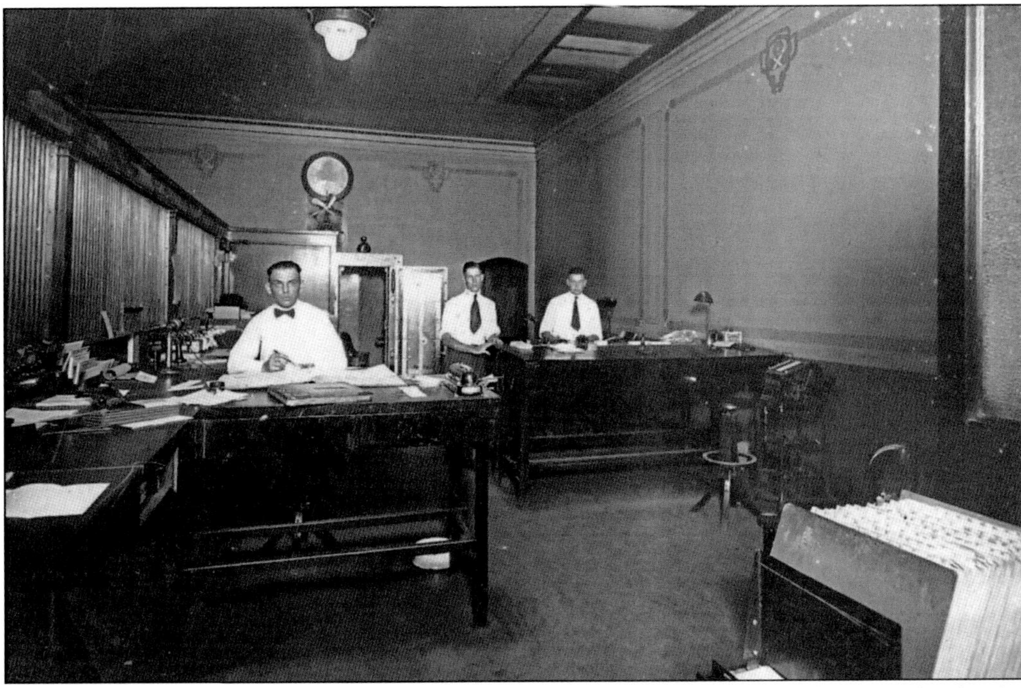

The oldest bank in Nebraska City, still in existence and the second oldest in the state of Nebraska, is Arbor Bank. When it was first organized in 1865, it was called Otoe County National Bank and intended to help finance freighting operations. This photograph is of the interior of Otoe County National Bank in 1922. (Courtesy of the Kimmel Foundation.)

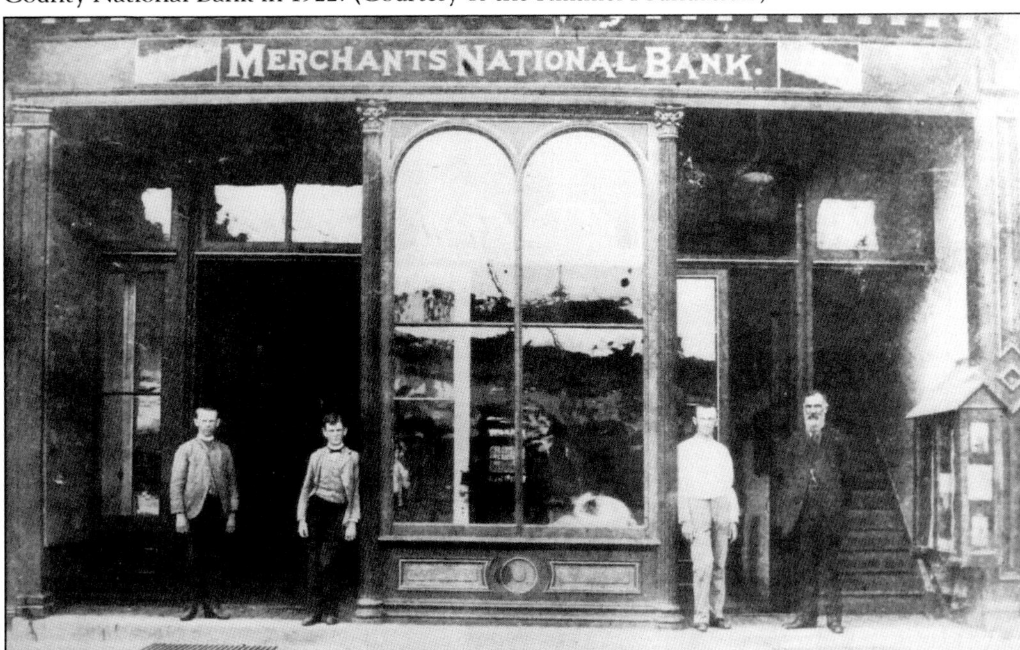

Merchants National Bank was another early bank of Nebraska City and was established in 1857. It is pictured here in August 1886. (Courtesy of the Nebraska City Historical Society.)

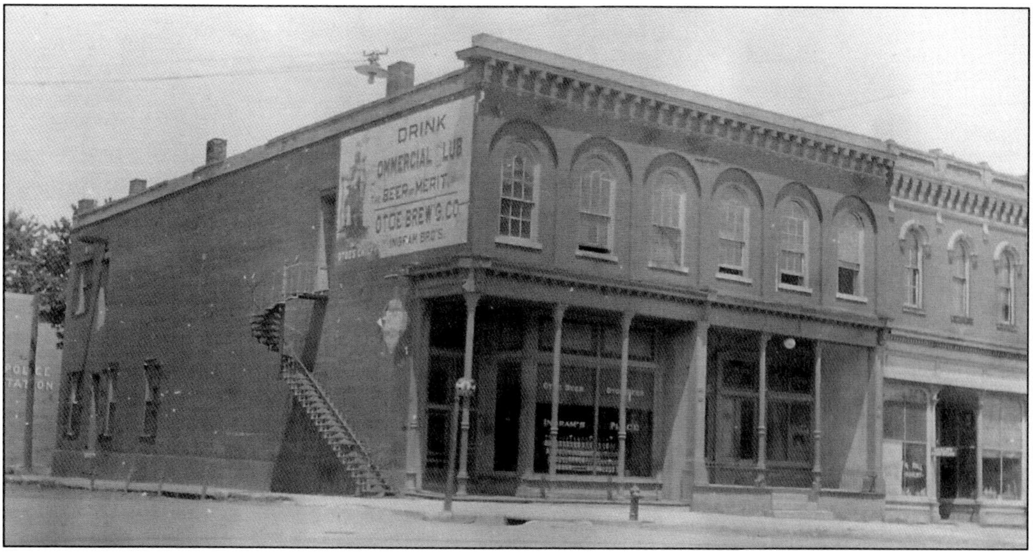

This 1900 photograph shows the building at 524 Central Avenue, home of the Otoe Brewing Company at the time. Decades later, the top floor of the building served as the city's roller rink. (Courtesy of the Nebraska City Historical Society.)

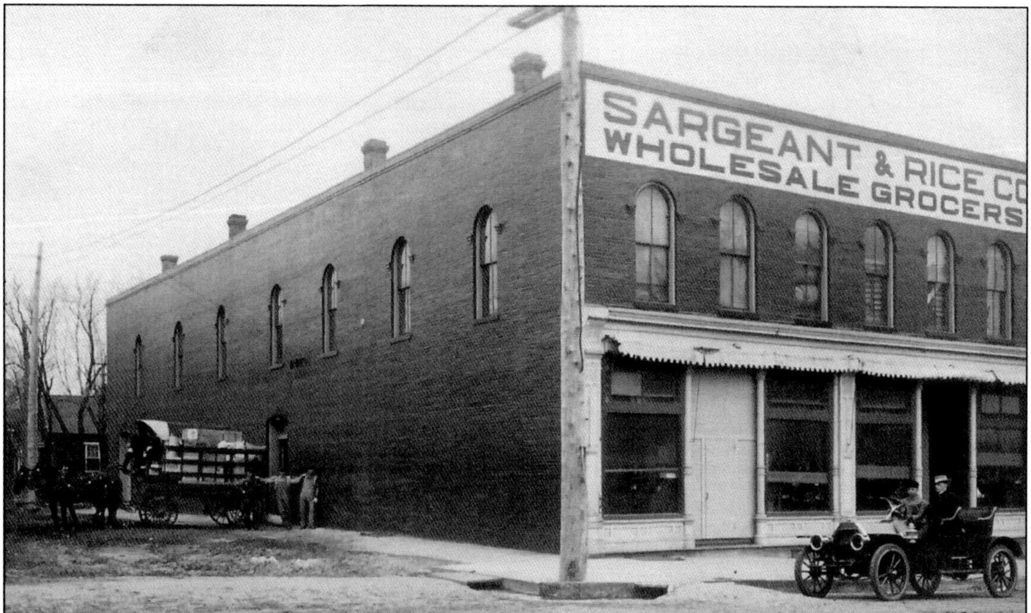

Wholesale Grocery at 424 Central Avenue was one of the many locally owned grocery stores in Nebraska City. (Courtesy of the Nebraska City Historical Society.)

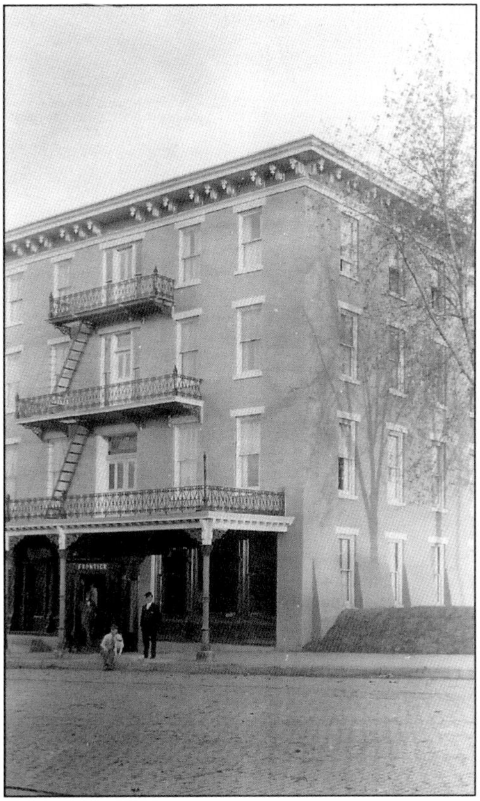

This Central Avenue structure, located between Fourth and Fifth Streets, opened as a four-story hotel called the Morton House in 1859. The name changed in the early 1860s to the Seymour House, then back to the Morton House for a time, and later became Frontier Hotel. The building was damaged by fire in 1919, then again in 1934; it was then demolished. (Courtesy of the Nebraska City Historical Society.)

Nebraska City often felt the pains of rapid growth. Businesses floundered and closed when periods of high traffic and strong economics were followed by statewide and nationwide depressions. Although many storefronts have been renovated in recent years, some succumbed to time and have been demolished. (Courtesy of the Nebraska City Historical Society.)

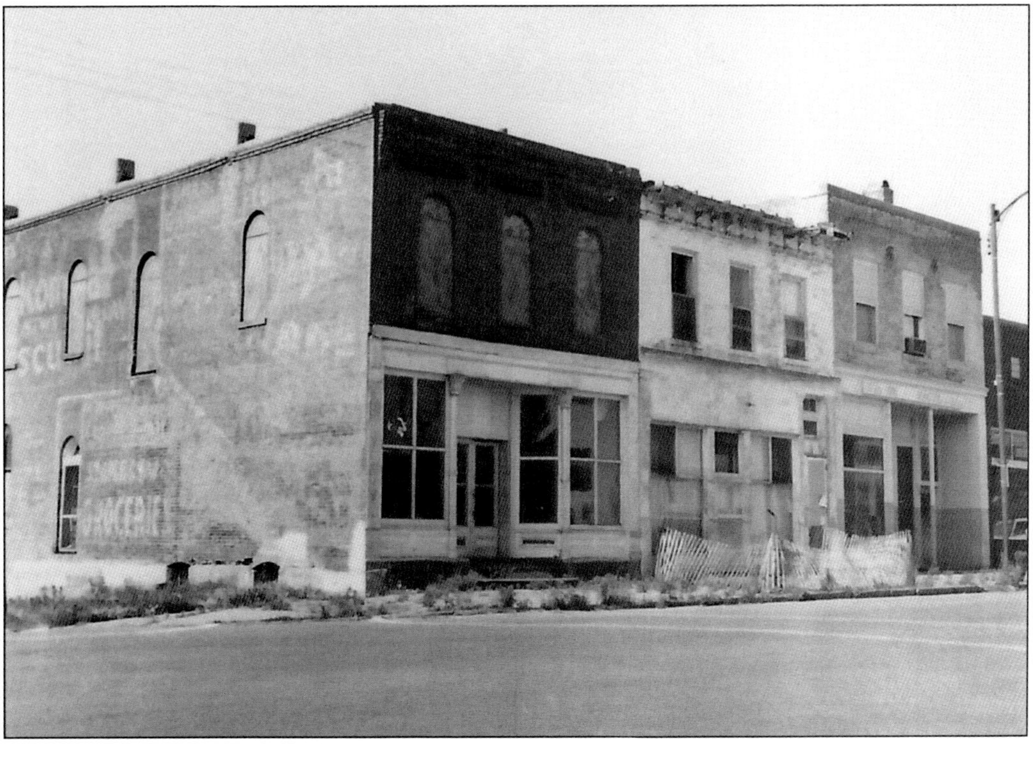

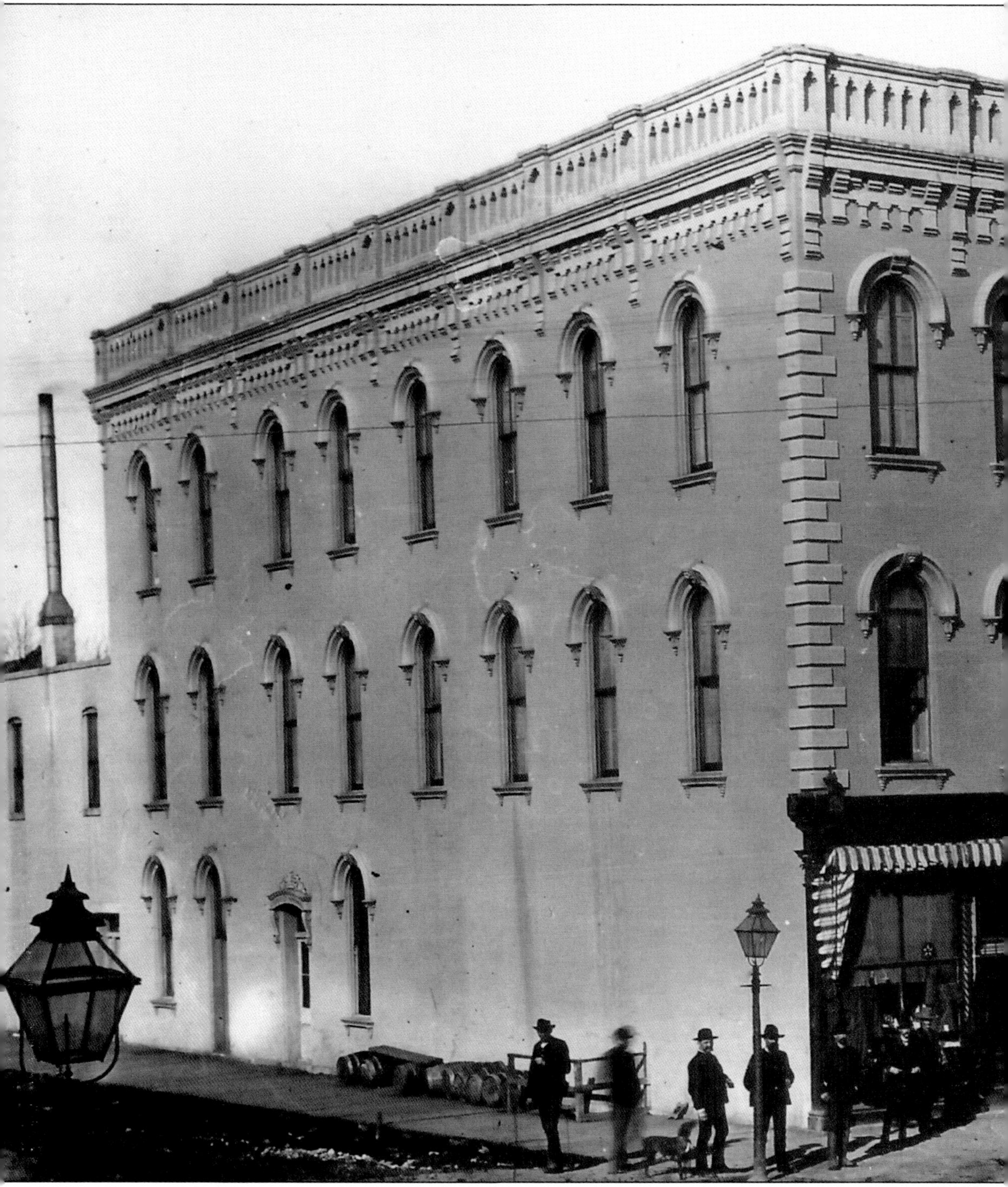

The Grand Hotel on the northeast corner of Tenth Street and Central Avenue was a downtown fixture for many years. Named the Schoff House when it opened in 1871, the hotel boasted 57

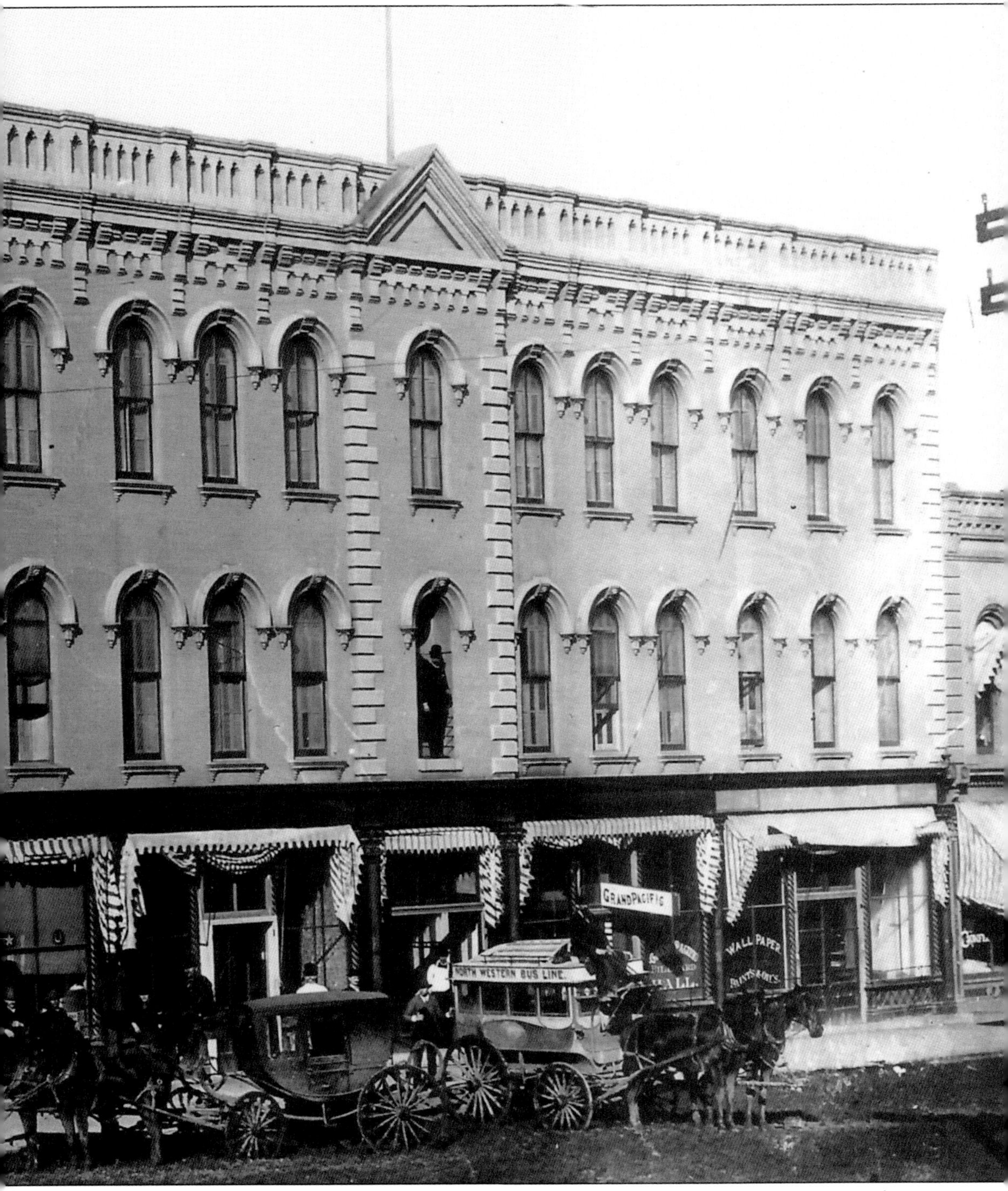

rooms and cost $50,000 to build. The Grand Hotel was gutted in a massive fire on December 6, 1970. (Courtesy of the Nebraska City Historical Society.)

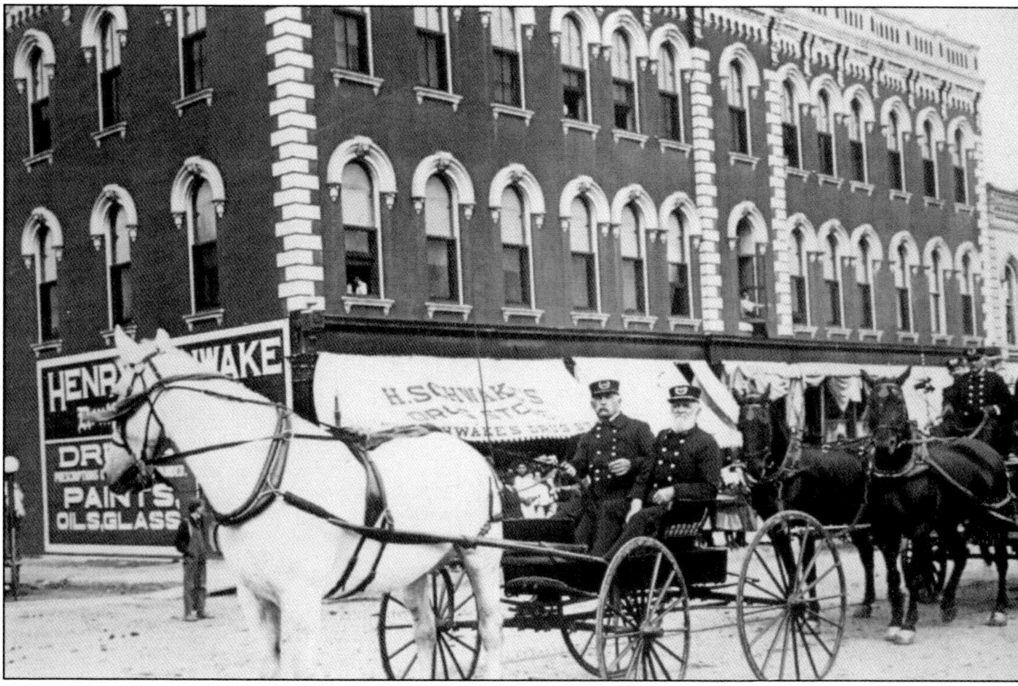

The Grand Hotel provided a spectacular background for every parade on Central Avenue, including the stock show parade in October 1908, pictured here. (Courtesy of the Arbor Day Foundation.)

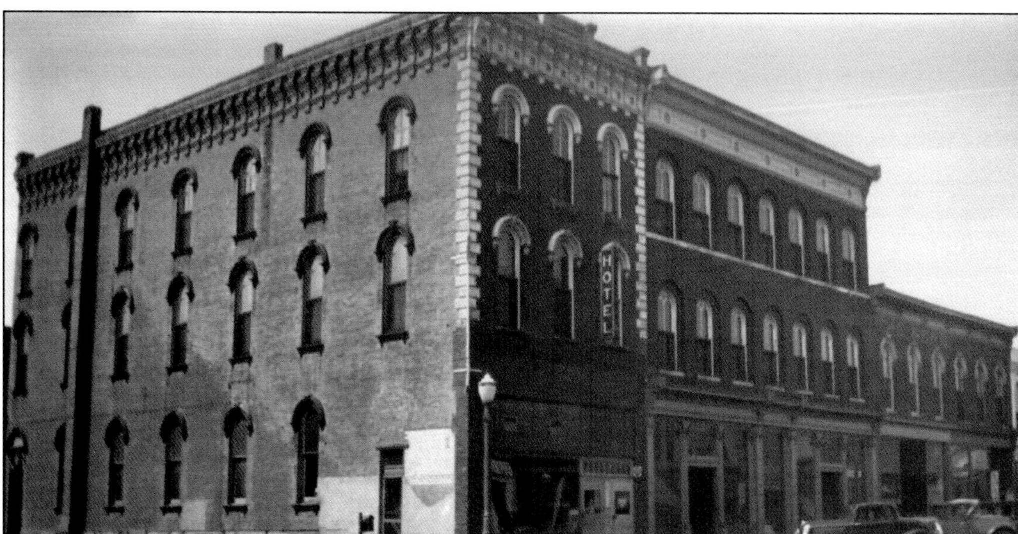

The Marcus Hotel at 601 Central also was destroyed by fire. It burned in 1936. (Courtesy of the Nebraska City Historical Society.)

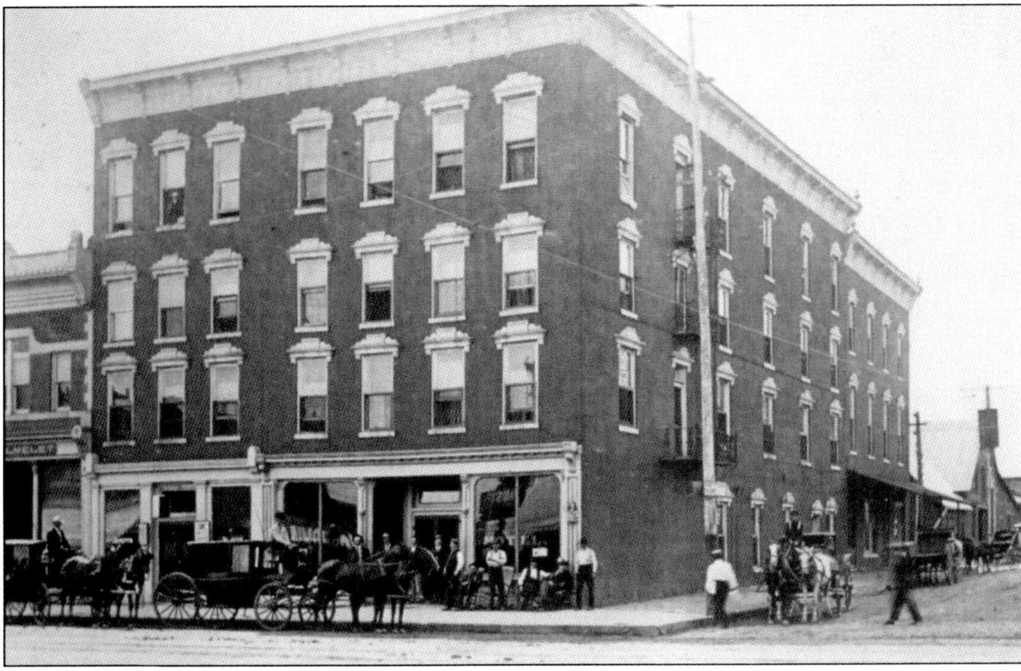

The Watson Hotel, on the southeast corner of Eighth Street and Central Avenue, is pictured above in the early 1900s. An 1897 advertisement for the hotel claimed it was the "best $2.00 house in the city!" The Watson Hotel was damaged in a fire in 1911 and subsequently condemned and razed. A new three-story retail shop, pictured below, was built in its place. Cleveland and Son Department Store was the first tenant (pictured). The store is showcasing white outfits in anticipation of the upcoming Chautauqua to be held in town. The Nebraska City Chautauqua Association was in existence from 1909 to 1919. (Above, courtesy of the Arbor Day Foundation; below, the Nebraska City Historical Society.)

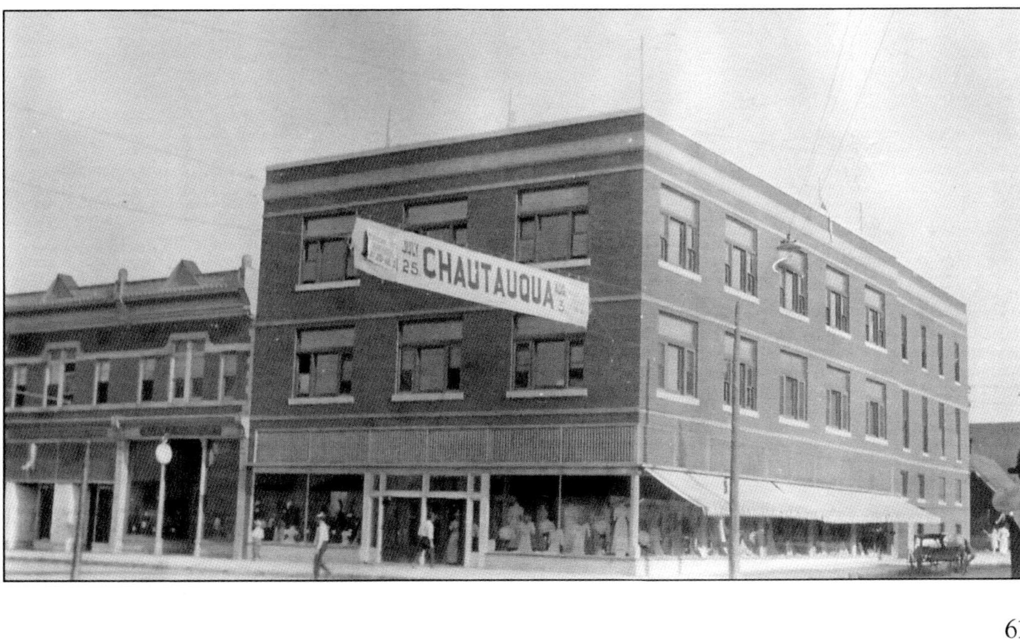

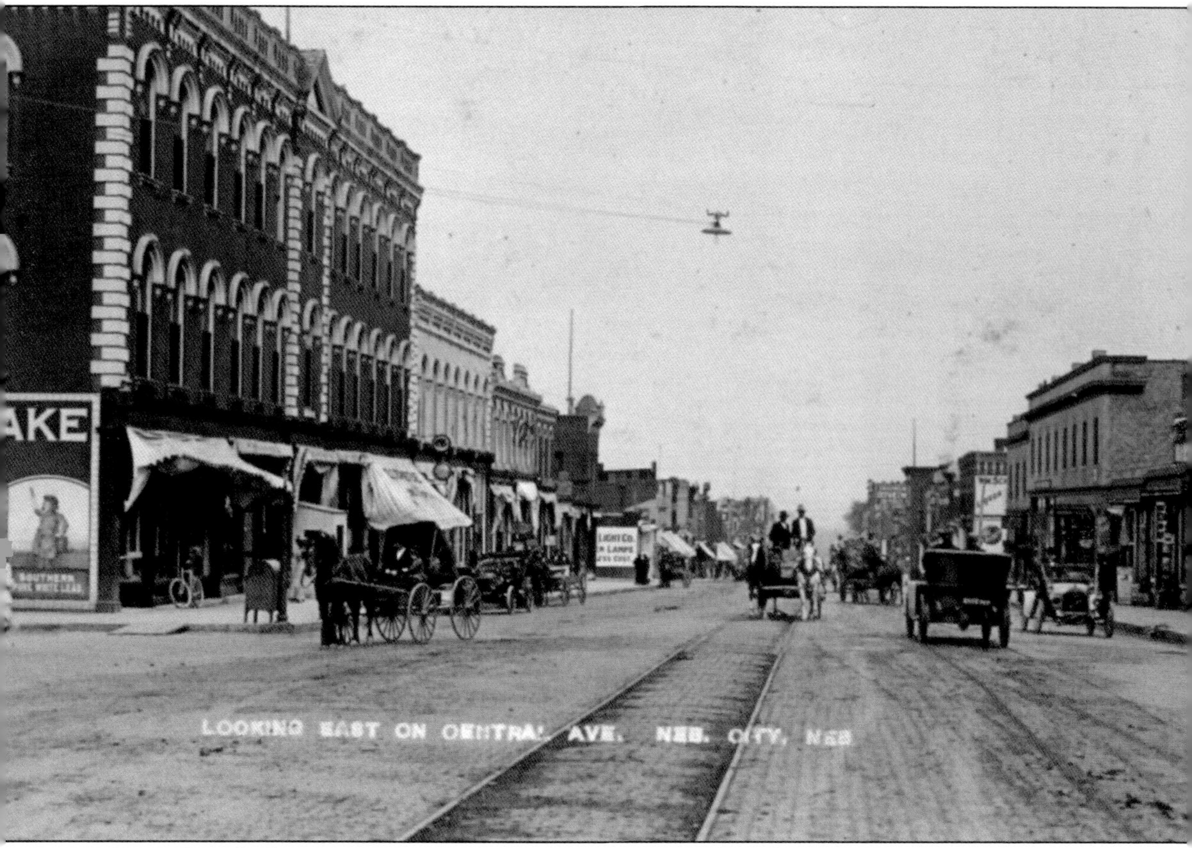

Even though the streetcars ceased operations in 1910, this photograph from Tenth Street and Central Avenue looking east shows that tracks remained a part of the downtown landscape for many years. The tracks are still embedded into the brick pavers, which make up the substructure of the current concrete overlay. (Courtesy of the Arbor Day Foundation.)

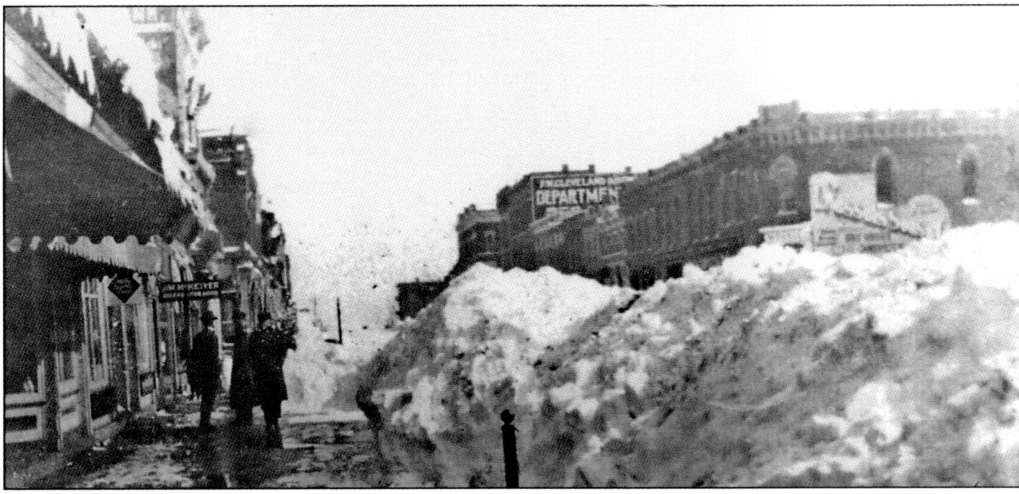

A massive snowstorm hit Nebraska City and the surrounding area on February 25, 1912. One resident said it was "more snow than I ever saw at one time." Shoppers downtown had to contend with large drifts on Central Avenue. (Both courtesy of Nebraska City Tourism and Commerce.)

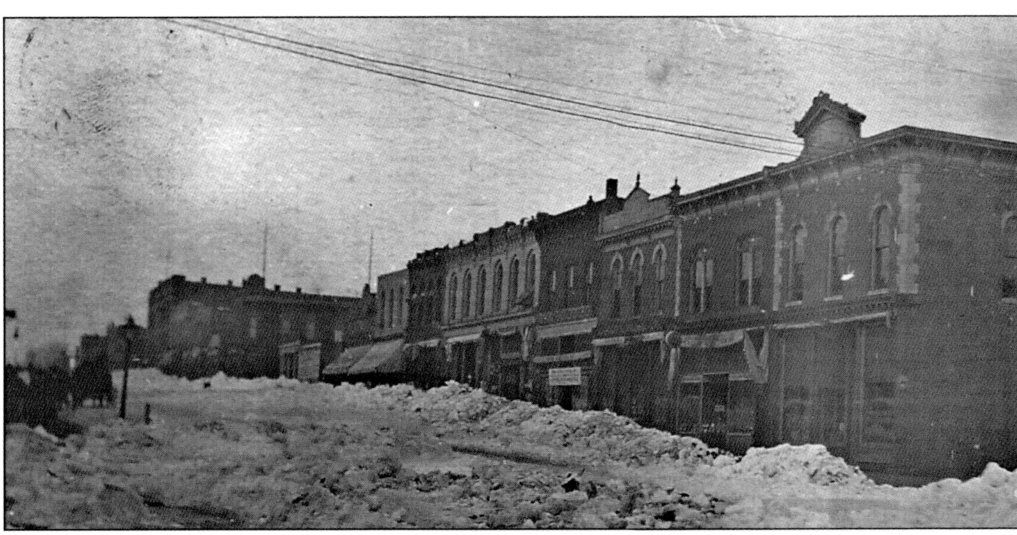

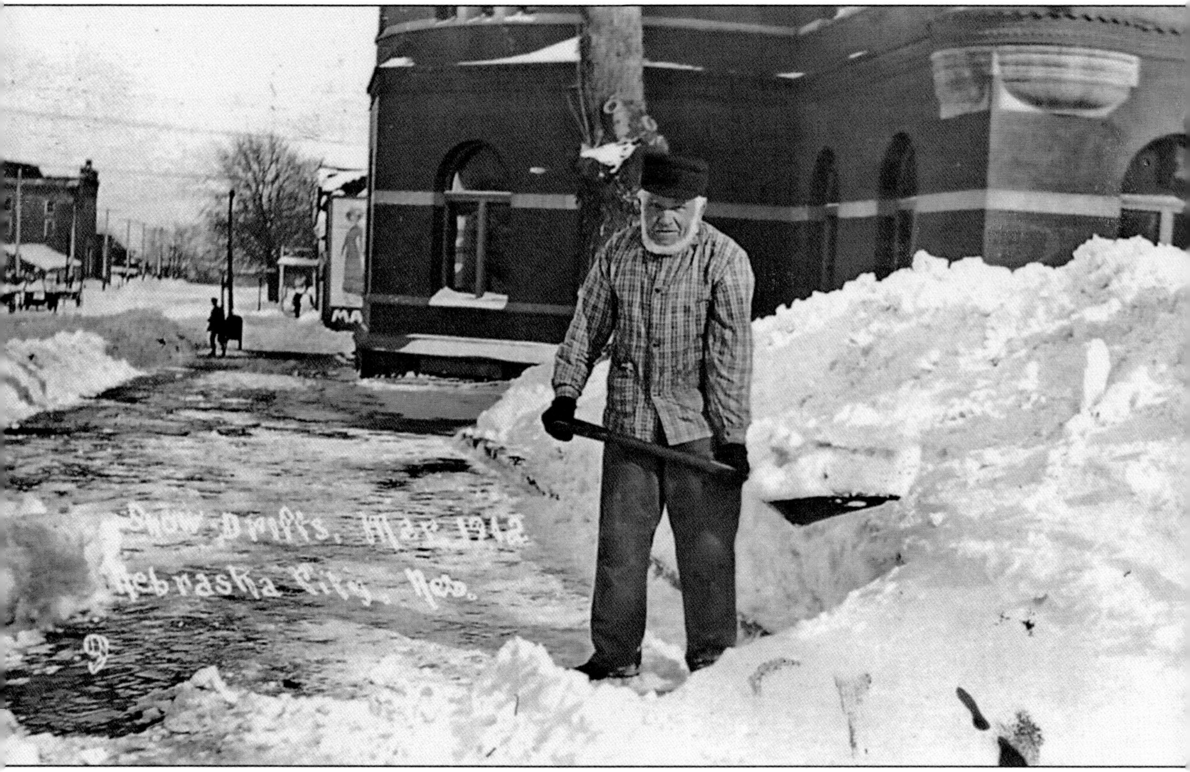

Mr. Dennis was the longtime janitor of the Nebraska City Post Office, pictured in the background. The post office was built in 1886 at a cost of $105,000 and was ornately designed because the town leaders were hoping to attract the federal court to locate there. When the court passed on the location, the postal service moved in. In the 1980s, the building was purchased and restored by Farmers Bank. (Courtesy of Nebraska City Tourism and Commerce.)

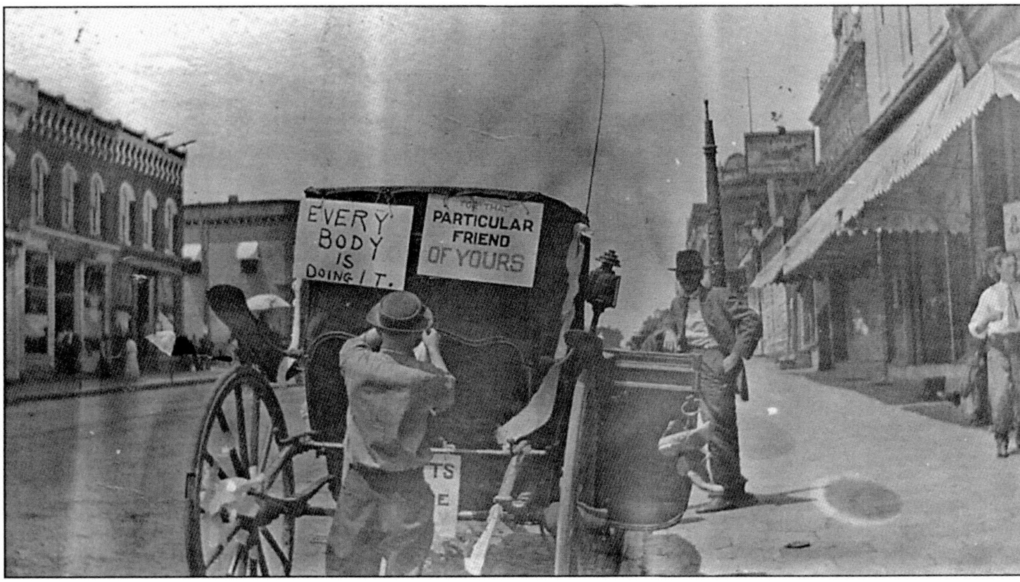

This June 1912 photograph captures a moment of lightheartedness as local folks celebrate a wedding by decorating the buggy of the lucky couple. (Courtesy of Nebraska City Tourism and Commerce.)

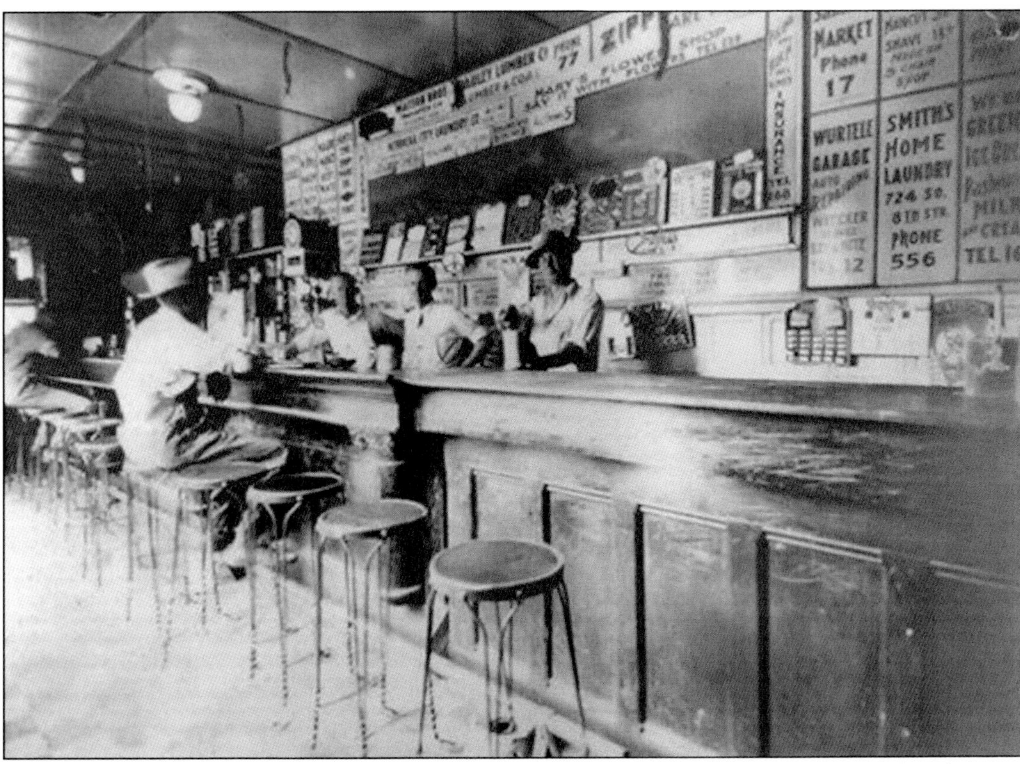

In 1906, Dinty Moore's bar and restaurant opened on South Eighth Street in Nebraska City. The bar remained open even during the Prohibition years, around the time this photograph was taken. (Courtesy of Tim Pendrell.)

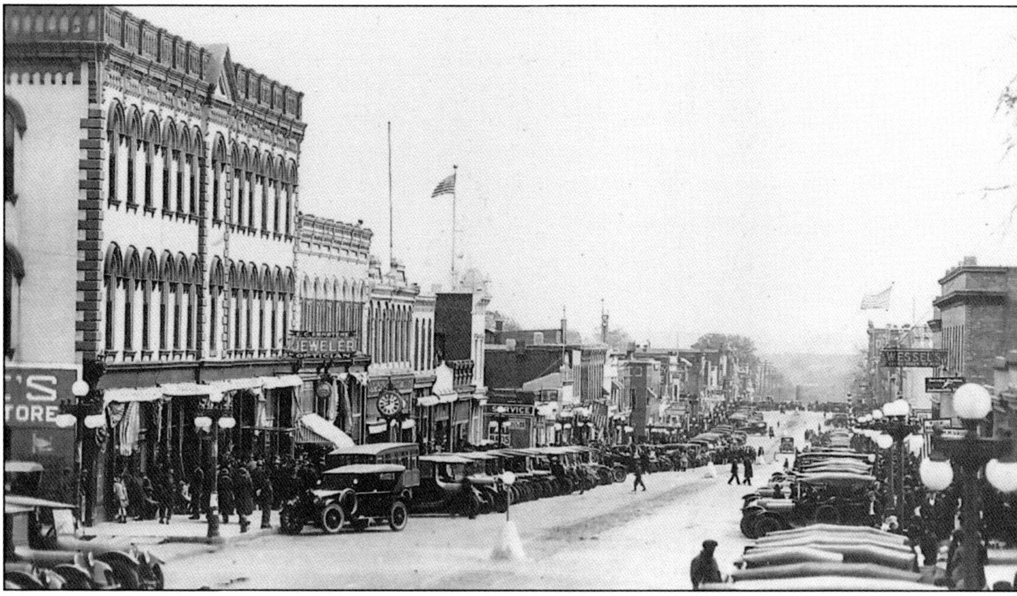

In the 1920s, downtown Nebraska City boasted hotels, drugstores, jewelry stores, and automobile repair shops. A pool hall, glass company, shoe store, and department store took up most of the south side of the 800 block of Central Avenue during that time. (Above, courtesy of the Morton James Public Library; below, the Nebraska City Historical Society.)

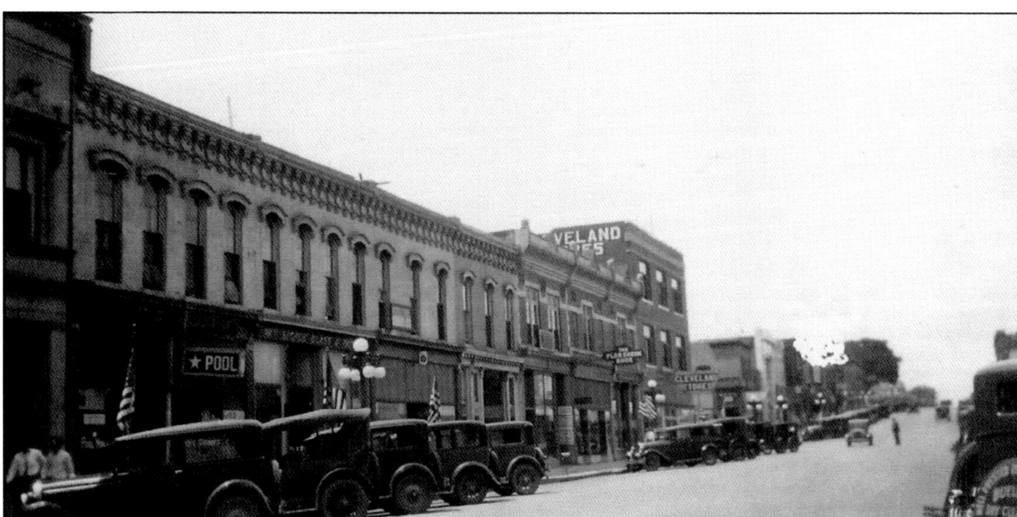

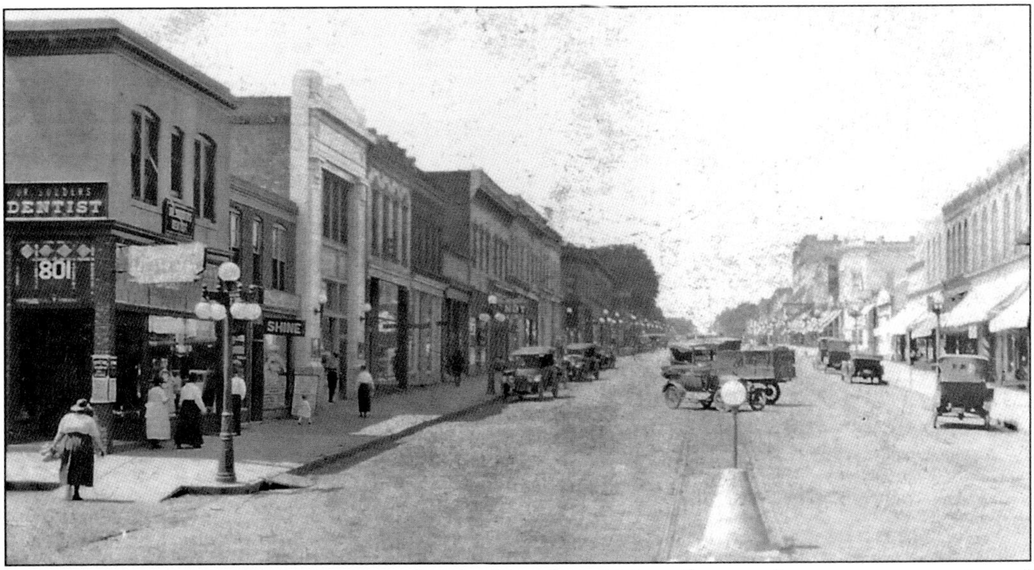

Nebraska City's muddy streets were bricked by the 1920s, allowing for easier navigation of automobiles. Cars could either park on the sides of the road or in the middle of the street. (Courtesy of Dorris Sackles.)

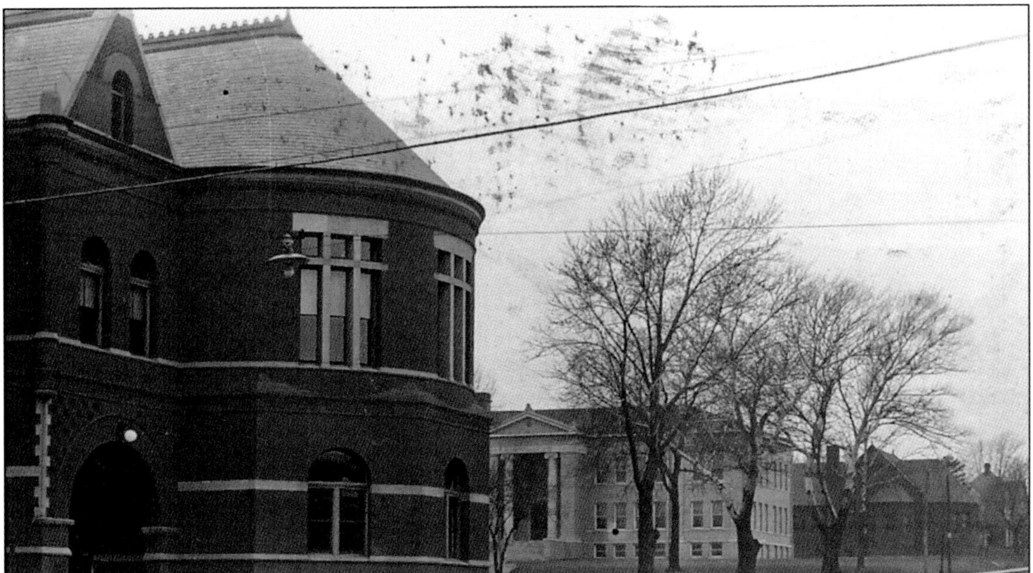

Pictured here around 1915, First Corso was often just as busy as Central Avenue, with the post office, the high school, and the Morton James Public Library all within two blocks of each other. (Courtesy of Nebraska City Tourism and Commerce.)

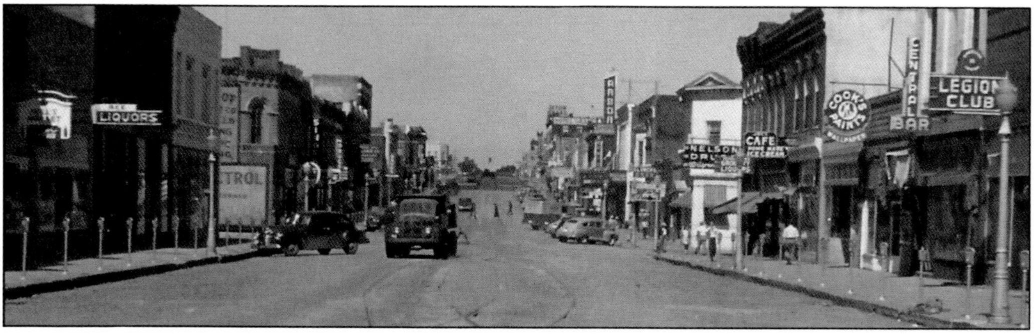

By 1925, automobiles were so common in Nebraska City that the town installed parking meters along Central Avenue. The business district, however, soon extended beyond the Otoe County Courthouse at Eleventh Street and Central Avenue. Shops like the Bartling Seed Company, Inc., and the Garden Café (below) popped up on Central Avenue between Fifteenth and Sixteenth Streets. Today, that block is home to the Rowe Memorial Public Safety Complex. (Both courtesy of the Nebraska City Historical Society.)

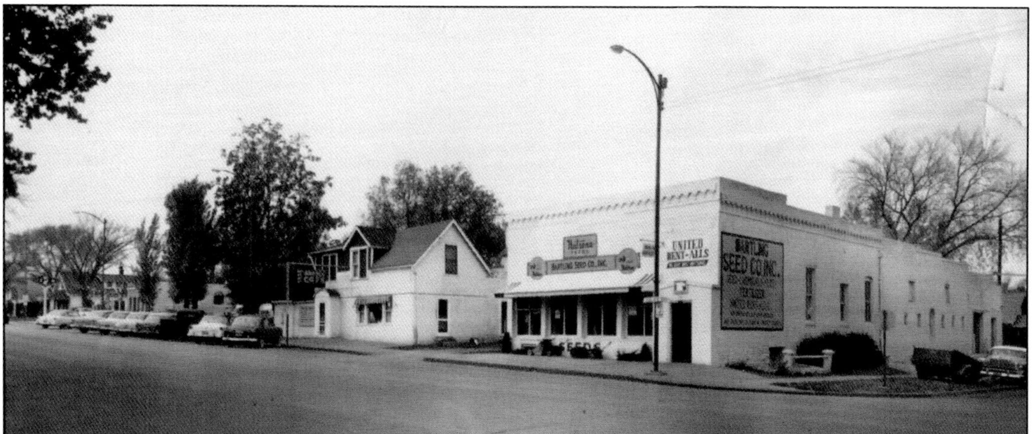

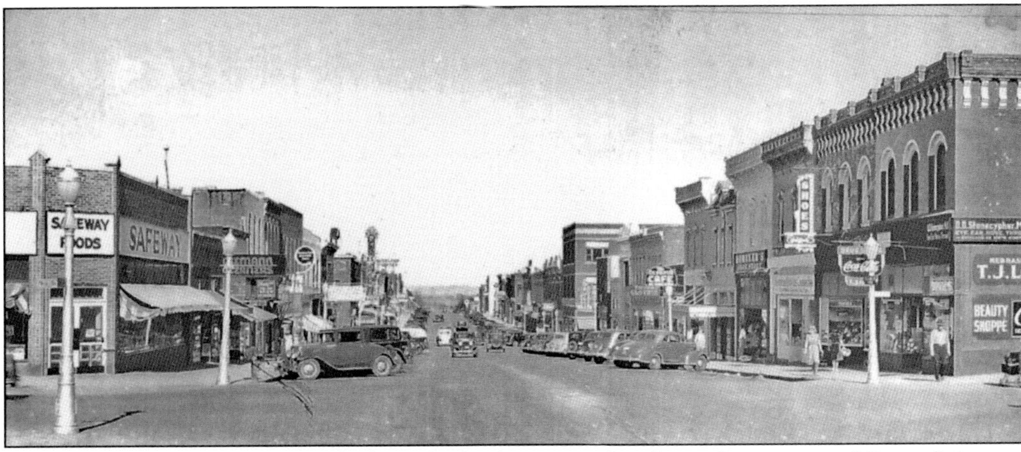

Although this 1940s photograph shows little change in the physical structure of Central Avenue and downtown Nebraska City, the businesses within those buildings came and went. This photograph, taken at Ninth Street and Central Avenue facing east, shows a grocery store, café, beauty shop, dry cleaners, drugstores, and even an ice cream parlor. (Courtesy of Nebraska City Tourism and Commerce.)

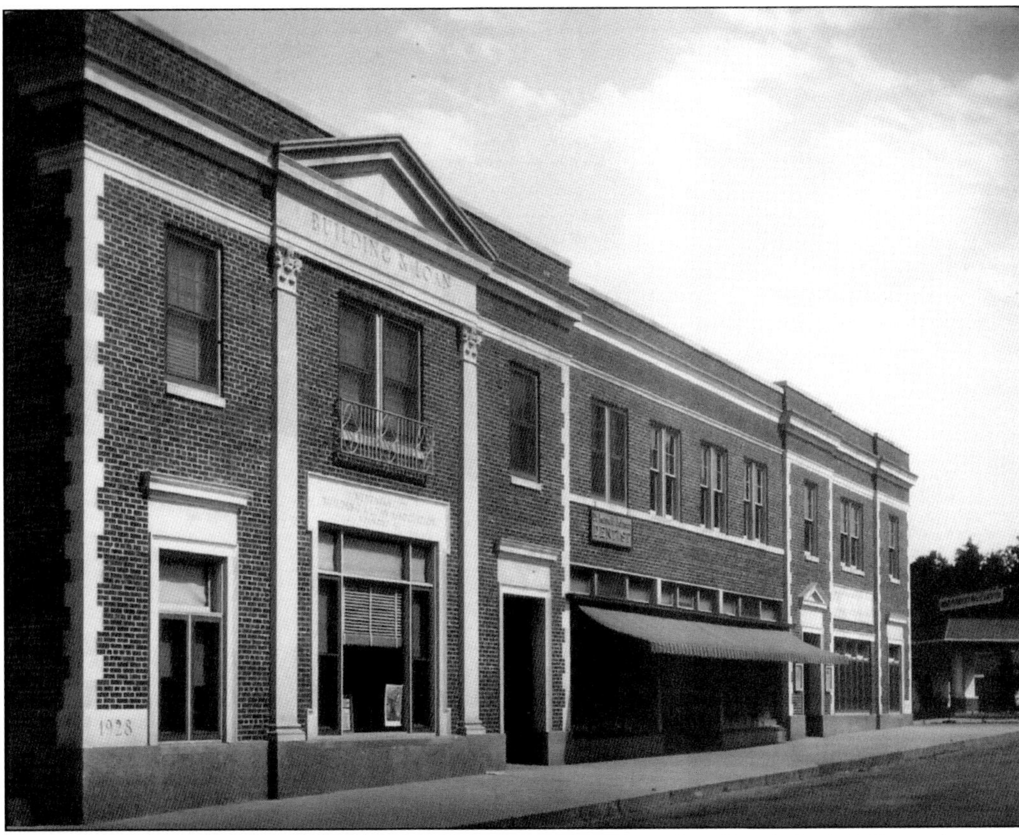

In 1928, the Nebraska City Building and Loan was constructed on South Eighth Street between Central Avenue and First Corso on a site previously home to a blacksmith shop and auto parts store. The building later housed the *Nebraska City News Press*. It is still in use today as a retail shop, corporate office, and a private residence. (Courtesy of the Nebraska City Historical Society.)

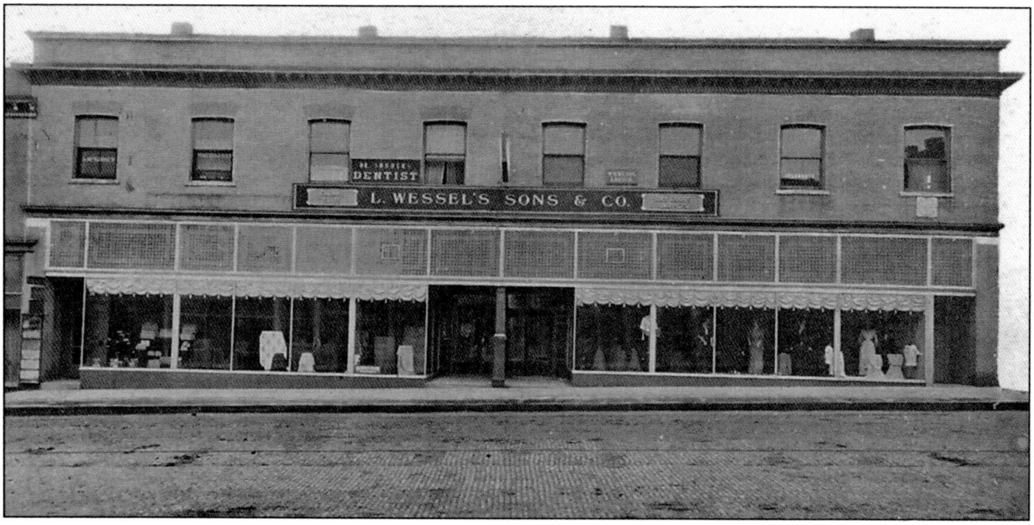

In 1855, Lewis Wessel opened a general store near Kearney Hill, and in 1869 he moved his store to Sixth Street and Central Avenue. Later, in 1890, Wessel moved to Seventh Street and Central Avenue. From 1913 until it burned down in 1964, Wessel's Sons and Company was located on the south side of Central Avenue between Ninth and Tenth Streets. This 1914 postcard advertised for Wessel's on the back by claiming it had "the largest and most complete stock of ladies and misses cloaks, suits, and dresses we have ever shown, all priced very moderately." (Courtesy of Nebraska City Tourism and Commerce.)

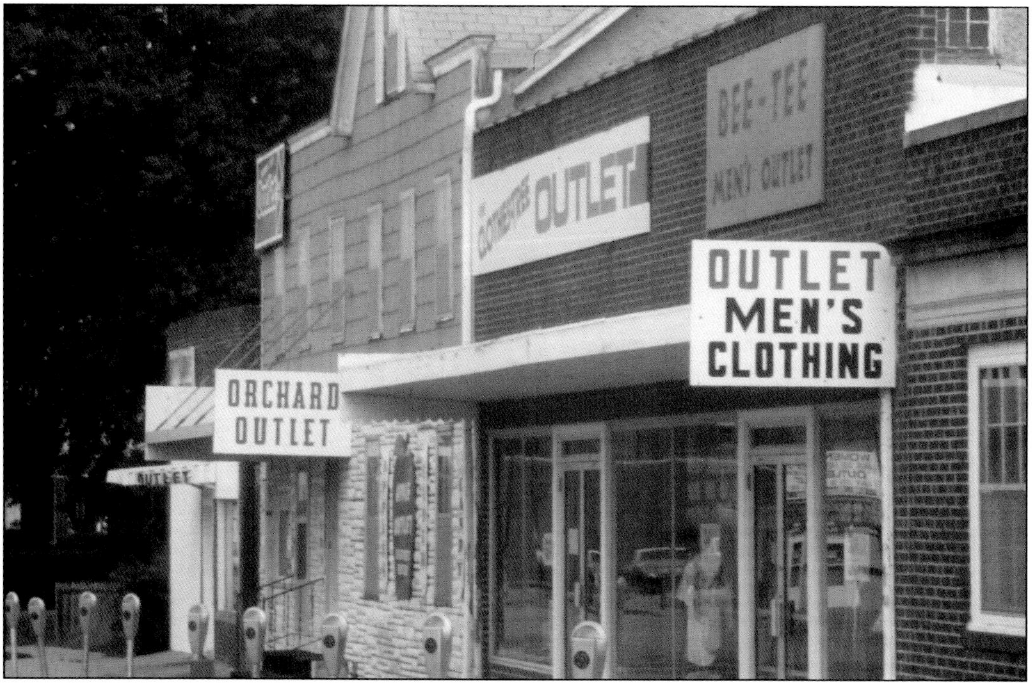

When shopping trends shifted, so did Nebraska City businesses. The 1970s and 1980s saw a strong presence of outlet stores in downtown Nebraska City. (Courtesy of the Arbor Day Foundation.)

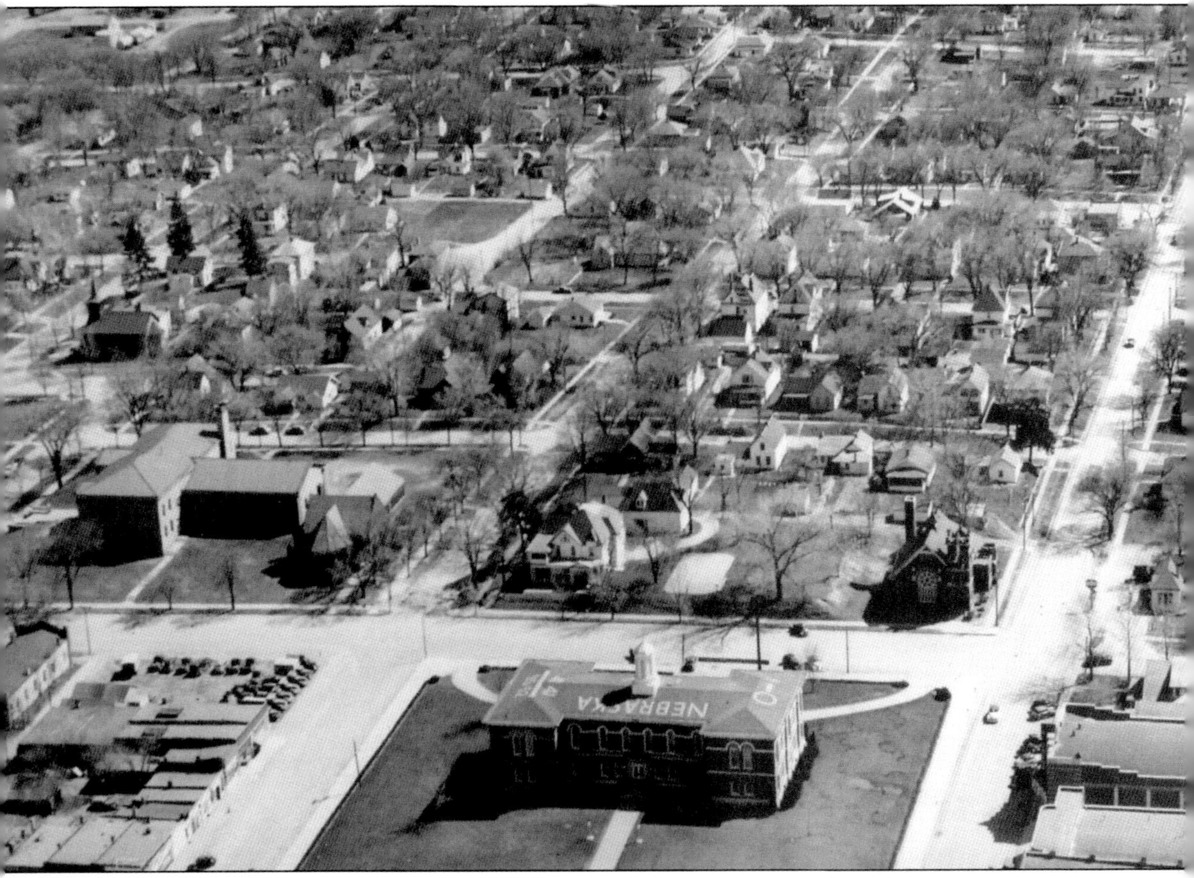

In this 1949 aerial view, the Otoe County Courthouse is easily spotted in the bottom center. The Morton James Public Library is on the opposite corner to the southeast of the courthouse, with the old Nebraska City High School beside it. South Eleventh Street, which stretches up the right side of the photograph, was still mostly residential at this time. (Courtesy of the Nebraska City Historical Society.)

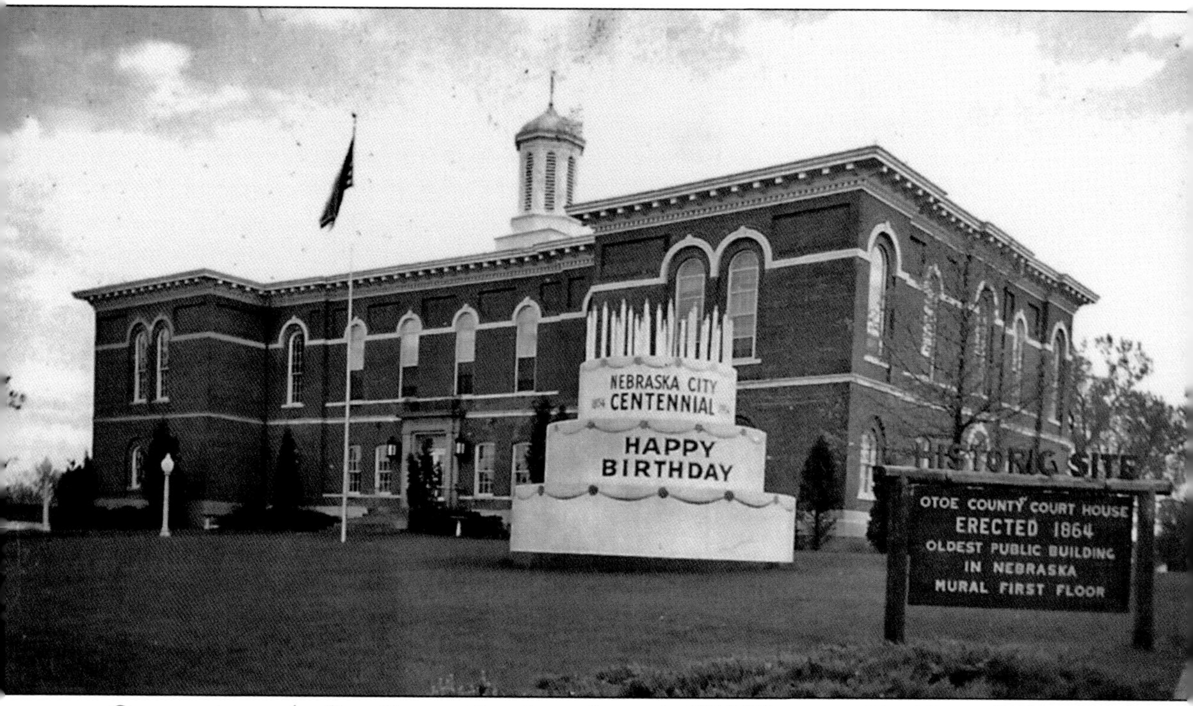

Construction on the Otoe County Courthouse began in 1864. The original building, which included a small cell in the basement to be used as a jail, was constructed for $22,500. The courthouse was enlarged over the years and is pictured here in 1954 during celebrations commemorating the 100th anniversary of the founding of Nebraska City. (Courtesy of Nebraska City Tourism and Commerce.)

Four

INDUSTRY

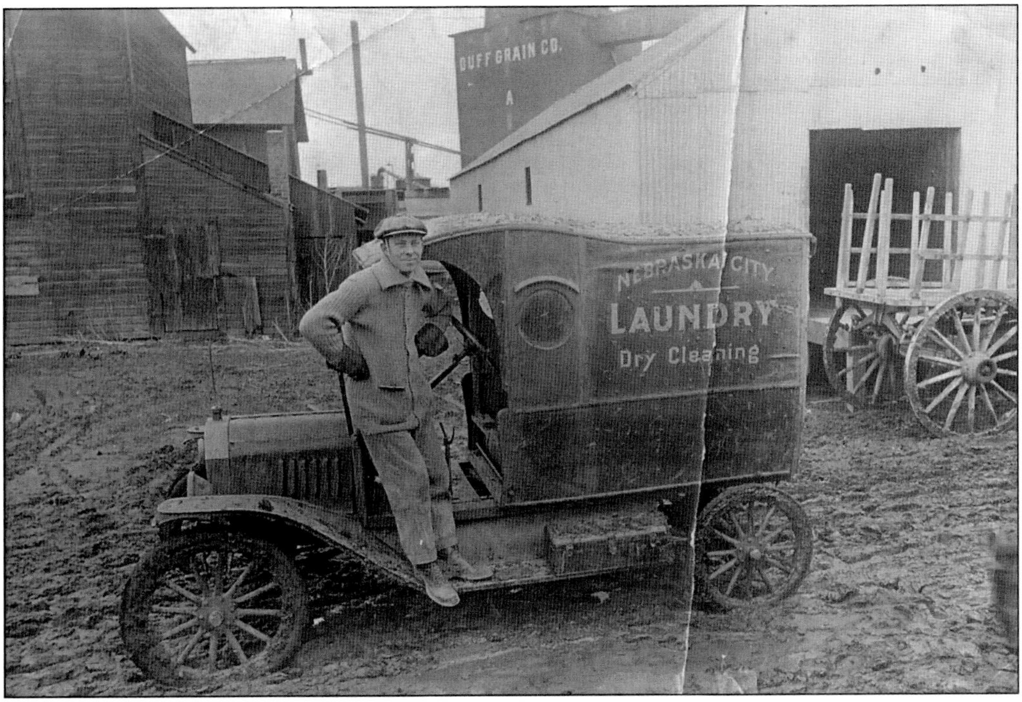

The Nebraska City Laundry Company was owned and operated by Eddie Wischmeyer. In this 1916 photograph, Wischmeyer is posing in front of the Duff Grain Company building. At the peak of its production, the Duff Grain Company held a capacity of 350,000 bushels. (Courtesy of the Morton James Public Library.)

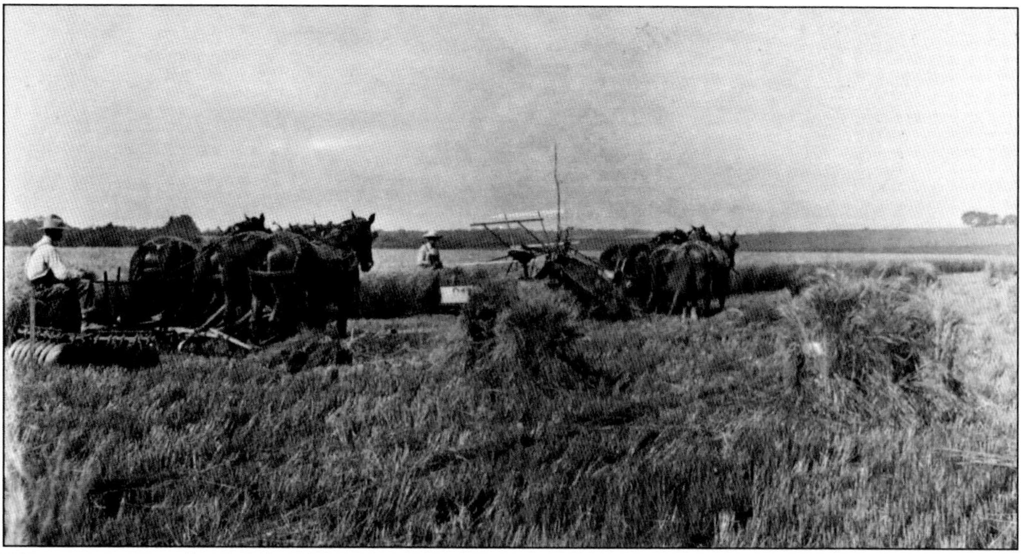

The area surrounding Nebraska City was cultivated as farmland. Farmers grew corn, wheat, beans, and hay. While the farmers in this early-1900s photograph are using horsepower to clear their fields, Nebraska City manufacturing wholly embraced technological advances, opening a steam flour mill in 1861 and a steam sawmill in 1864. Other industries included the introduction of a soap-making company and a carriage-manufacturing business in 1869. (Courtesy of Arbor Lodge.)

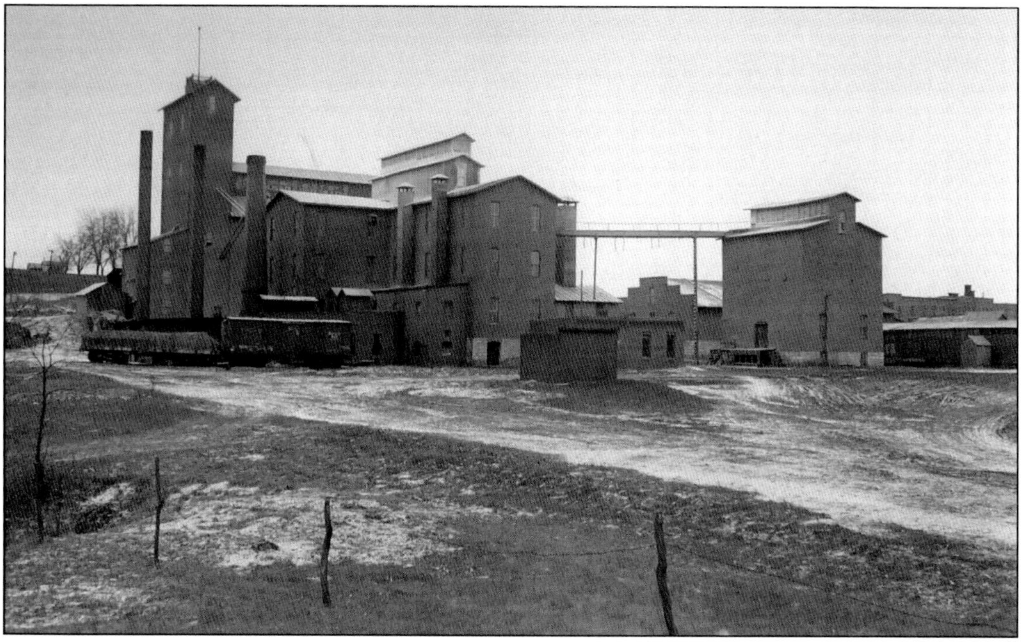

The Nebraska City Cereal Mills opened in 1886, joining the Nebraska City Canning Company as a major food products manufacturer. The Nebraska City Canning Company was organized in 1880, and it became the Otoe Canning and Preserving Company in 1901 before being named Otoe Food Products Company in 1914. In 1950, it was known as the Morton House Kitchens. Morton House Kitchen packed corn, beans, tomatoes, pumpkins, apples, peanut butter, cider, and more. It regularly employed 350 people and, by 1963, had a payroll of $1.6 million. (Courtesy of the Morton James Public Library.)

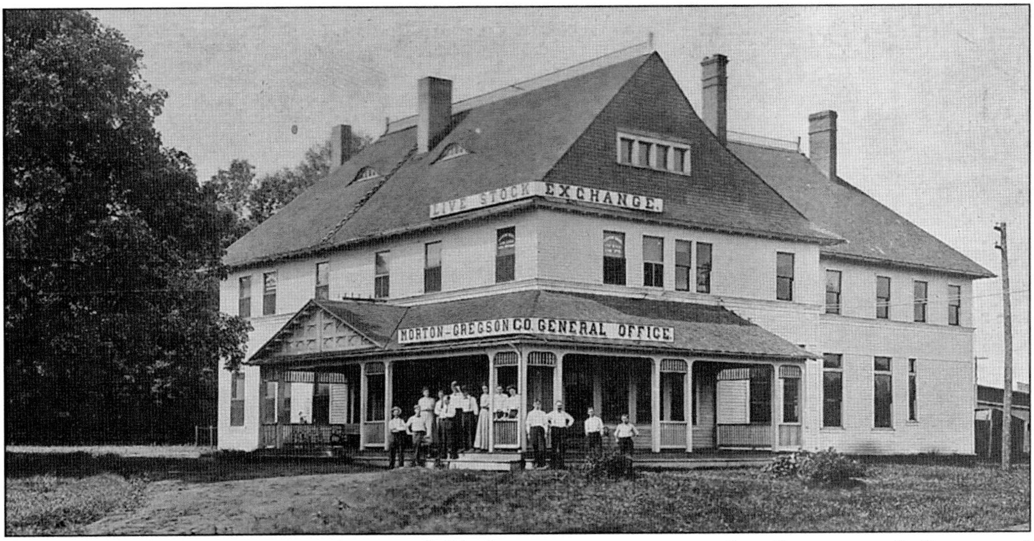

In 1888, the Morton Gregson Livestock Exchange was constructed at Seventeenth Street and Eleventh Corso, just south of Wyuka Cemetery. The structure burned down on January 15, 1934, and there were reports that the blaze could be seen in Lincoln, some 50 miles to the west. (Courtesy of Nebraska City Tourism and Commerce.)

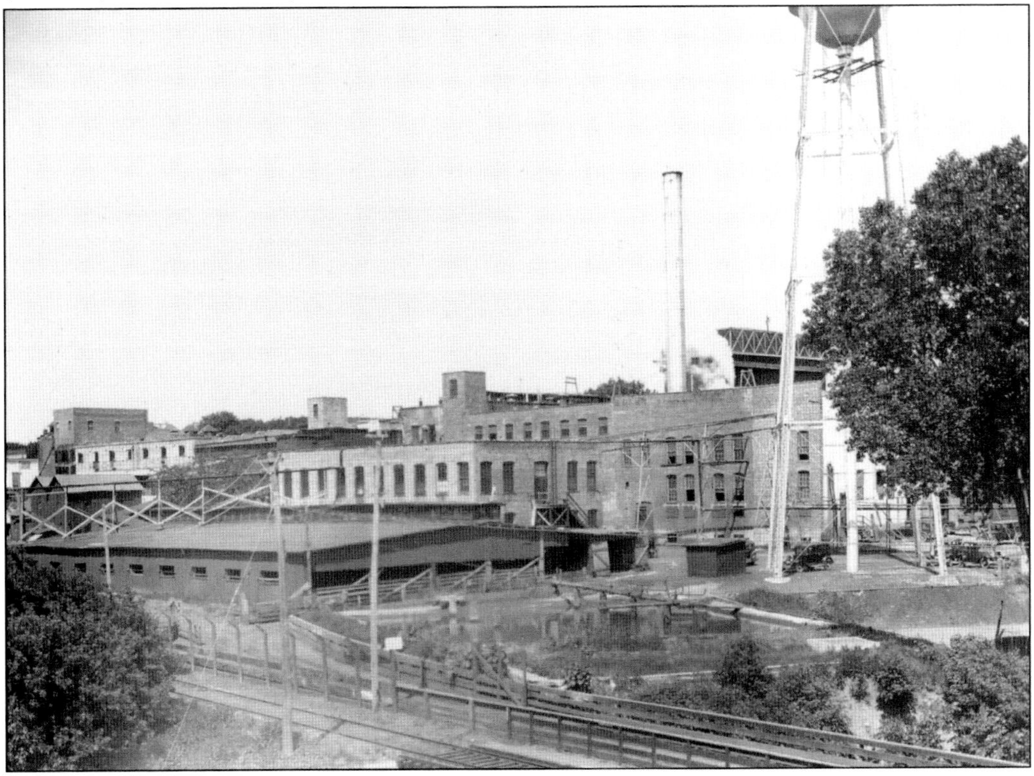

Originally known as the Trans-Missouri Packing Plant, the Morton Gregson Packing Plant, founded in 1901, employed 250 to 350 people and produced 50,000 pounds of pork products annually. One notable building on the property was the five-story cold-storage structure. The plant closed in 1932. (Courtesy of the Morton James Public Library.)

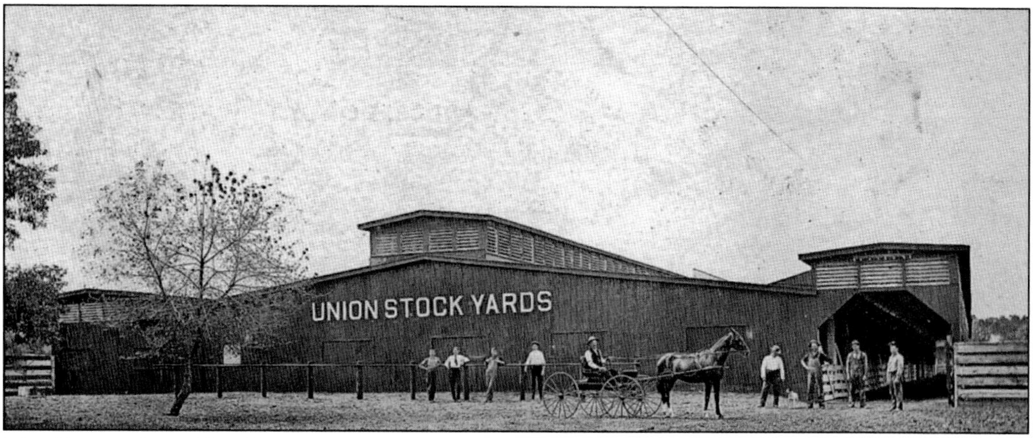

The Union Stock Yard Company was located next to the Morton Gregson Livestock Exchange building at Seventeenth Street and Eleventh Corso. The stockyards were destroyed by fire in March 1920. (Courtesy of Nebraska City Tourism and Commerce.)

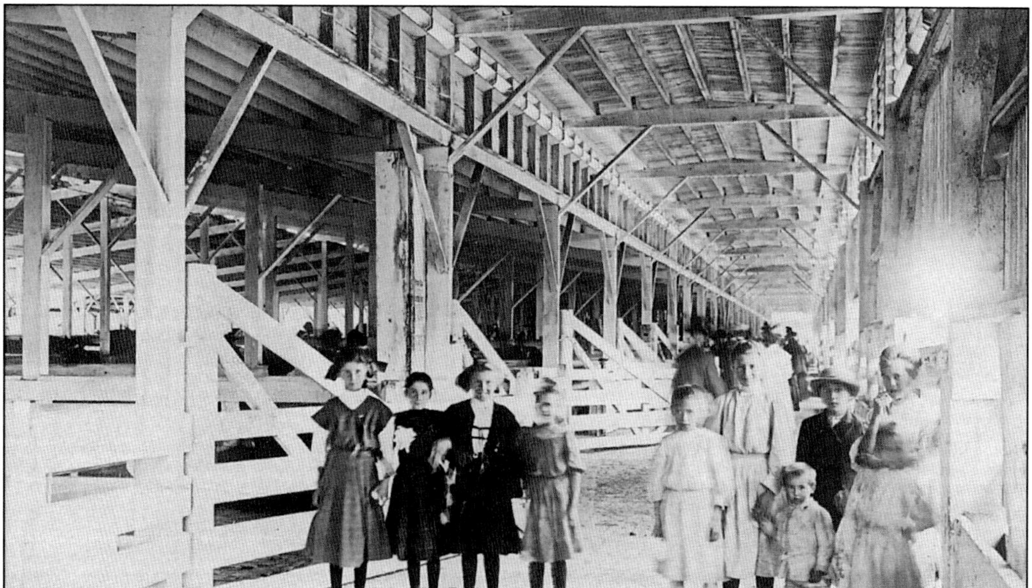

During the stock show parades of 1908 and 1909, the Union Stock Yard Company opened its doors to the public. More than 600 heads of hog were lost when the structure burned in 1920. (Courtesy of Dorris Sackles.)

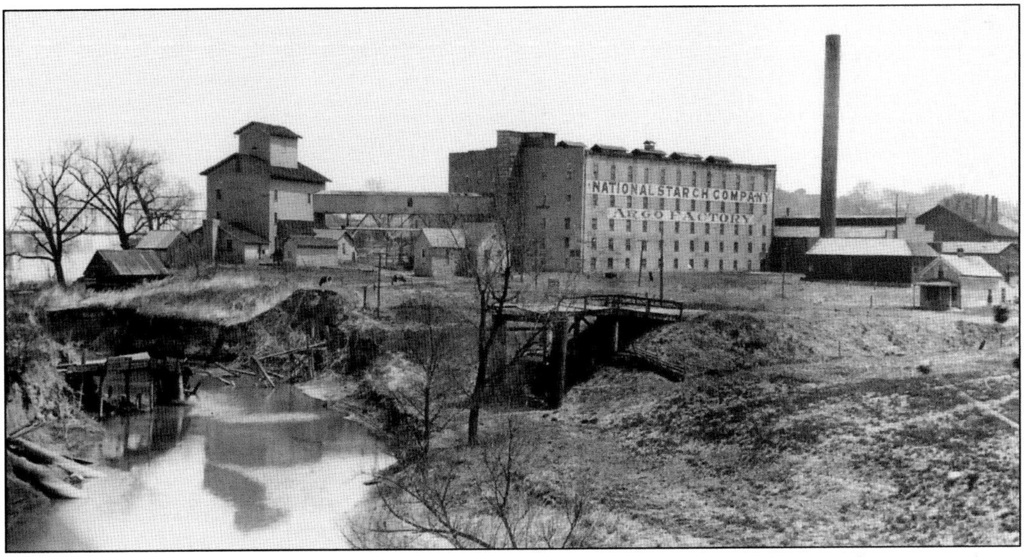

In 1887, a corn-milling factory was built right on the Missouri River. It became known as Argo Starch Company and was under the direction of J. Sterling Morton's youngest son, Carl. After Carl's death, the plant closed and, in 1912, burned to the ground. The railroad bridge spanning the Missouri River is visible in the background of this photograph. (Courtesy of the Nebraska City Historical Society.)

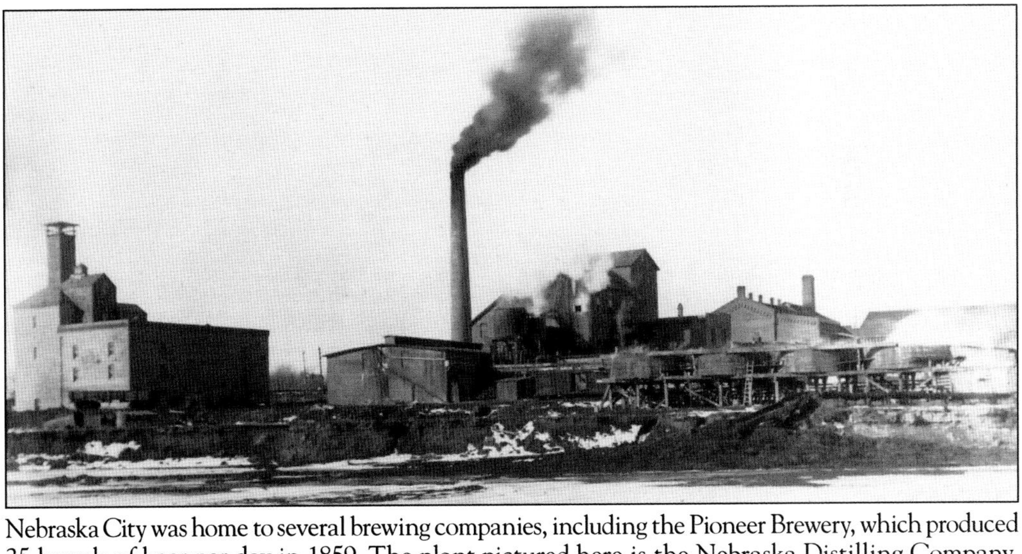

Nebraska City was home to several brewing companies, including the Pioneer Brewery, which produced 25 barrels of beer per day in 1859. The plant pictured here is the Nebraska Distilling Company, which was damaged in an 1881 flood. (Courtesy of the Nebraska City Historical Society.)

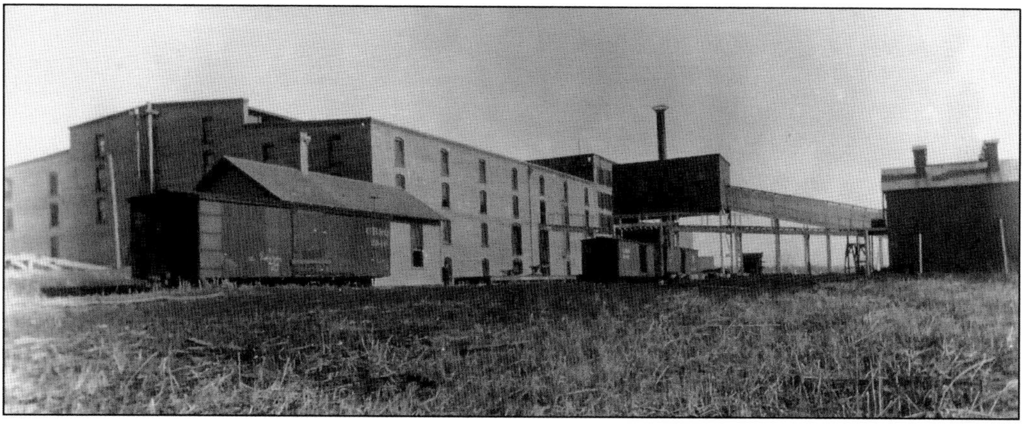

Meatpacking has long been a part of Nebraska City's industrial makeup. Nebraska City Packing, later known as the Nebraska Iowa Packing Company, started in 1881. It was joined in 1885 by the Trans-Mississippi Packing and Provision Company, and both were purchased by the Morton Gregson Firm. (Both courtesy of the Nebraska City Historical Society.)

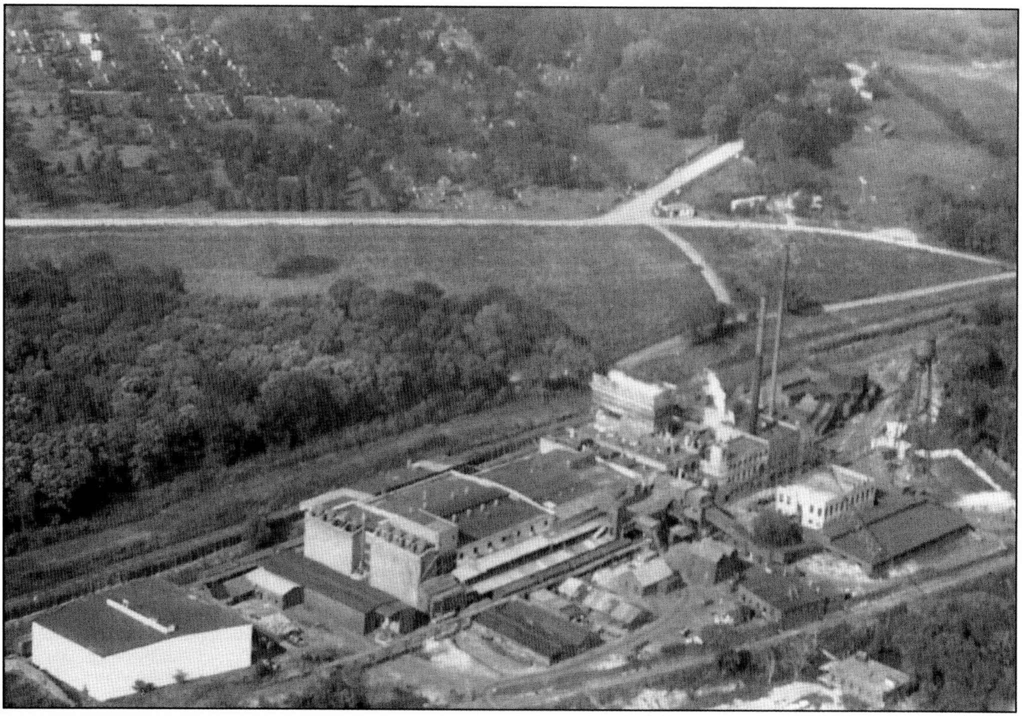

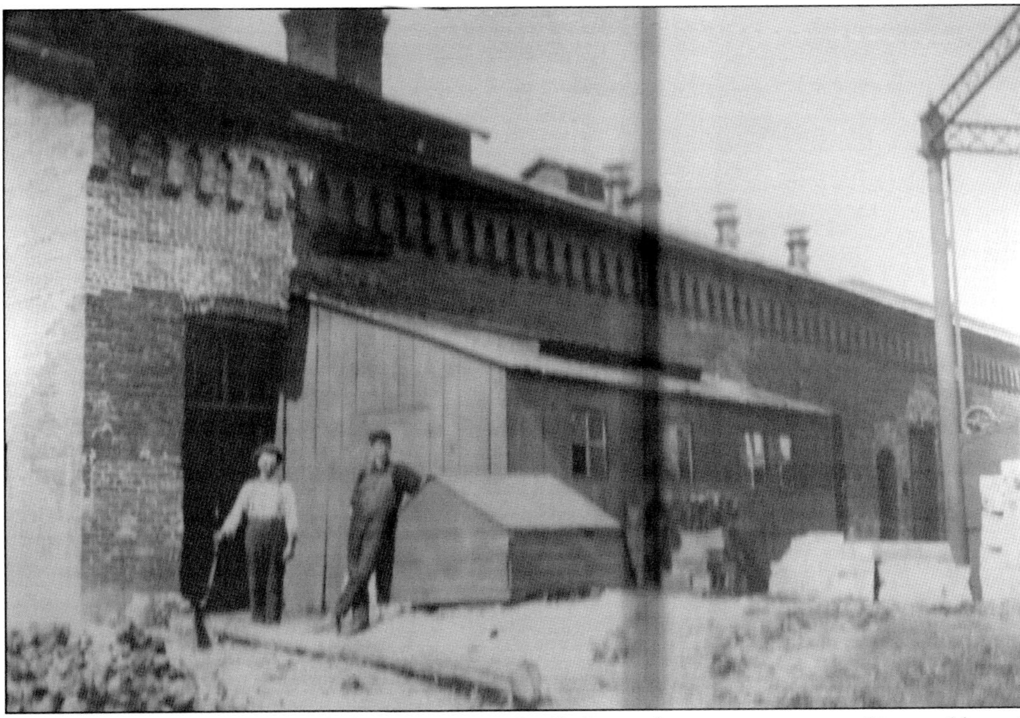

By 1903, Nebraska City provided its citizens with all the modern conveniences. Pictured here is the gas works company. (Courtesy of the Nebraska City Historical Society.)

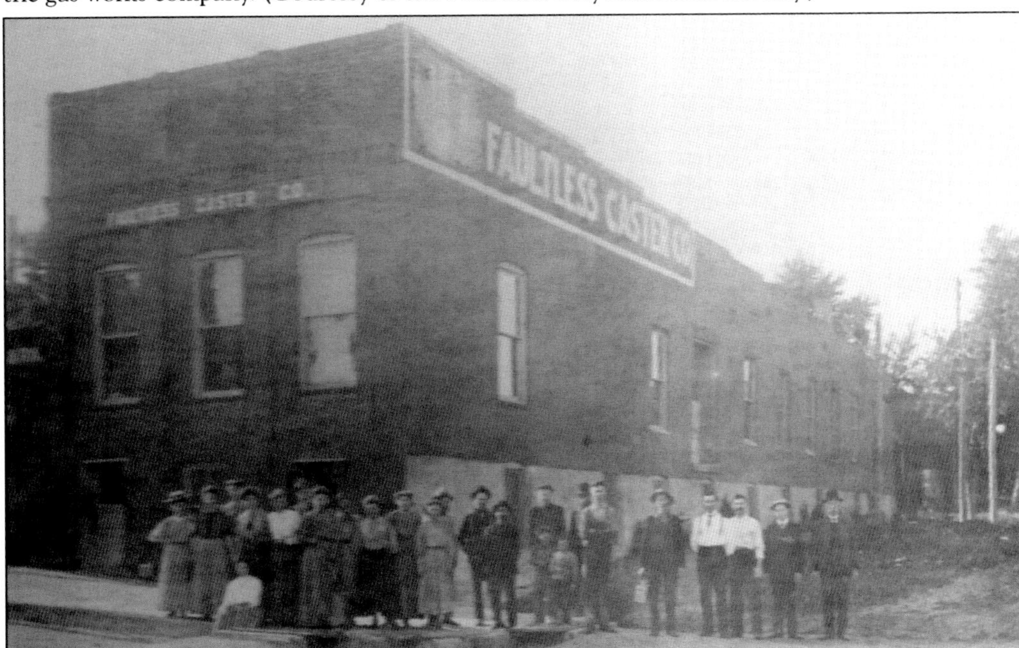

The Faultless Caster Company was located at Fourth Street and Central Avenue. Specializing in creating rolling furniture, it earned recognition at the St. Louis World's Fair in 1904. Soon after, it closed the Nebraska City store and moved to Indiana. (Courtesy of the Nebraska City Historical Society.)

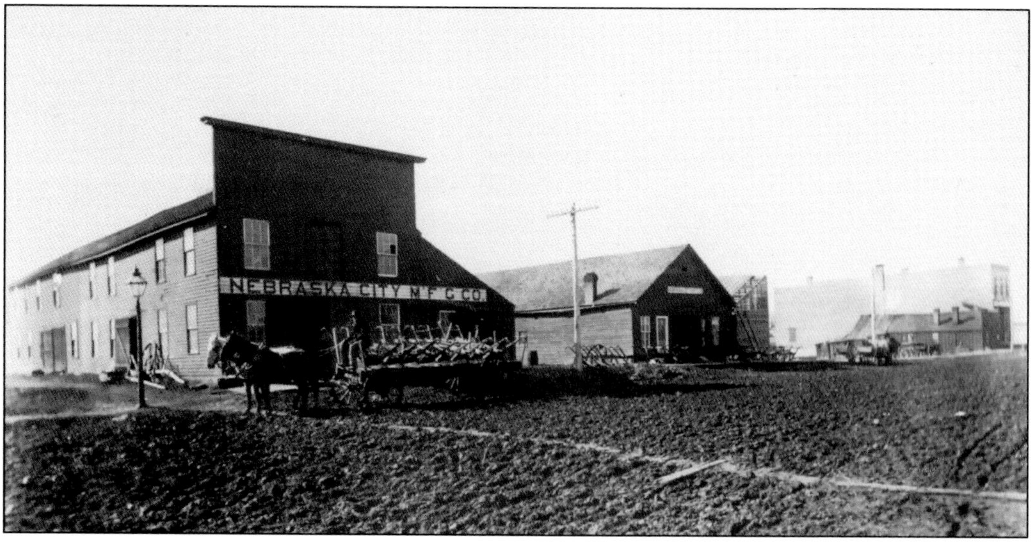

The Nebraska City Manufacturing Company started in 1870. Its warehouse (above) was located at 1401 Central Avenue, the current site of the Nebraska City Volunteer Fire Department. The company specialized in making grasshopper plows. (Above, courtesy of the Nebraska City Historical Society; below, the Kregel Windmill Factory Museum.)

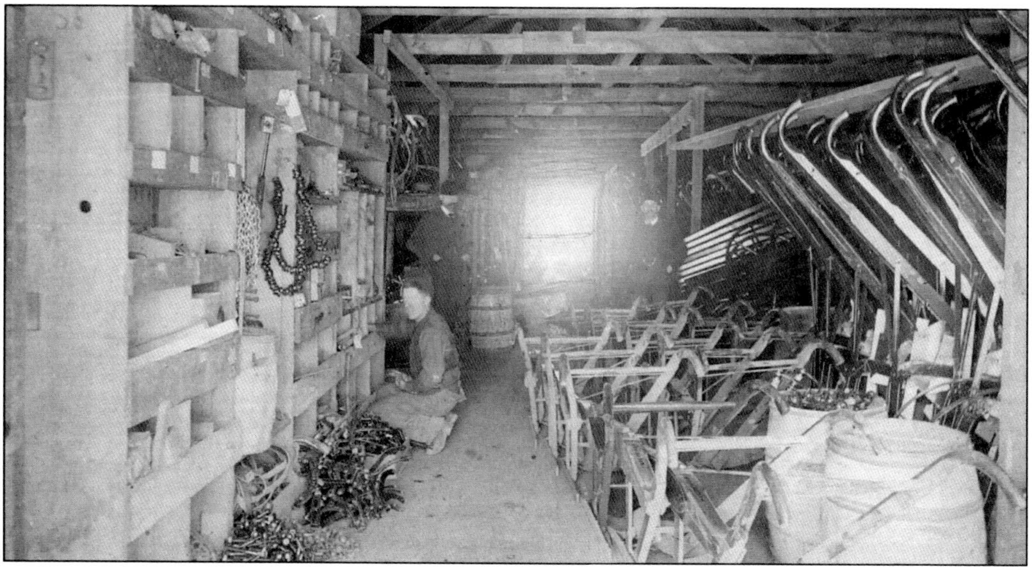

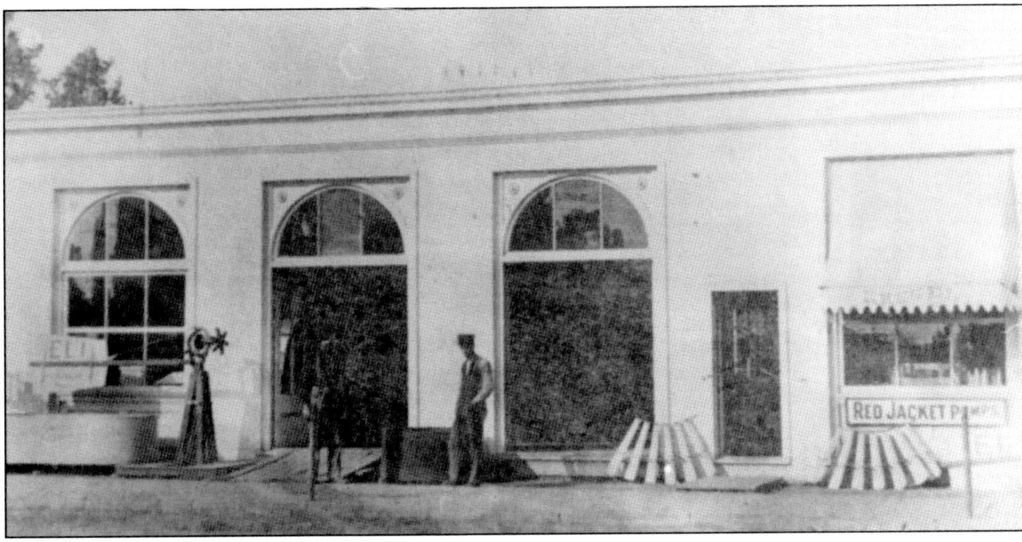

In 1879, cousins George and Louis Kregel, partners in the Nebraska City Manufacturing Company, bought out the business and opened the Kregel Windmill Factory in the same facility. In 1903, they built a new facility across the street. George's son Art Kregel took over the business in the 1940s and ran it until his death in 1991 at age 93. Now preserved as a museum, it offers a unique look at manufacturing life in the early 20th century. (Both courtesy of the Kregel Windmill Factory Museum.)

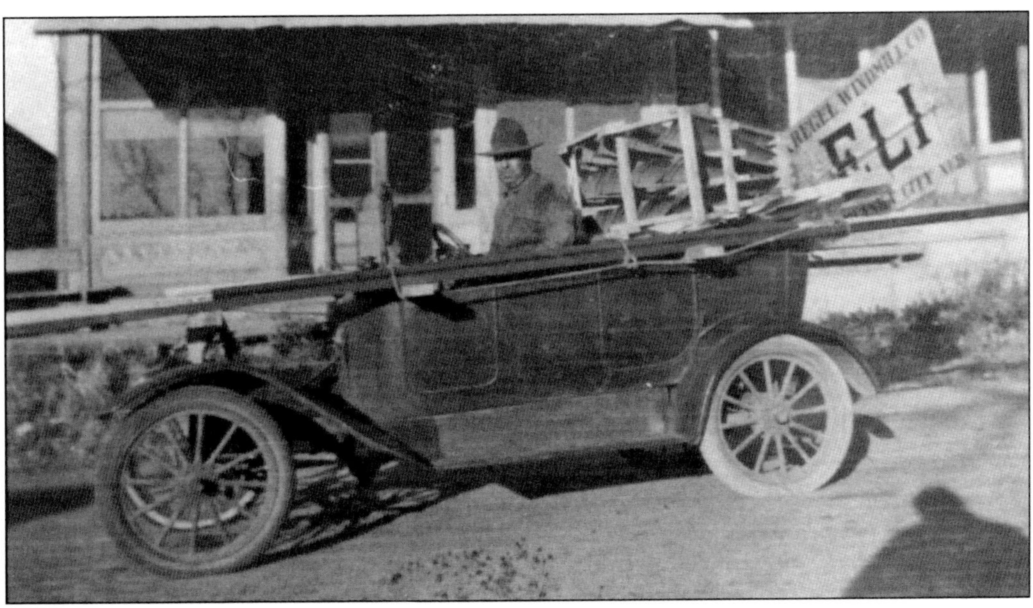

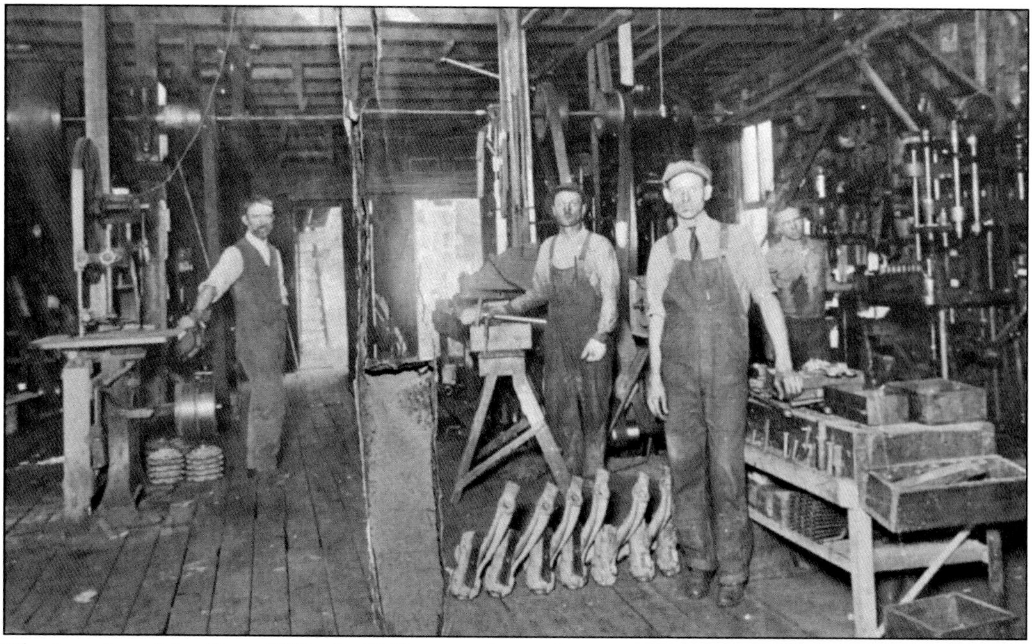

The interior of the Kregel Windmill Factory, shown here around 1920, has not changed much in the past 100 years. The company started out creating wooden windmills before changing to all steel by the early 1900s. Material rationing during World War II stopped windmill production, and the company shifted its focus to maintenance and servicing, never going back to full-scale windmills. Art Kregel, owner of the company from the 1940s until his death in 1991, is second from the right. (Courtesy of the Kregel Windmill Factory Museum.)

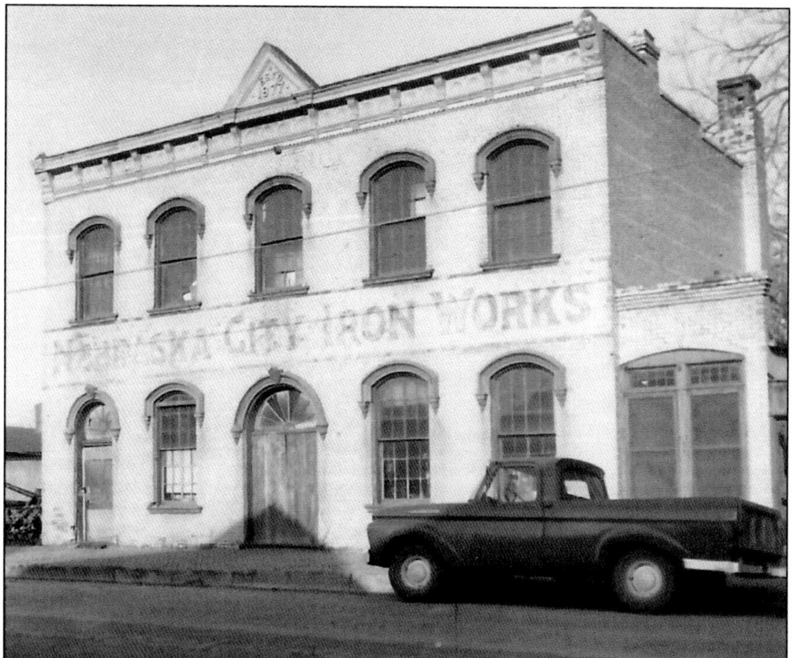

Nebraska City Iron Works was located on the southeast corner of Sixth Street and First Corso. Starting out as a machine shop in 1877, a foundry was added in the 1880s. (Courtesy of the Nebraska City Historical Society.)

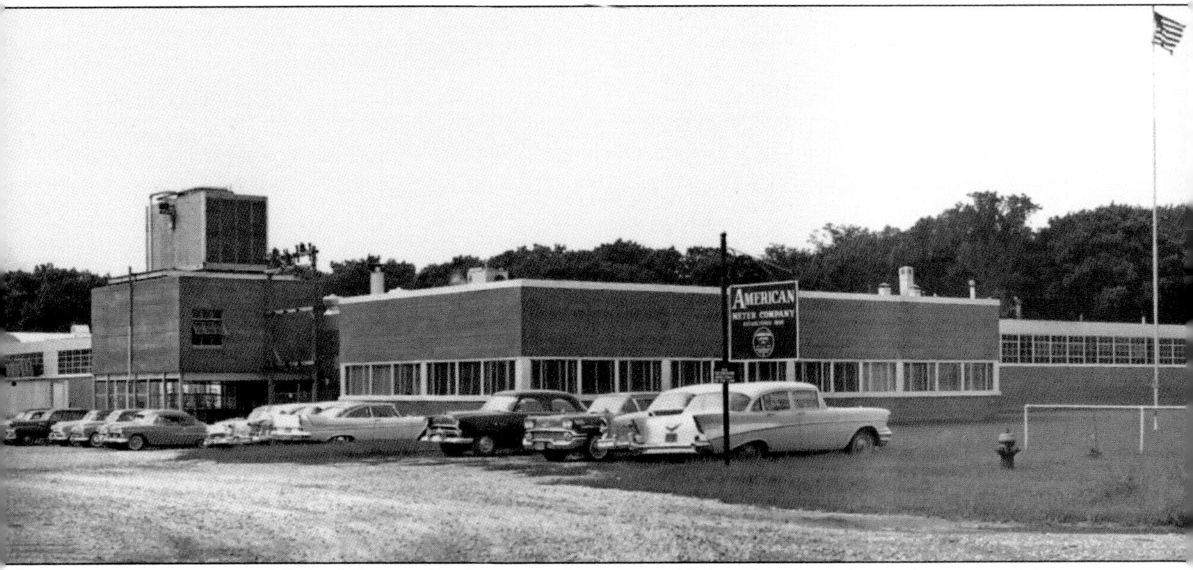

In May 1952, an established factory broke ground on a new Nebraska City plant. American Meter was founded in New York City in 1836 and by the mid-1900s had plants in Pennsylvania, Canada, California, and Texas. More than 300 Nebraska City residents bought $200,000 in bonds to help fund the construction. Constructed on 12 acres on Industrial Road, the building cost $350,000. The grand opening in June 1953 featured exhibits, lunches, speeches, a concert, and a dance. This 1958 photograph was taken five years after the plant opened. (Courtesy of Nebraska City Tourism and Commerce.)

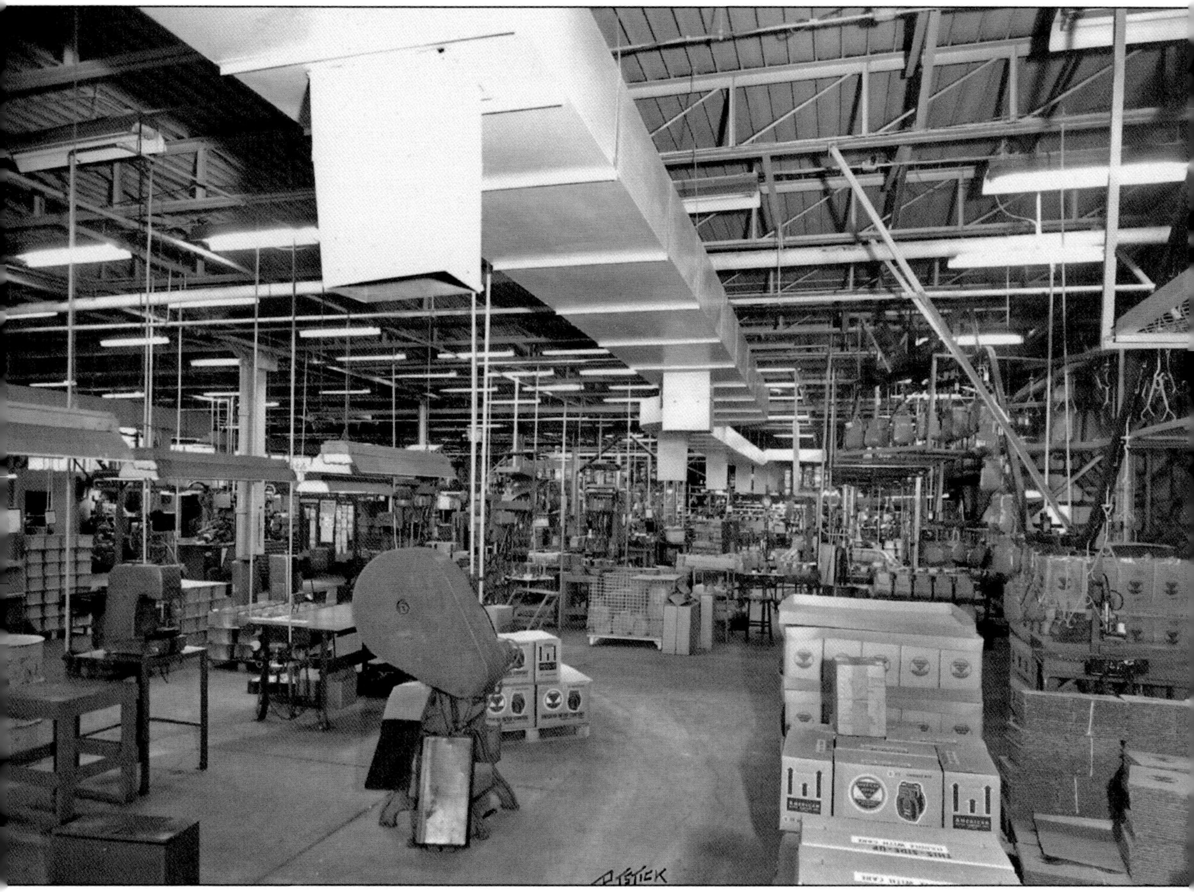

In its first 10 years in existence, American Meter produced over one million utility meters from the Nebraska City plant, employing an average of 100 people. Workers took part in annual family picnics, which often included entertainment such as elephant rides, Ferris wheels, and roller coasters. The American Meter campus also had a picnic area, softball field, tennis courts, outdoor grills, swings, and seesaws. In writing about why they chose Nebraska City as a place to build their plant, American Meter executives commented that they found Nebraska City to be an ideal place, saying, "An amazing number of families are home owners and great churchgoers; even men in less-skilled occupations hold offices in the city administration and take great interest in civic affairs. Nebraska City schools are among the best in the state and the recreational facilities are quite unusual for a town of its size. The attitude of the city and the citizens was friendly and cooperative." (Courtesy of Nebraska City Tourism and Commerce.)

Five

FIGHTING FIRE

When not fighting fire, Nebraska City firefighters would show off their strength, agility, and bravery in competitions throughout the Midwest. This 1883 photograph shows Ira Goldin (left) and William Lasher of Company No. 1 as the champion hose couplers at a competition in Omaha. Goldin owned a confectionery and ice cream parlor in downtown Nebraska City, and Lasher was chief engineer at Great Western Cereal Mills. (Courtesy of the Nebraska City Museum of Firefighting.)

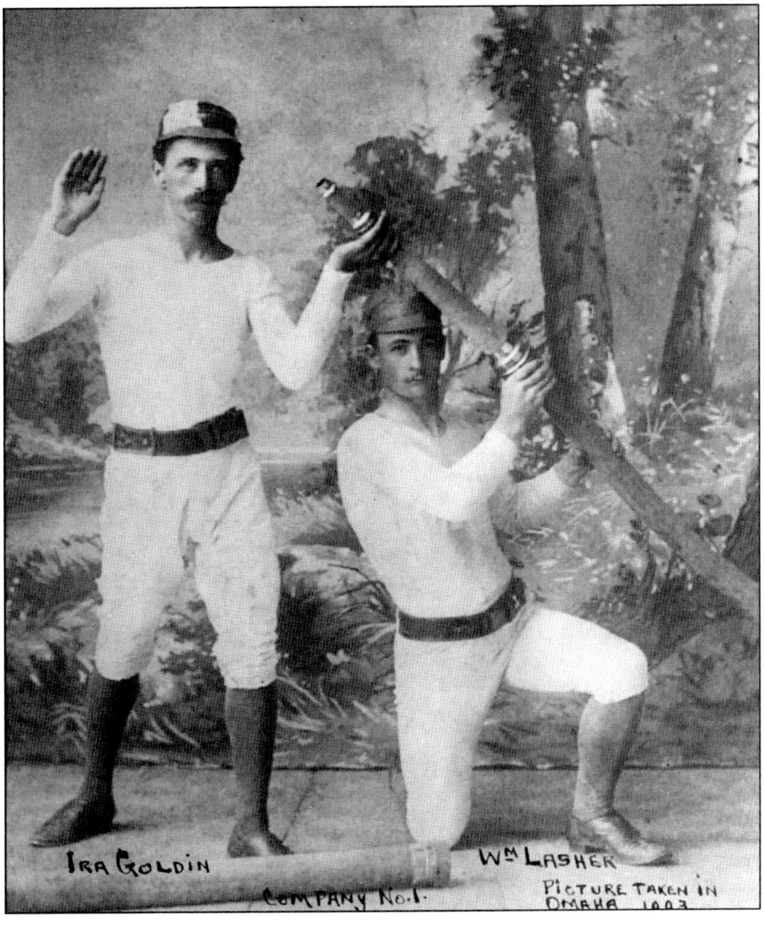

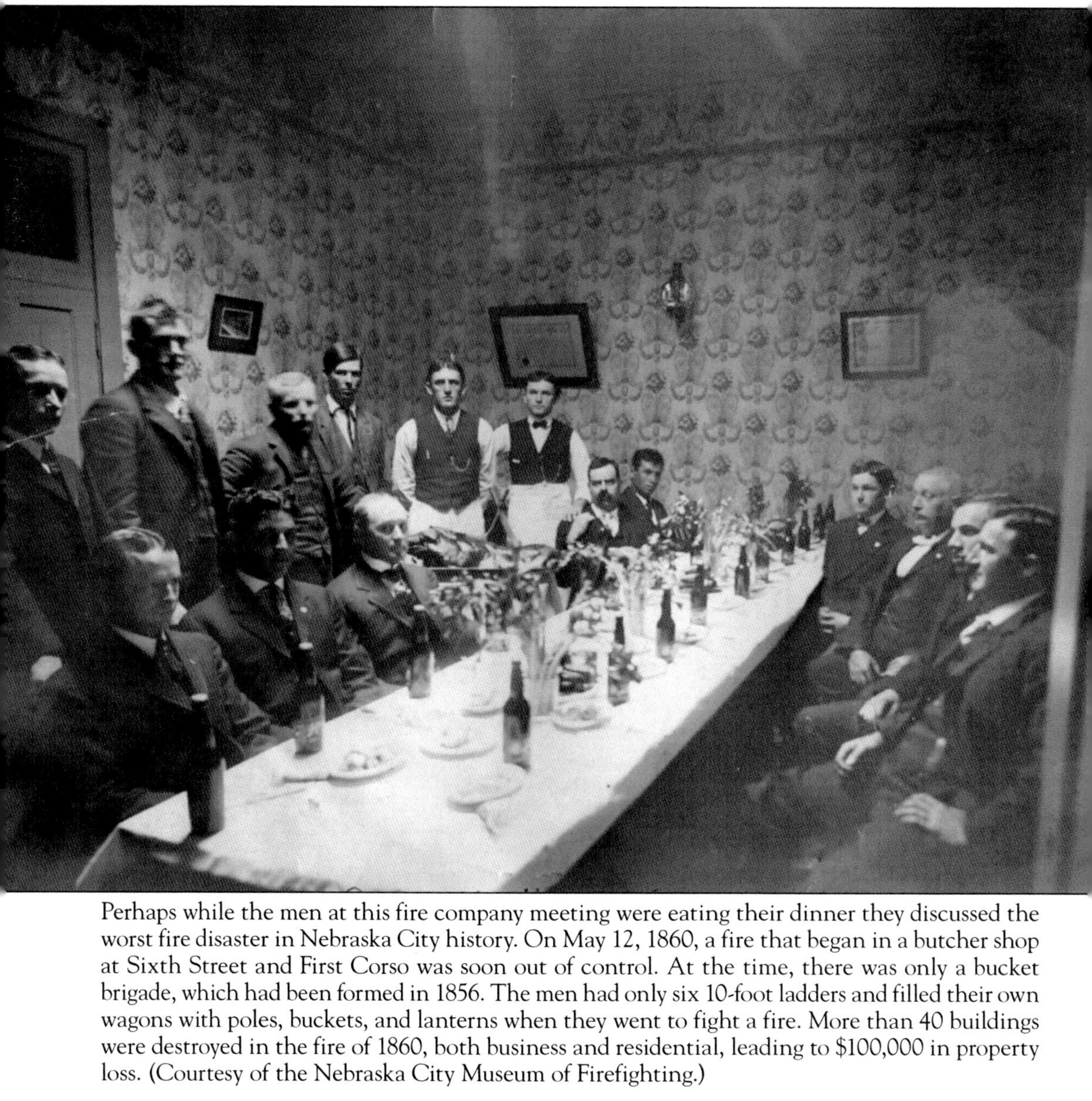

Perhaps while the men at this fire company meeting were eating their dinner they discussed the worst fire disaster in Nebraska City history. On May 12, 1860, a fire that began in a butcher shop at Sixth Street and First Corso was soon out of control. At the time, there was only a bucket brigade, which had been formed in 1856. The men had only six 10-foot ladders and filled their own wagons with poles, buckets, and lanterns when they went to fight a fire. More than 40 buildings were destroyed in the fire of 1860, both business and residential, leading to $100,000 in property loss. (Courtesy of the Nebraska City Museum of Firefighting.)

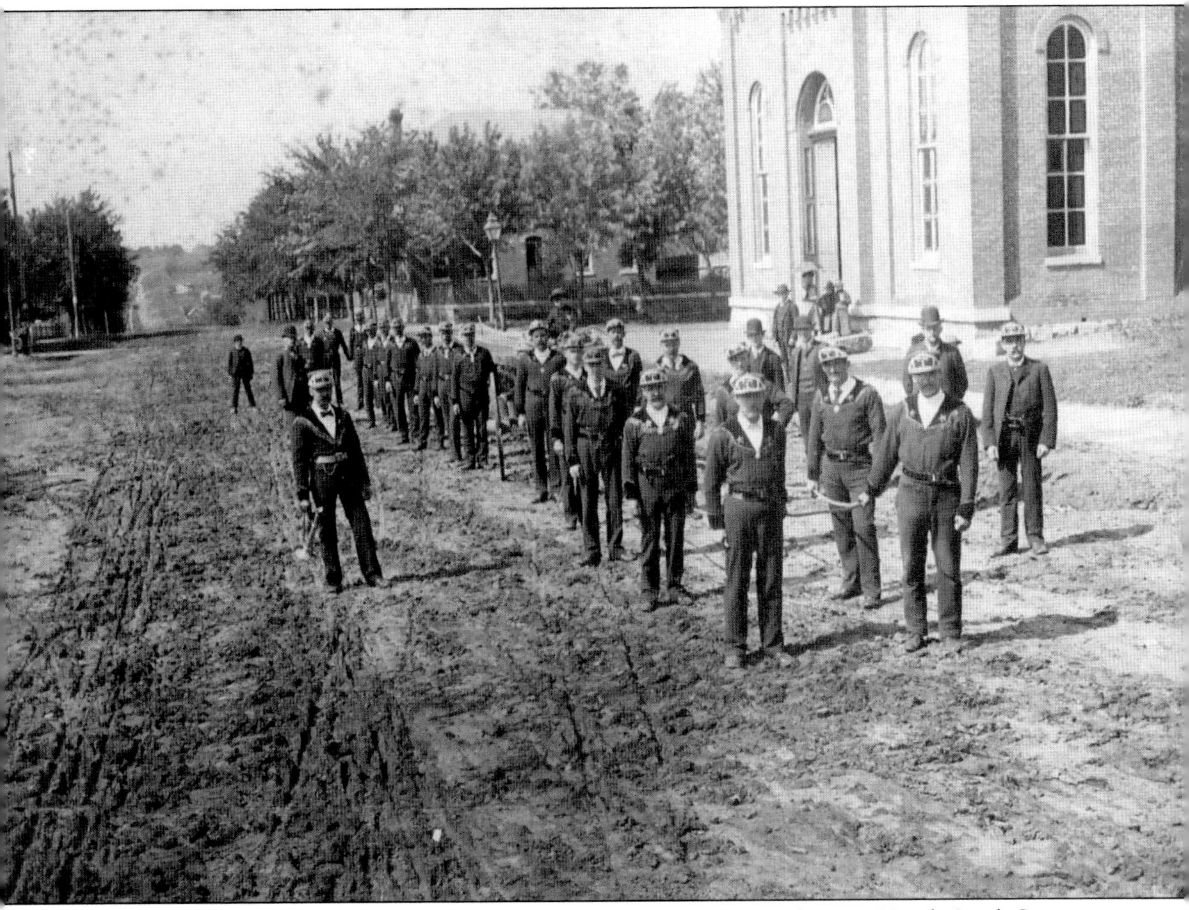

This 1887 photograph of the Otoe Hook and Ladder Company was taken on North Sixth Street between Central and First Avenues. The old St. Mary's Catholic Church is behind the men, and the unpaved Sixth Street is visible through the trees as it heads north. Nebraska City is home to the oldest fire department in the state; the Otoe Hook and Ladder Company No. 1 officially formed on November 28, 1861. The Nebraska City Fire Company No. 1 began in 1865, and the Great Western Fire Company No. 1 organized in 1869. (Courtesy of the Nebraska City Museum of Firefighting.)

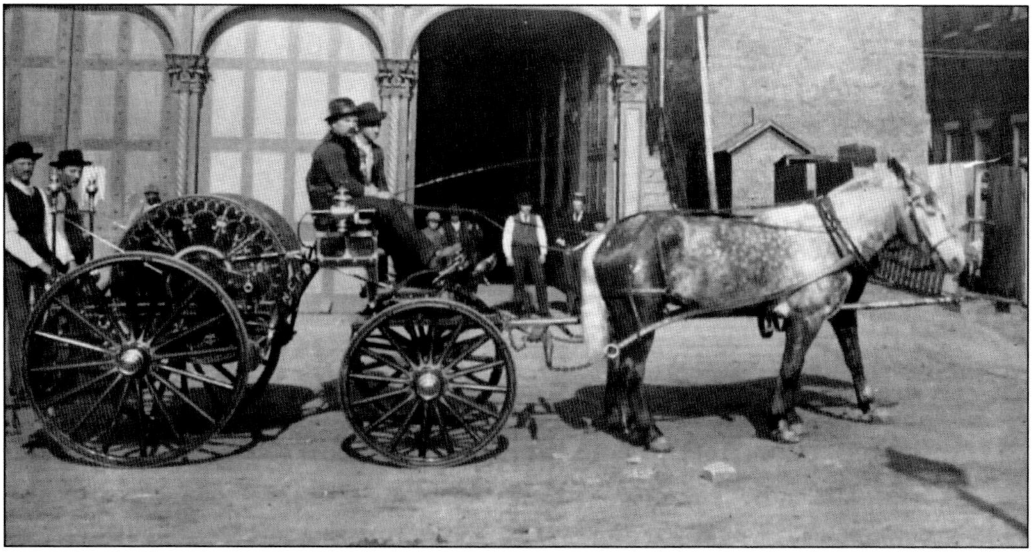

In 1888, a hydrant system was installed throughout town, and this horse-drawn reel was hooked to the hydrant. In the background is the original fire hall, built in 1872. It burned in 1901, and a new hall was constructed on the same spot. The current Nebraska City Museum of Firefighting at 1320 Central Avenue was designed to look like the original fire hall. (Courtesy of the Nebraska City Museum of Firefighting.)

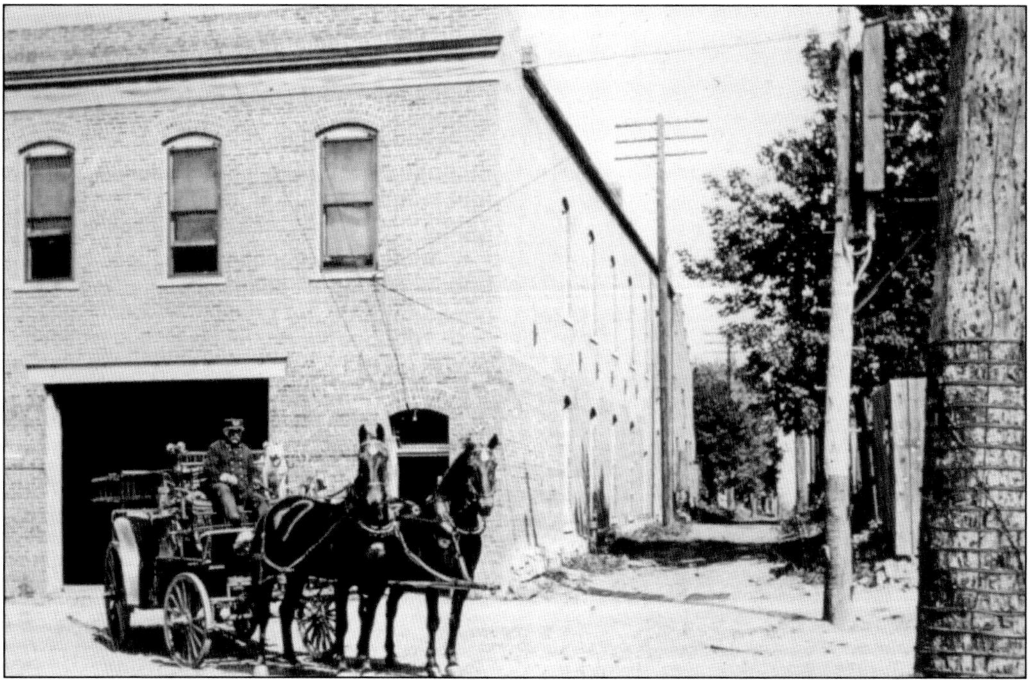

The 1901 fire hall also housed city hall. The brick building was located on the east side of Sixth Street between Central and First Avenues. (Courtesy of the Nebraska City Museum of Firefighting.)

This 1900 parade on the 900 block of Central Avenue shows two longtime fixtures of the fire department. Driving the wagon is White Handley, and next to him is Chief Mike Bauer. Bauer was in the department for 67 years and served as chief for 31 years. The fire department purchased its first motorized vehicle in 1916, and its fleet of horses was officially retired in 1923. (Courtesy of the Nebraska City Museum of Firefighting.)

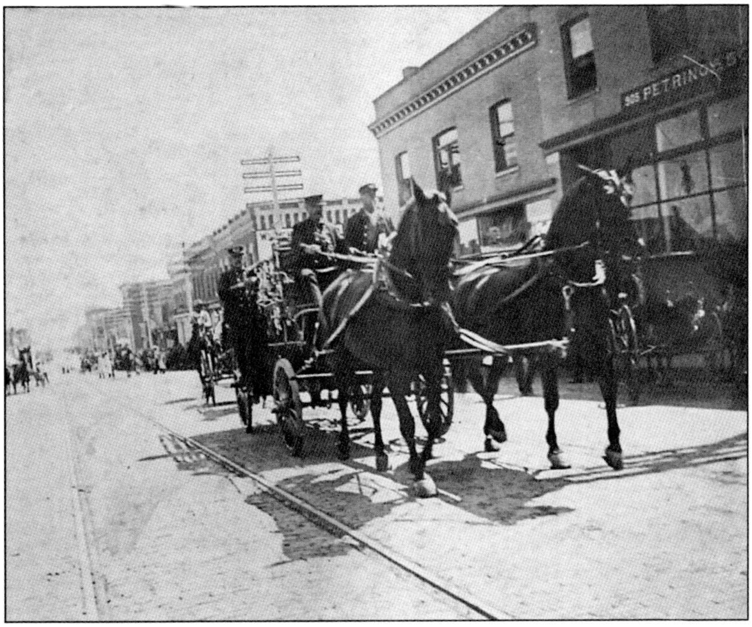

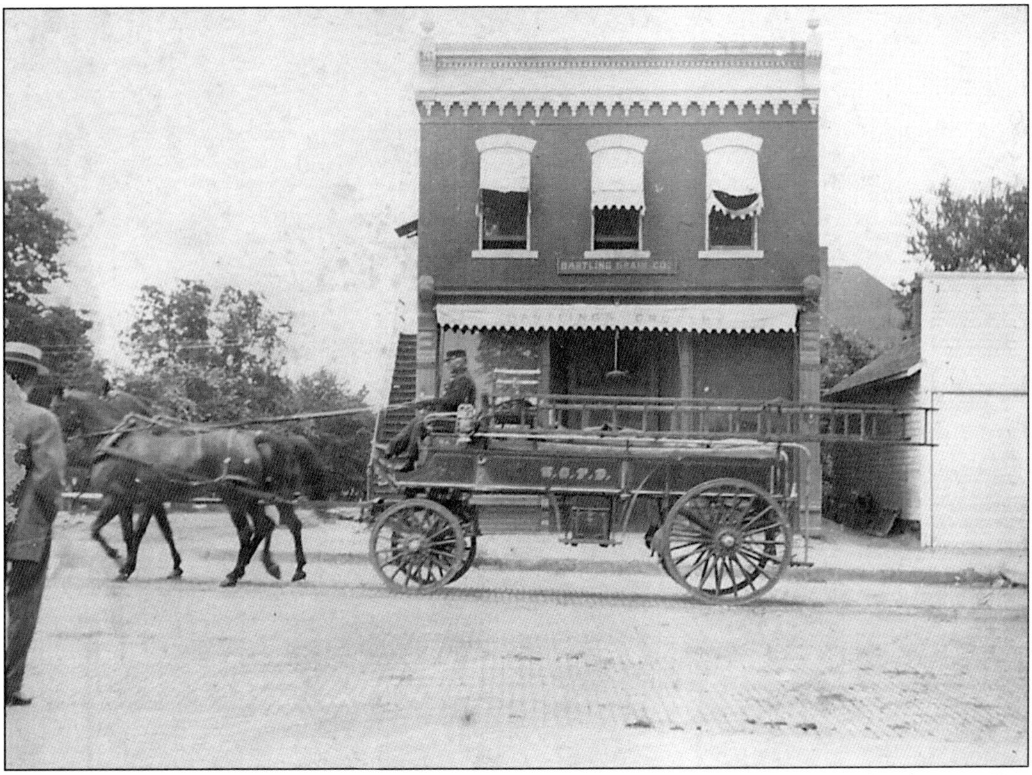

In 1906, all three fire companies (Otoe Hook and Ladder Company No. 1, the Nebraska City Fire Company No. 1, and Great Western Fire Company No. 1) joined together to create the Nebraska City Volunteer Fire Department. This photograph from a 1907 parade shows a fire wagon in front of the Bartling Grain Company at Central Avenue and Eleventh Street. (Courtesy of the Nebraska City Museum of Firefighting.)

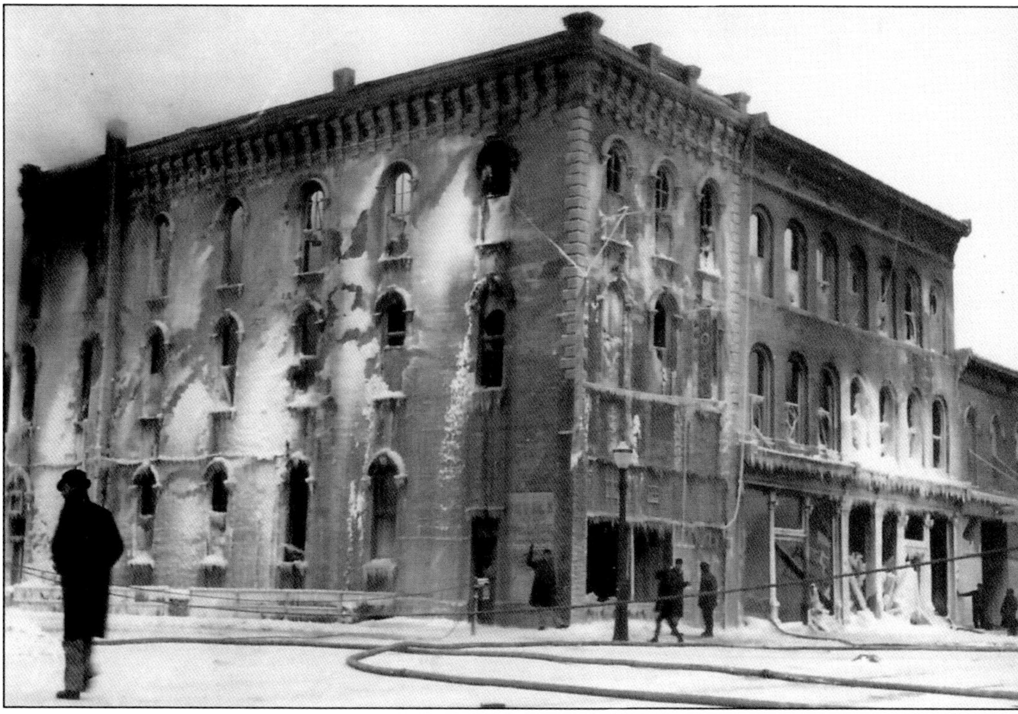

The Marcus Hotel at the southwest corner of Sixth Street and Central Avenue was built in 1871 and later irreparably damaged in 1936. Nine firemen were injured fighting the blaze. After the fire, bricks from the Marcus Hotel were gathered and reused in other building projects. (Both courtesy of the Nebraska City Museum of Firefighting.)

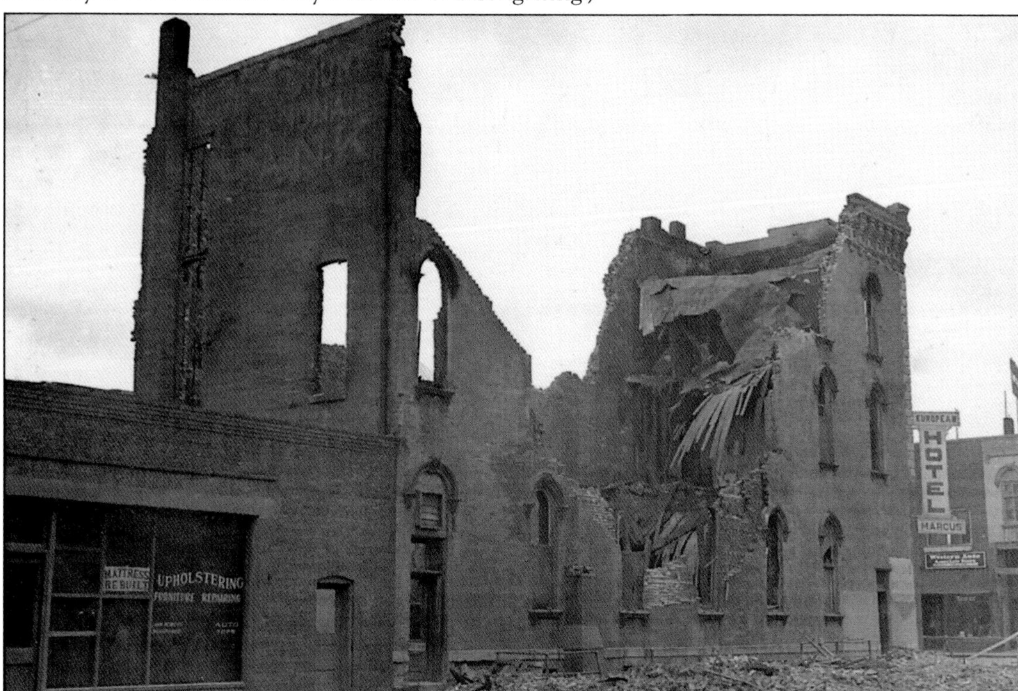

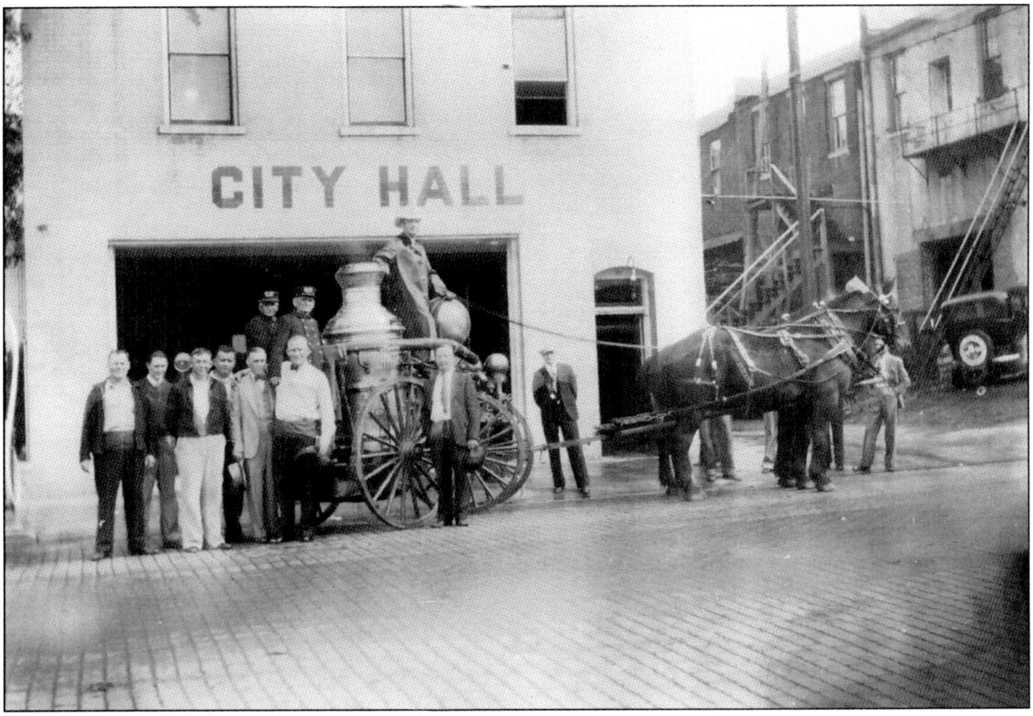

Nebraska City firefighters welcomed the first steam pumper in 1884. Used for many years, the contraption was pulled by hand, although the firemen did hook it up to horses when displaying it in parades. (Courtesy of the Nebraska City Museum of Firefighting.)

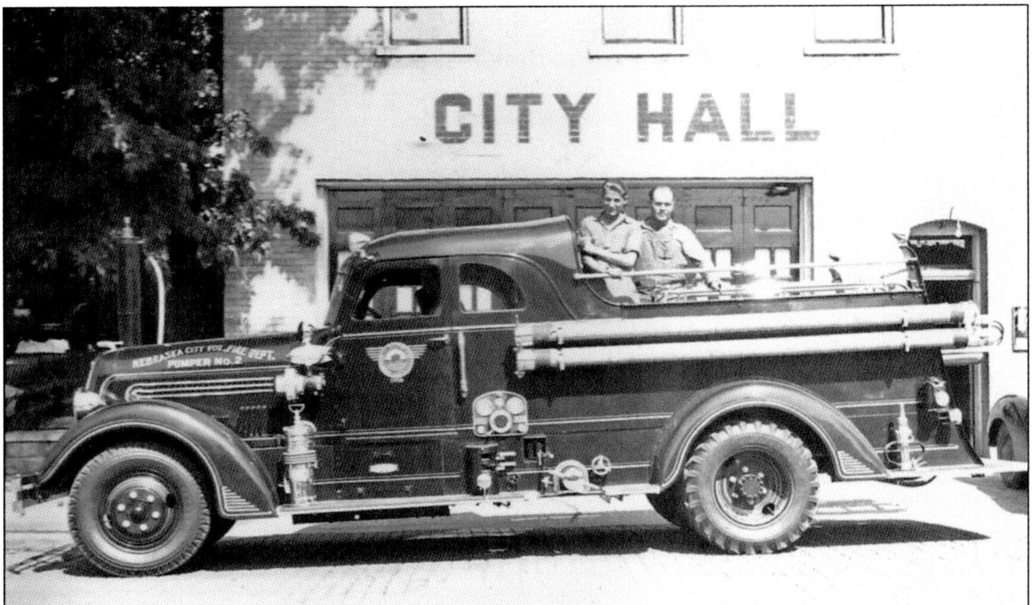

Costing just under $7,000, the Nebraska City Volunteer Fire Department welcomed the Seagrave Fire Engine Pumper No. 2 to its arsenal in July 1938. (Courtesy of the Nebraska City Museum of Firefighting.)

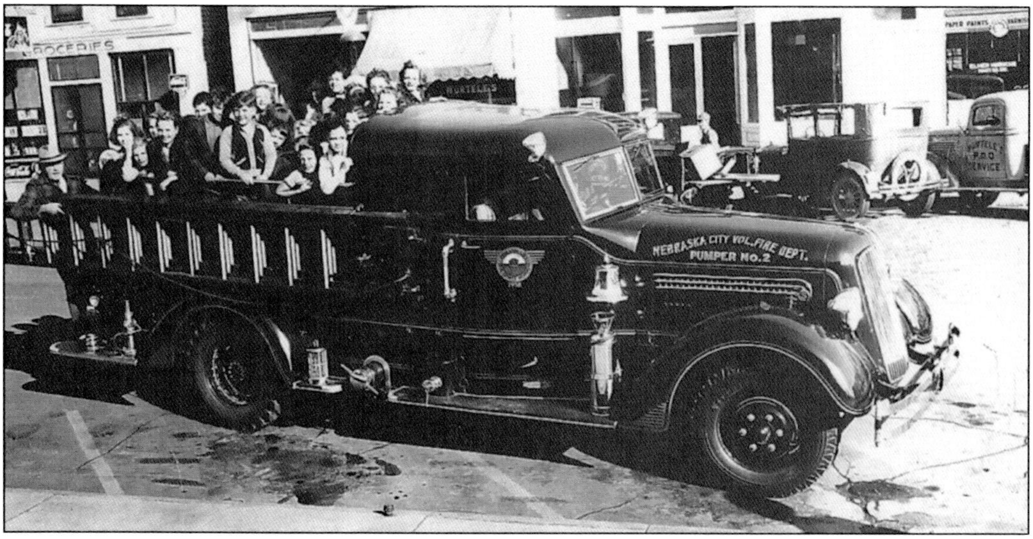

Firefighters invited children to ride around town in the Seagrave during Fire Prevention Week. Since its inception, the Nebraska City Volunteer Fire Department has focused much of its energy on educating the public about fire safety and fire prevention. Although the Seagrave has been retired from service for many years, it joins the first steam pumper and other apparatus on display at the Nebraska City Museum of Firefighting, which opened to the public in 2008. (Both courtesy of the Nebraska City Museum of Firefighting.)

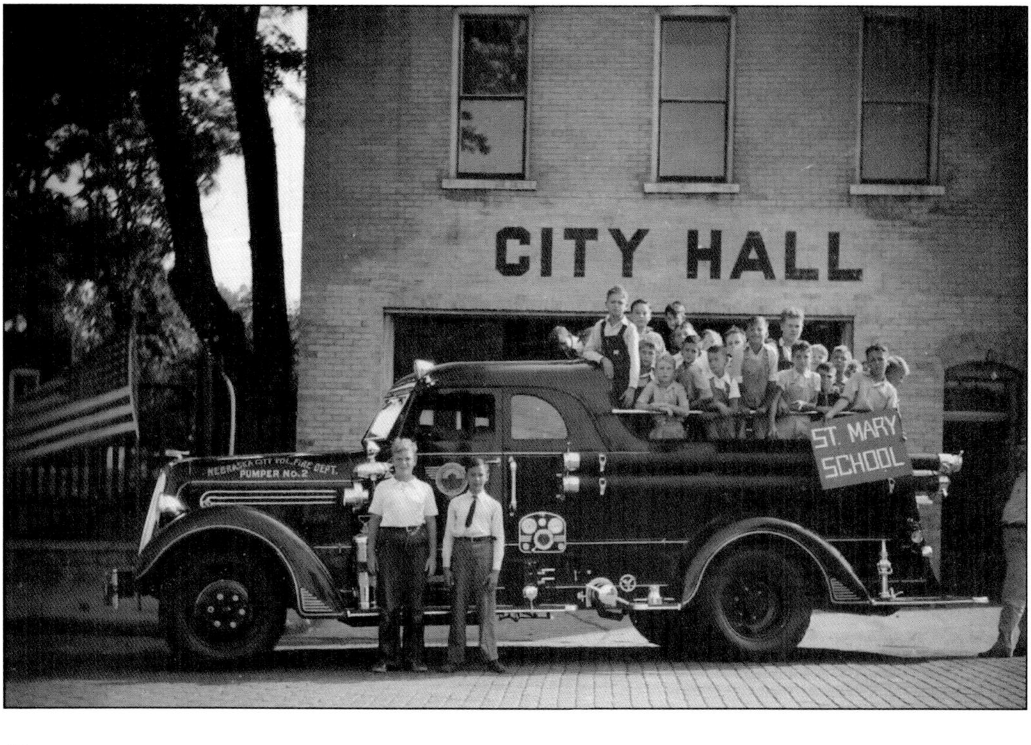

Six

Daily Life

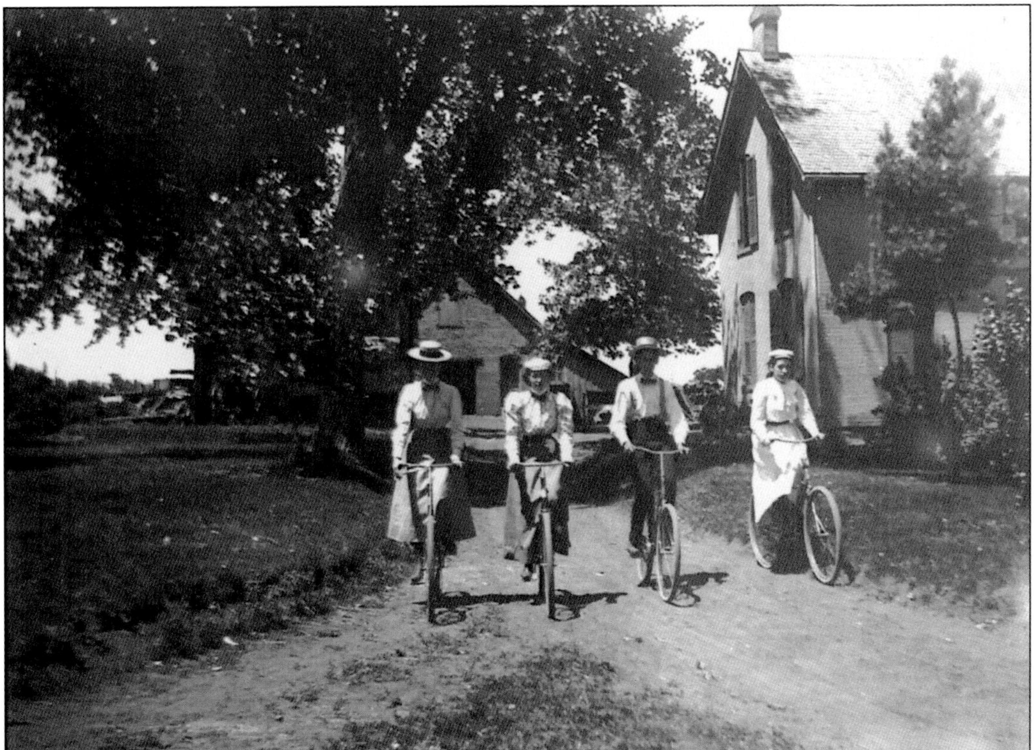

Florence, Nell, Grace, and Norton Ware are pictured here riding bicycles at their home, named Wildwood. Jasper and Ellen Ware, their parents, moved to Nebraska City in 1869. The town was already home to several schools, public entertainment venues, and fraternal lodges. In September 1859, ten acres south of town had been cordoned off to create grounds for the first Territorial Agriculture and Mechanical Fair. Nebraska City even hosted the first Nebraska State Fair in 1868. (Courtesy of the Wildwood Period House.)

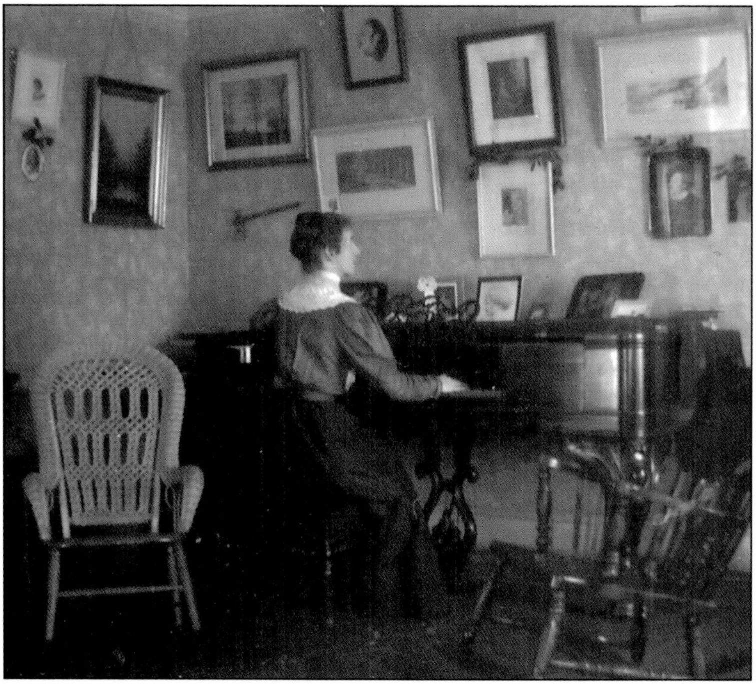

Reading was a popular hobby in the 1800s; the Ladies Round Table and Literary Club was organized in 1869 and collected 100 books to start the town's first library. That led to the construction of the Morton James Public Library in 1896. Another hobby was music. Grace Ware, daughter of Jasper and Ellen, is pictured here at her home, Wildwood. Ware trained in music at Juilliard in New York City. (Courtesy of the Wildwood Period House.)

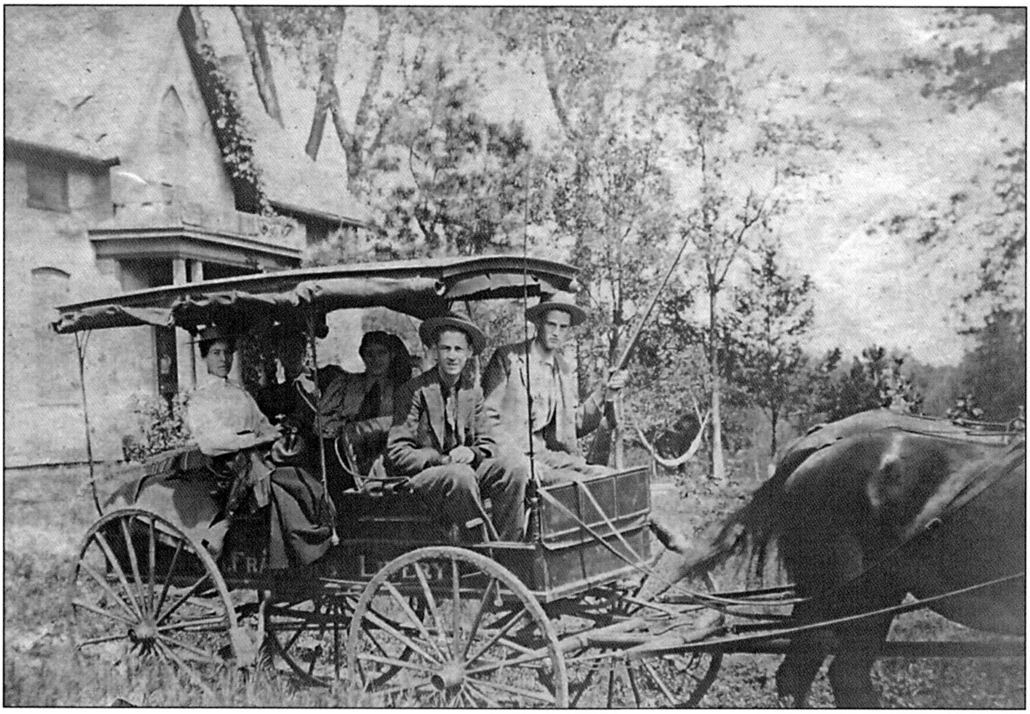

The four Ware children and a friend loaded up a livery wagon in preparation for a three-day trip in the late 1890s. Their home, Wildwood, is pictured in the background. In the late 1960s, the Ware's historical home and grounds were given to the City of Nebraska City to serve as a park, increase the size of the city-owned golf course, and preserve the house as a museum. (Courtesy of the Wildwood Period House.)

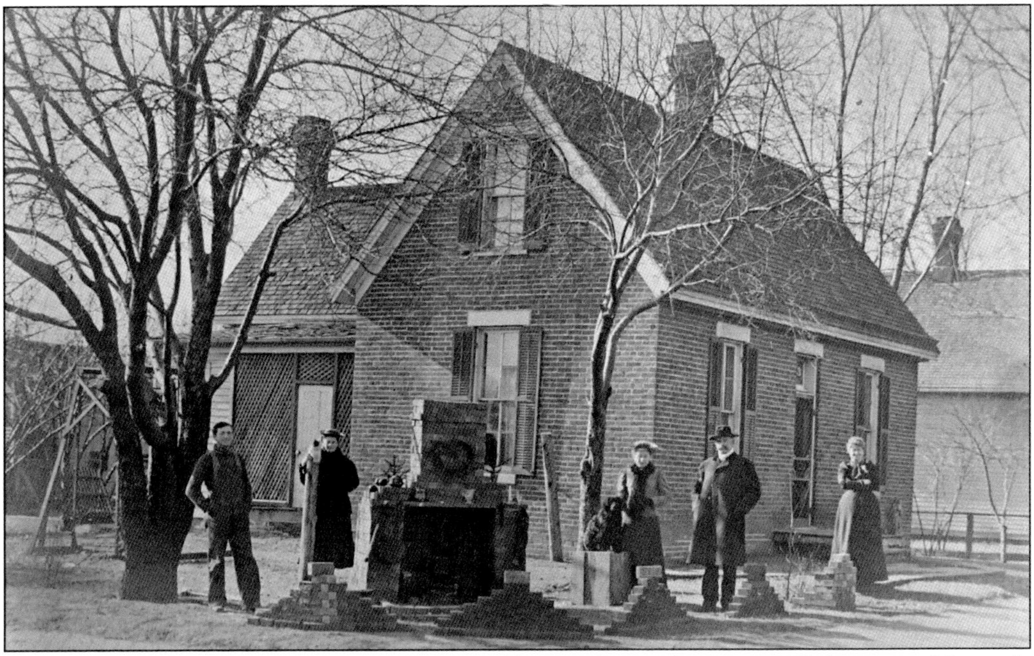

The Bickel home at 703 Third Corso is pictured here in December 1906. While many of the early structures in Nebraska City were built of wood, the founding of local brick factories increased the number of brick homes and businesses. Brick was favored over wood mainly because of its durability and fire-resistant nature. (Courtesy of Brett and Robyn Gay.)

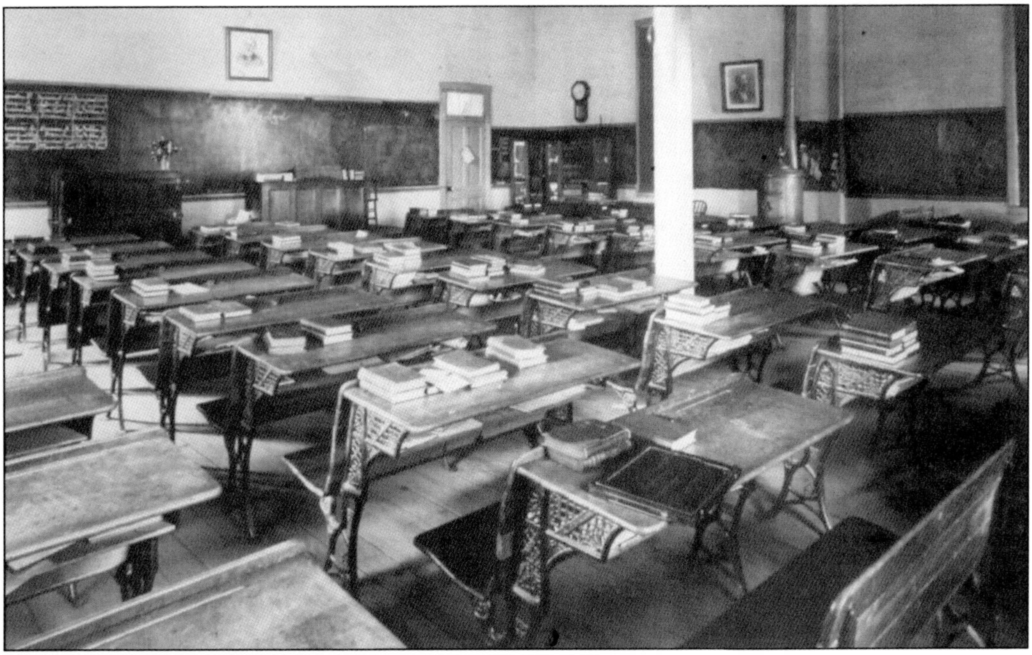

Nebraska City's first teacher was Margaret Martin. She began teaching in 1855 and earned $1.50 per month. Lucy Bowen taught at the second school opened in Nebraska City, beginning in the spring of 1856. It was a private school on Third Rue and Sixth Terrace. Bowen taught there 25 years. (Courtesy of the Nebraska City Historical Society.)

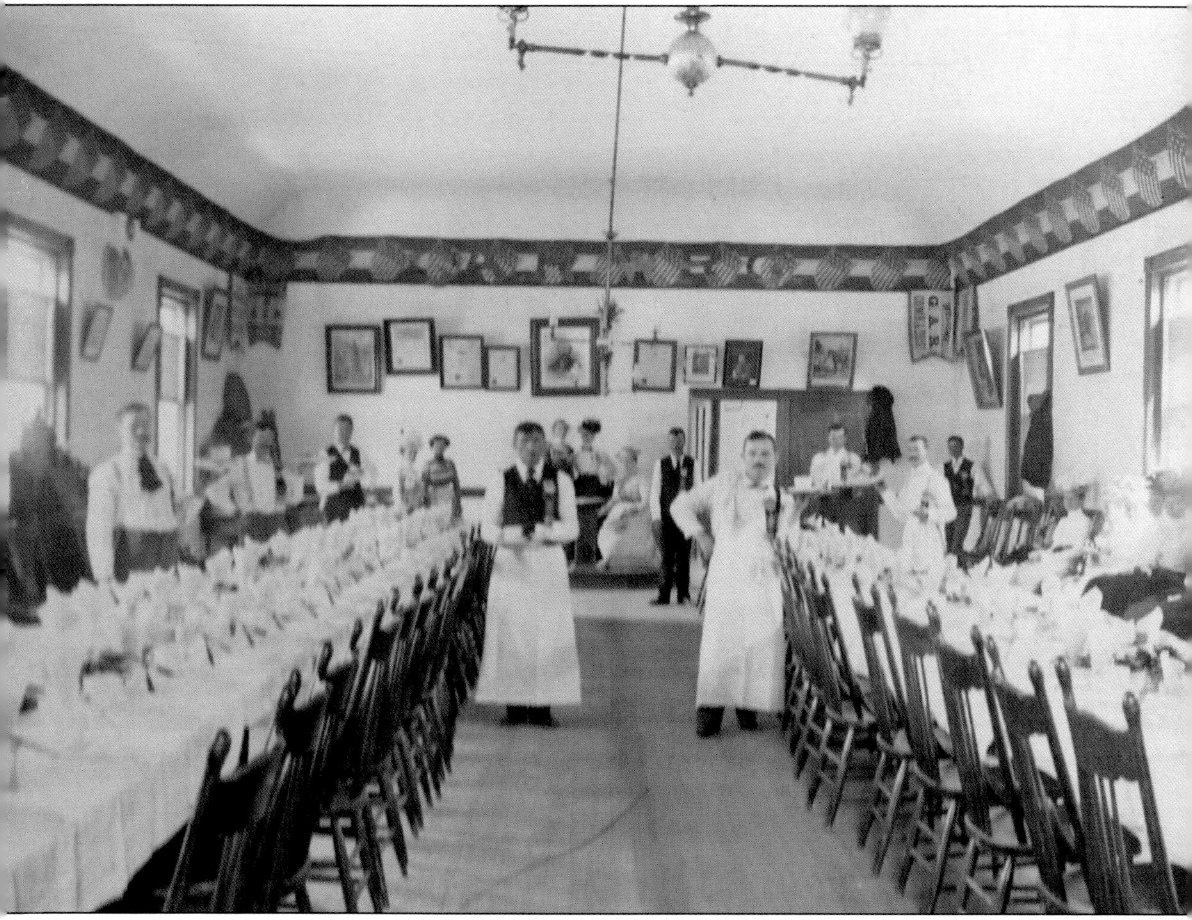

Nebraska City's Grand Army of the Republic Hall at 910 First Corso was built in 1894 to honor local veterans of the Civil War. The hall was used for meetings and special events, like the one in this 1898 photograph. (Courtesy of the GAR Hall.)

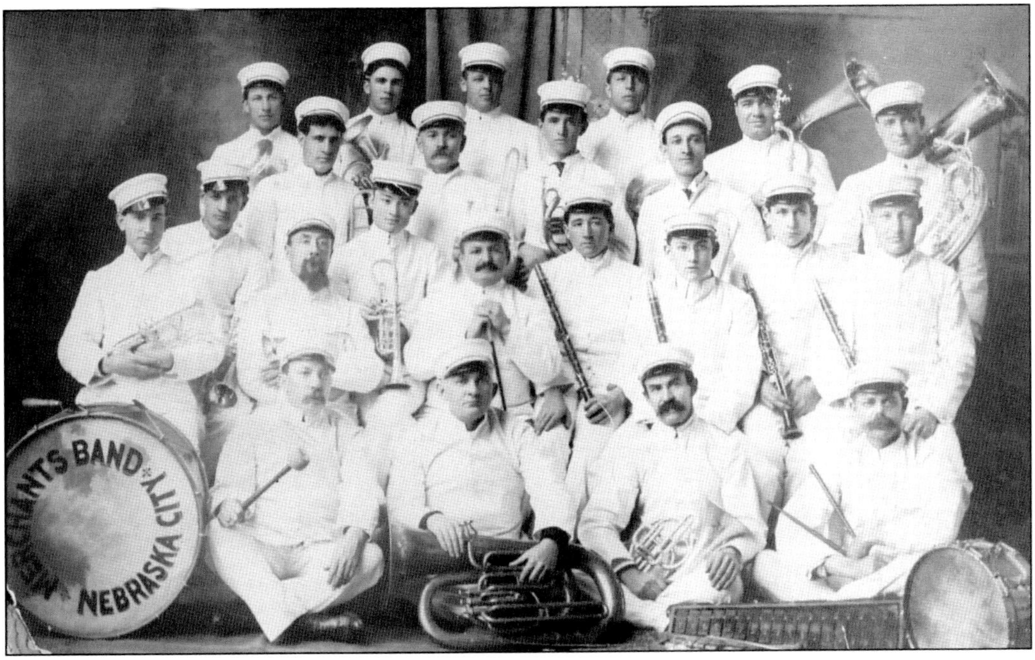

Early settlers tended to be civic-minded people. Local merchants started a band, seen above, and even held parades. The photograph below was taken on May 30, 1908. Residents also were quick to hold posts in the city government and introduced many fraternal lodges, including a Masonic lodge and the Independent Order of Odd Fellows. (Both courtesy of Nebraska City Tourism and Commerce.)

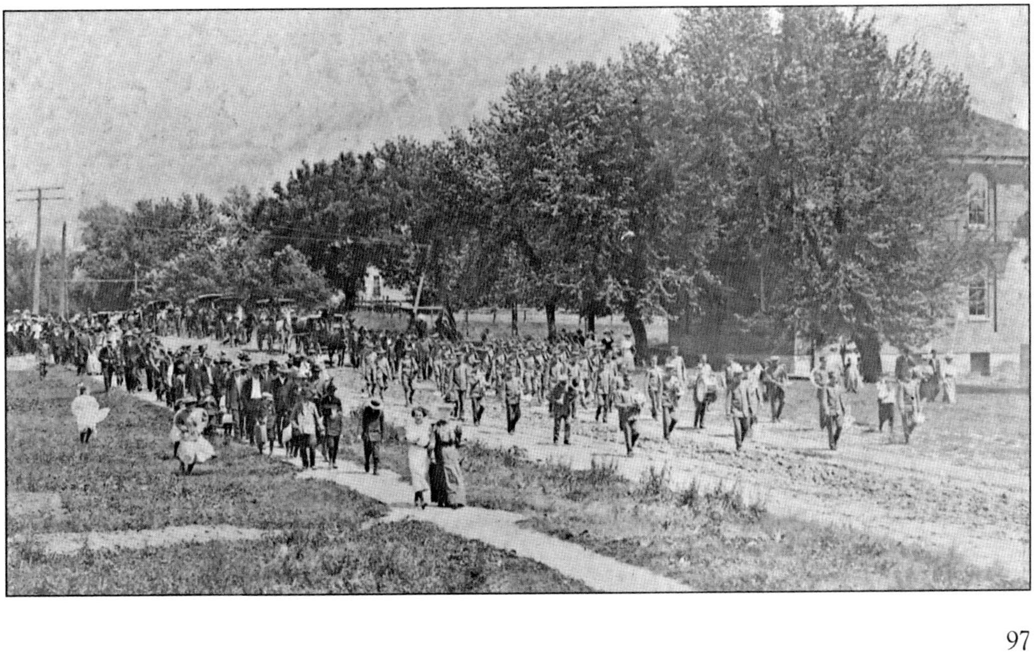

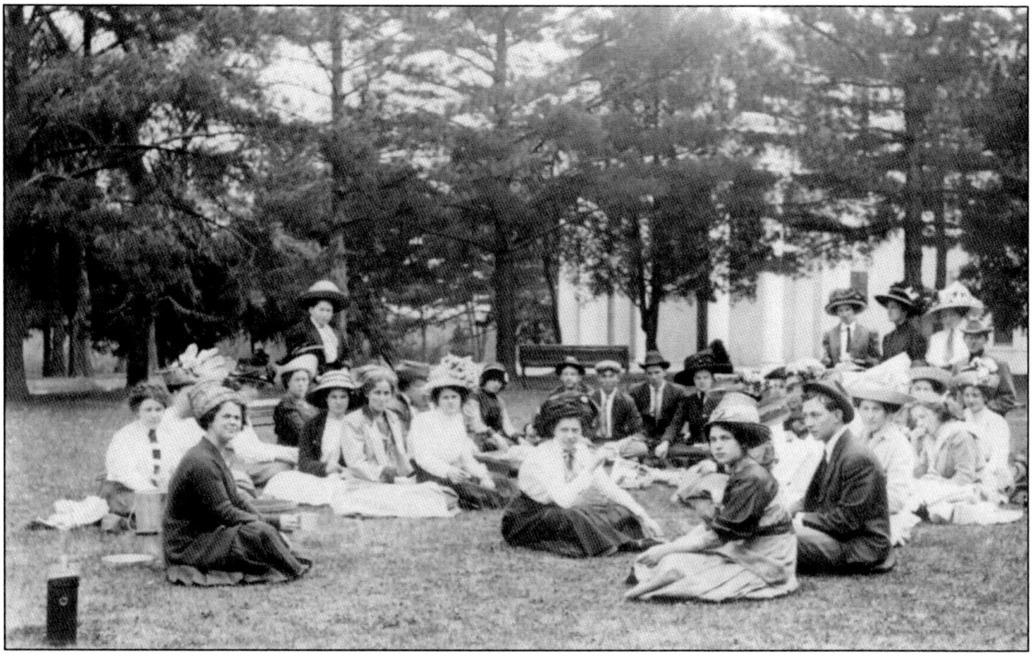

Nebraska City residents enjoy a picnic on the lawn of Arbor Lodge. Other leisure activities included concerts, parades, gun clubs, tennis, horse racing, and bicycling. (Courtesy of Arbor Lodge.)

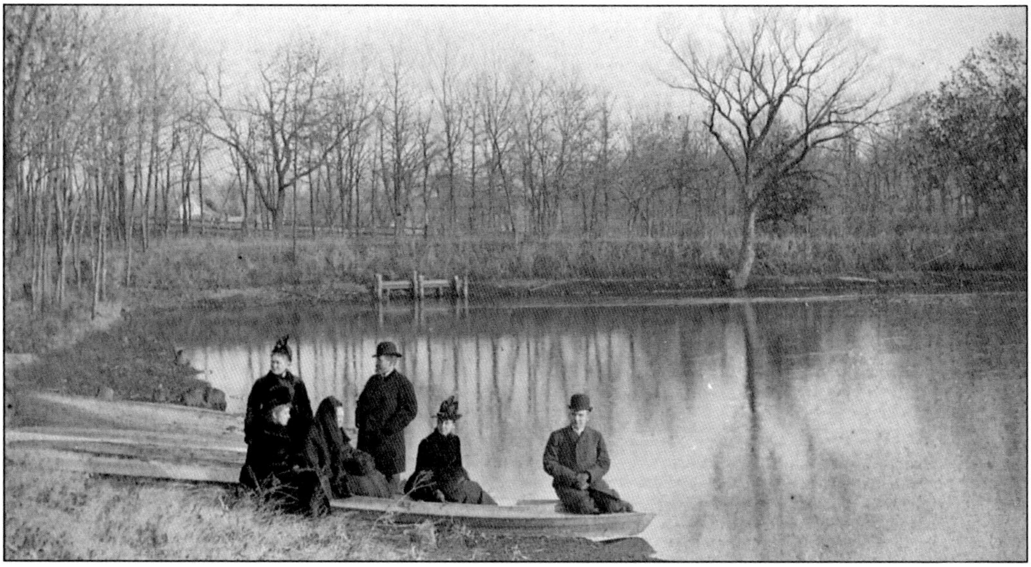

At the east end of Arbor Lodge Park, along Second Avenue, was Morton Lake. It was located in a 23-acre tract of land that had been ceded to Nebraska City by J. Sterling Morton. Morton asked the city to tend to the land as a public park, and when Joy Morton donated Arbor Lodge to the state in 1923, Morton Park was included in the transaction. The lake was eventually filled in. (Courtesy of Arbor Lodge.)

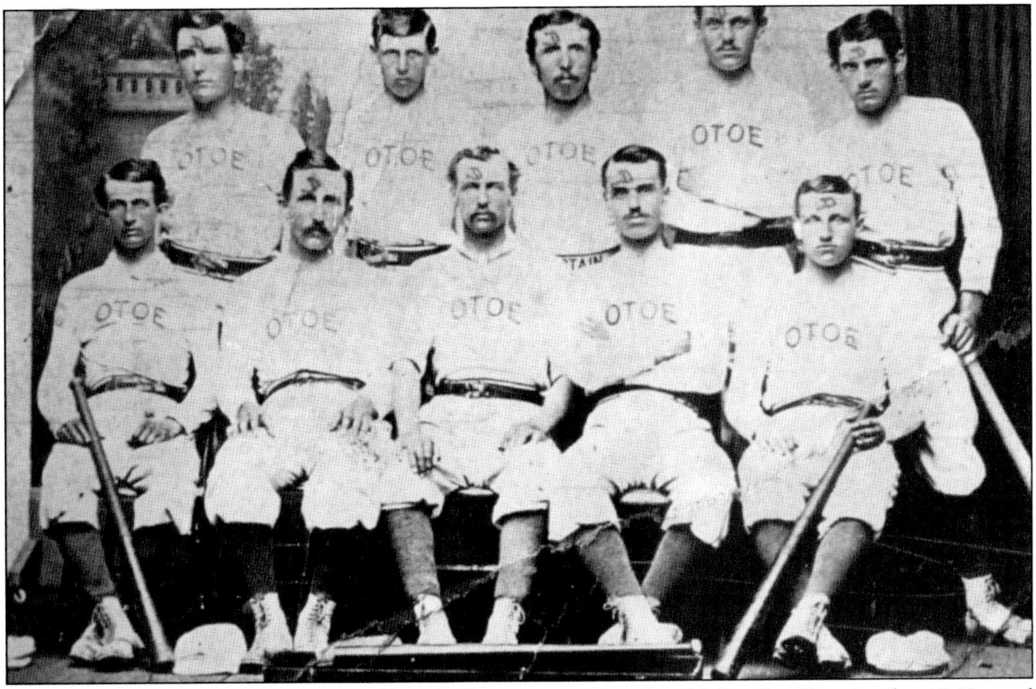

The thoroughly American sport of baseball was introduced to Nebraska City in the 1860s and proved to be very popular. The town's team, called the Otoes, even played a game against the Cincinnati Reds in 1869. The Reds went undefeated that season; the team is often considered the first professional team in baseball. (Courtesy of the Arbor Day Foundation.)

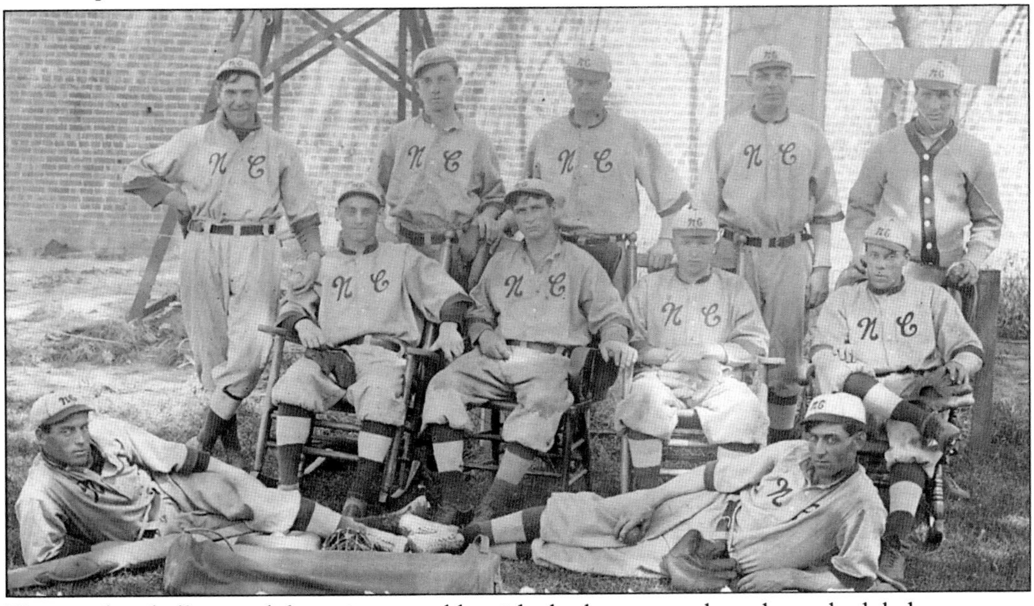

The city baseball team did run into trouble with the law once when they scheduled a game on a Sunday afternoon. The local sheriff came armed to stop the game, but the crowd interfered, giving the visiting team from Omaha time go into hiding until they could catch the next train home. Sunday baseball was not played again for a long time, perhaps not even by these players in 1910. (Courtesy of the Nebraska City Museum of Firefighting.)

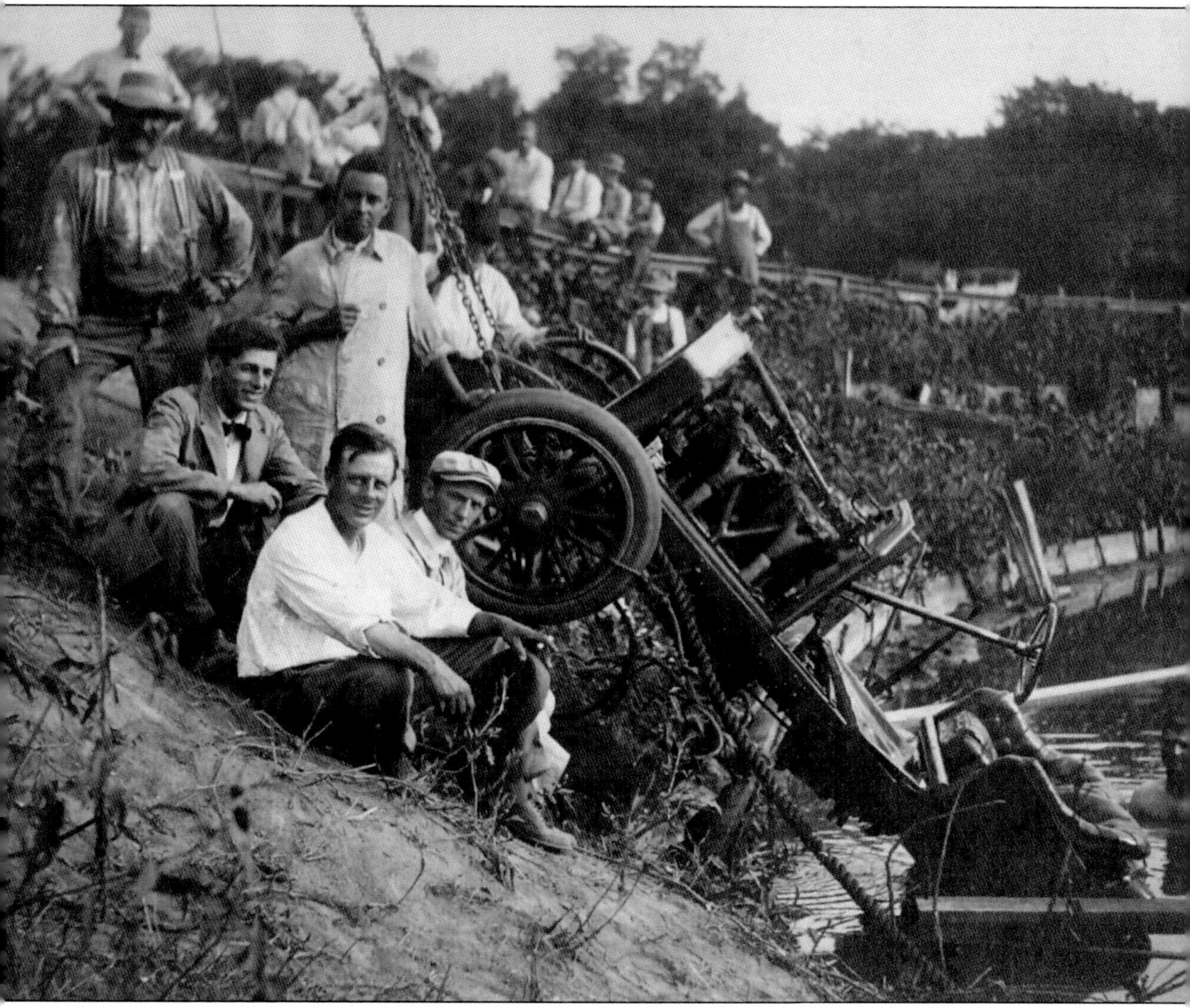

On July 4, 1910, Eddie Rickenbacker, who was well on his way to becoming a famous race-car driver, participated in a car race in Nebraska City's Steinhart Park, nicknamed Driving Park. Rickenbacker blew a tire and ended up in Steinhart Pond. He later competed several times in the Indianapolis 500 and became a top fighter pilot during World War I. (Courtesy of the Nebraska City Museum of Firefighting.)

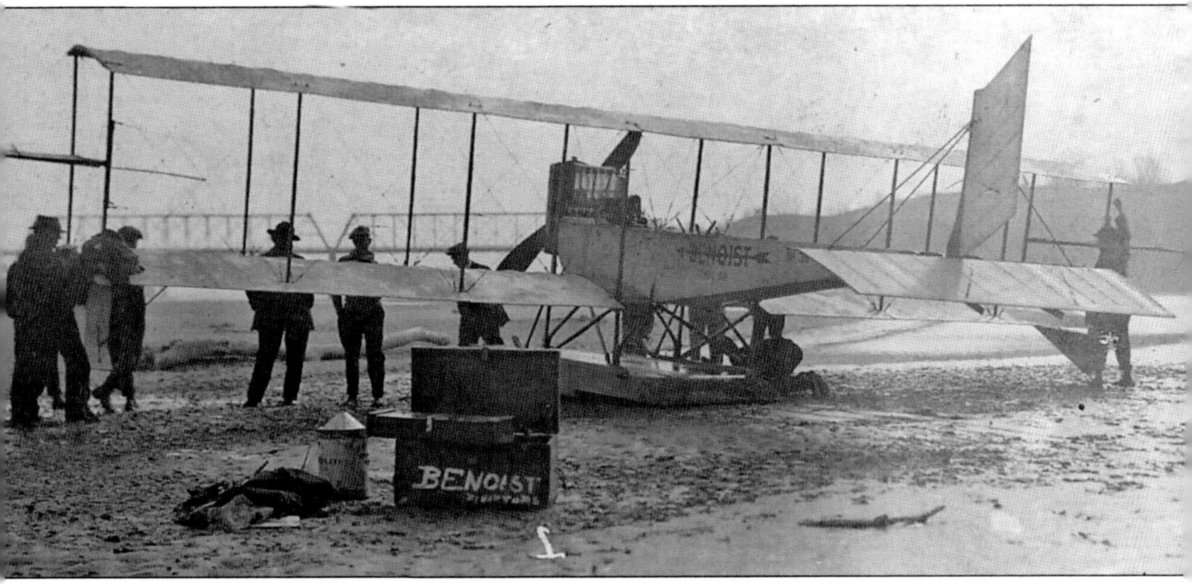

On a cold day in November 1912, Benoist Aviators landed a tractor biplane on the flats of the Missouri River. The plane was in route from Omaha, Nebraska, to New Orleans, Louisiana. (Courtesy of Nebraska City Tourism and Commerce.)

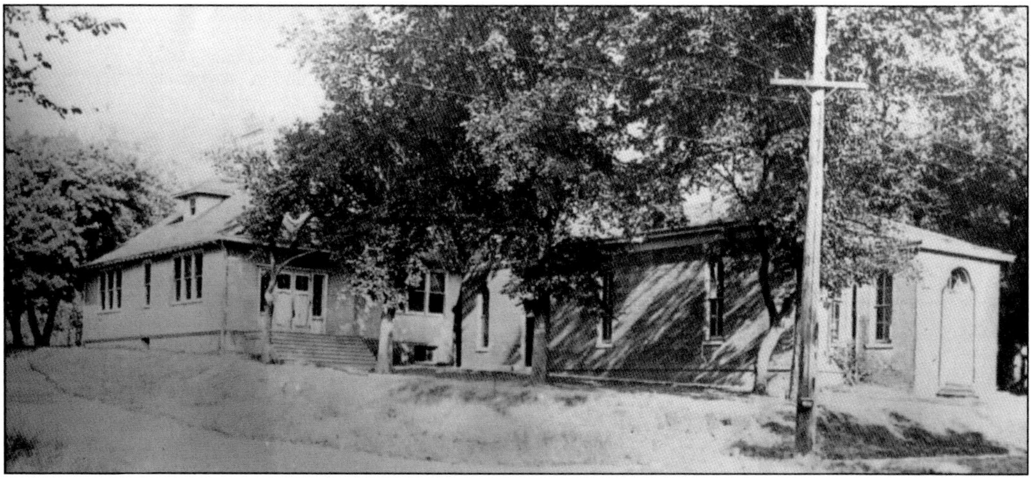

Nebraska City opened the first high school in the state in 1865. While not consistently used due to many options of private schooling in the community, residents did front the $31,000 to build the structure. The first NCHS graduate is recognized as Mary Cornelia Petring, in 1880. (Both courtesy of the Nebraska City Historical Society.)

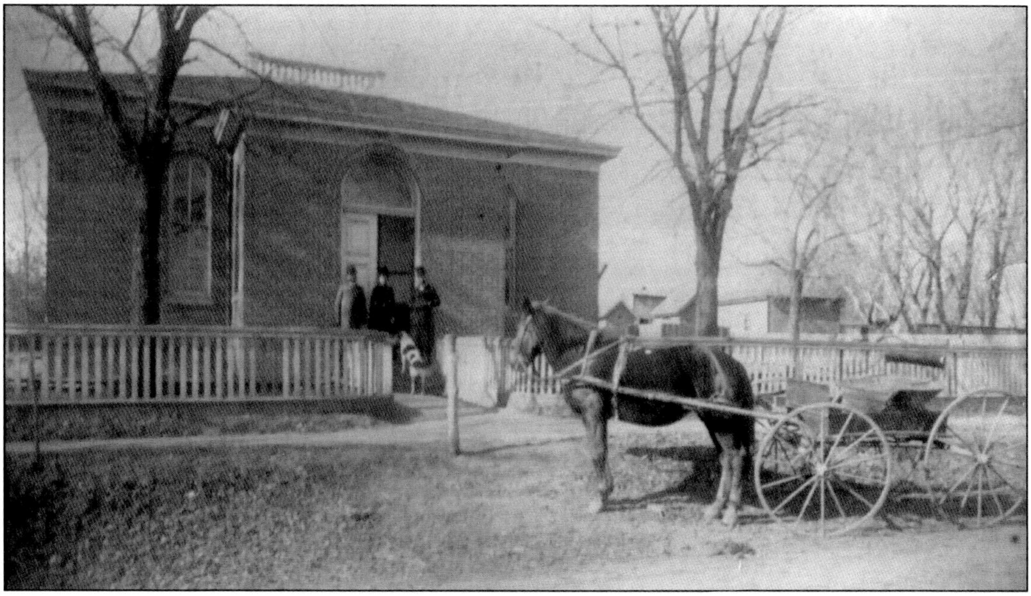

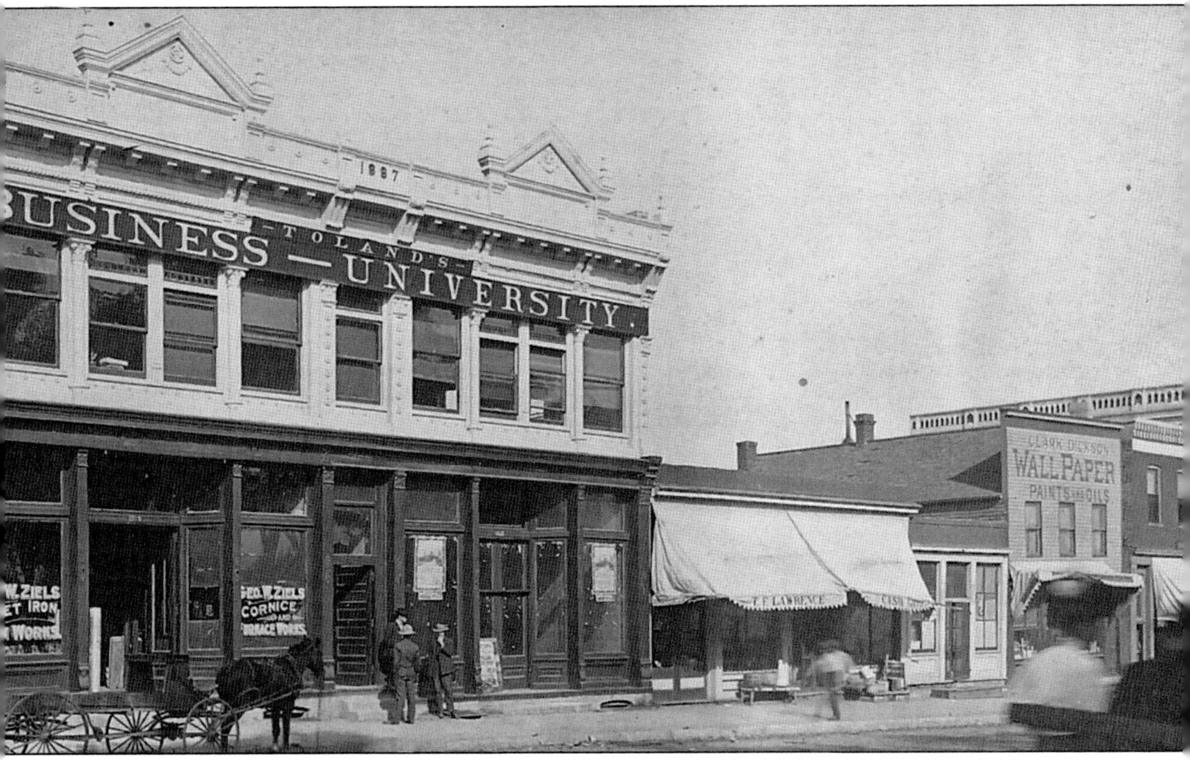

After completing high school, there were several opportunities for higher education in Nebraska City, including Toland's Business University on Central Avenue across from the Otoe County Courthouse. Another school, Otoe University, opened in 1859 at the corner of Fourteenth Street and Fourth Avenue. Classes were offered in languages, moral science, mathematics, natural science, German, French, music, painting, gymnastics, physiology, pathology, and the nature and laws of the mind. Otoe University was sponsored by the Presbyterian Church and had about 100 students annually. Nebraska College bought the Otoe University property in 1872 and closed it in 1885. (Courtesy of Dorris Sackles.)

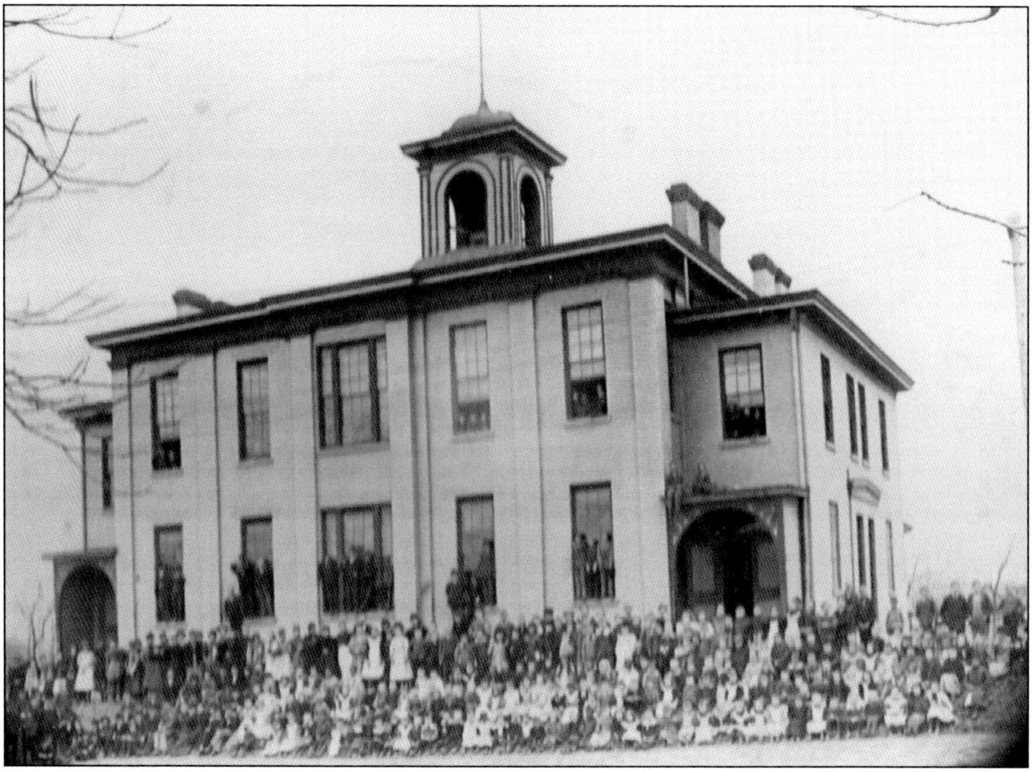

Local students gather outside the Sixth Street School at the corner of Sixth Street and Fourth Corso in 1895. Other schools included a female seminary in operation from 1861 until 1863. The Benedictine Sisters opened an academy for young ladies in 1865, and in 1868, the Nebraska Legislature chartered Nebraska College and Divinity School at Talbot Hall, located a couple of miles outside of town. In 1888, the Nebraska City Academy opened at that site and, within six months, reached an enrollment of 85 students. The Prairie Institute at Thirteenth Street and Second Avenue opened in 1869 with music, language, and general studies in its curriculum. Finally, Schoenberger Hall opened in 1870. The school for girls taught French, German, drawing, music, Latin, and more. It closed in the late 1880s. (Courtesy of the Nebraska City Historical Society.)

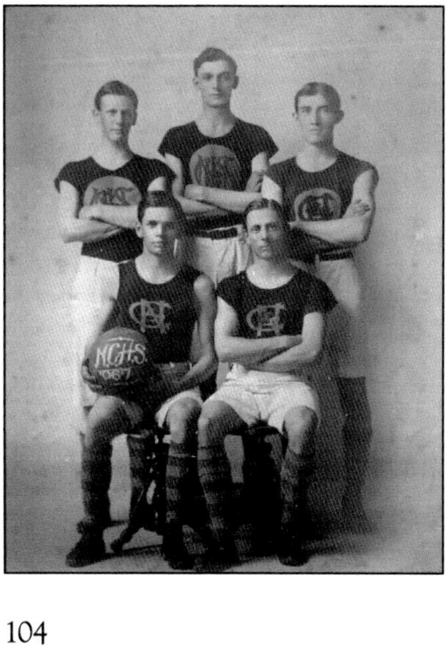

Students at Nebraska City High School took advantage of opportunities to participate in extracurricular activities such as basketball. Pictured here is the 1906–1907 basketball team. (Courtesy of the Morton James Public Library.)

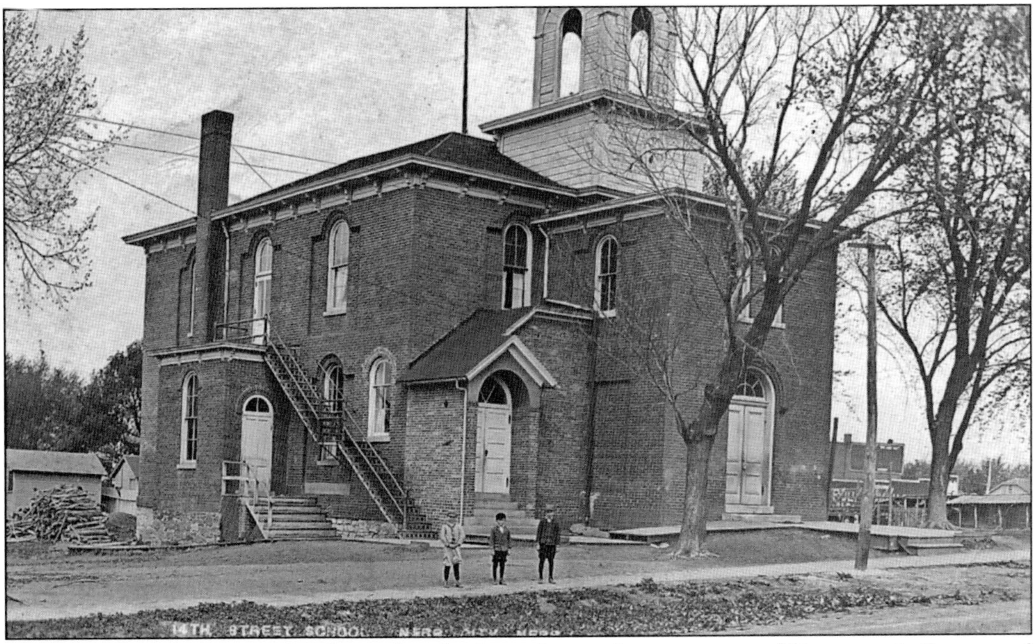

The Fourteenth Street School was first built at the southeast corner of Fourteenth Street and First Corso in 1869. The building was destroyed by fire in 1874 and rebuilt the following year at the same location. (Courtesy of the Nebraska City Museum of Firefighting.)

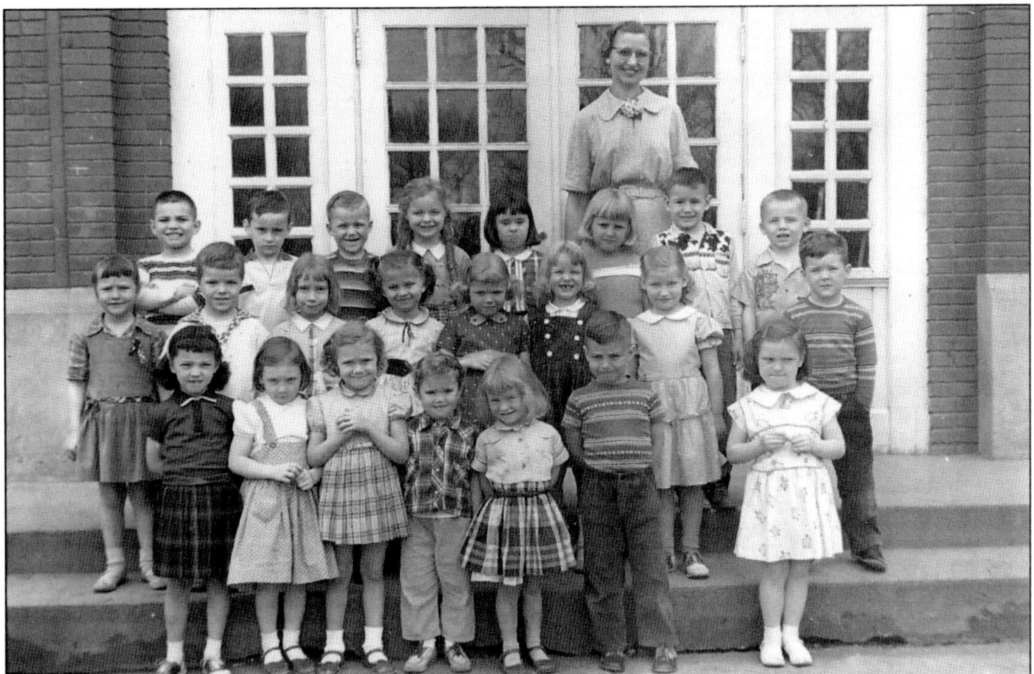

Lilly Sorensen was a longtime teacher at the Sixth Street School. She is pictured here with the morning kindergarten class of 1956–1957. (Courtesy of the Morton James Public Library.)

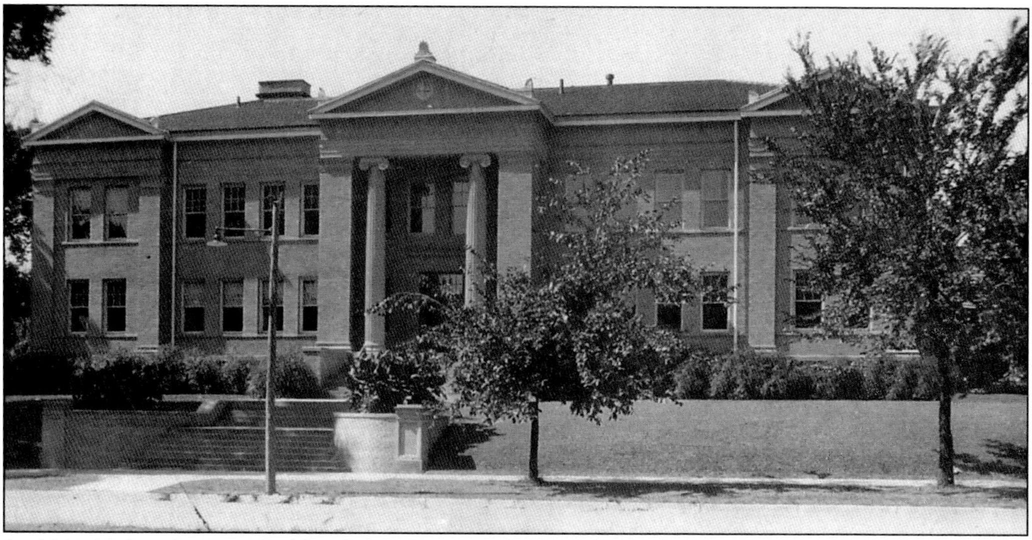

In 1911, Nebraska City Public Schools erected a new high school on the southwest corner of First Corso and Ninth Street. Thousands of students graduated from that building before it was demolished in 1964. (Courtesy of the Morton James Public Library.)

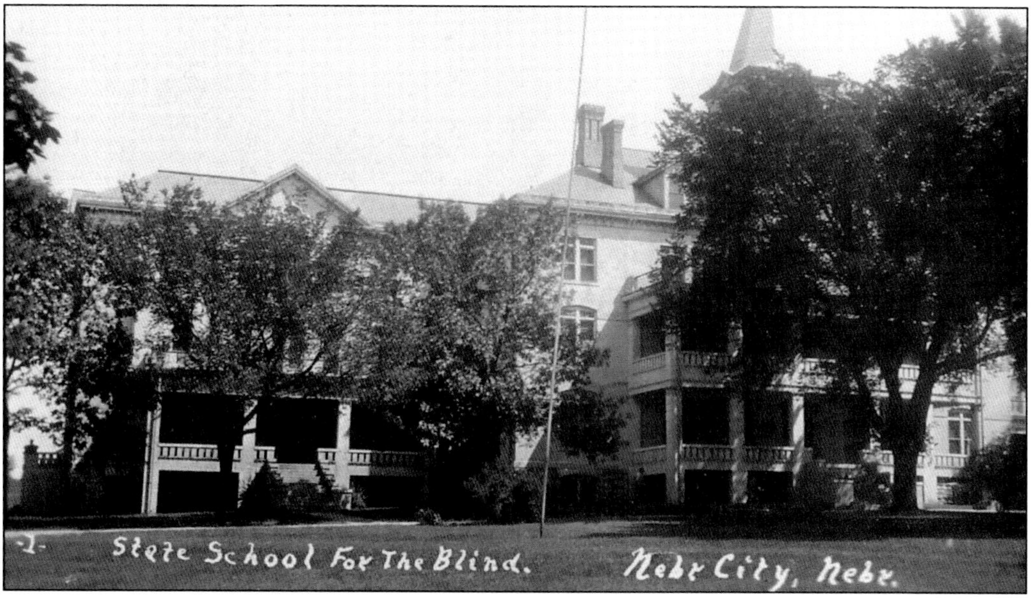

Nebraska City has been home to the state's school for the blind since March 1875. When the school first opened, it had an enrollment of three students, and annual tuition for one student was $250. The original building was constructed for under $1,000 and had no indoor plumbing. By the 1900s, the school averaged 60 to 80 students and boasted a gymnasium, stables, and an orchard. Music was a high priority for educators at the school. The institution has been in continuous operation and is now known as the Nebraska Center for the Education of Children Who Are Blind or Visually Impaired. (Courtesy of the Morton James Public Library.)

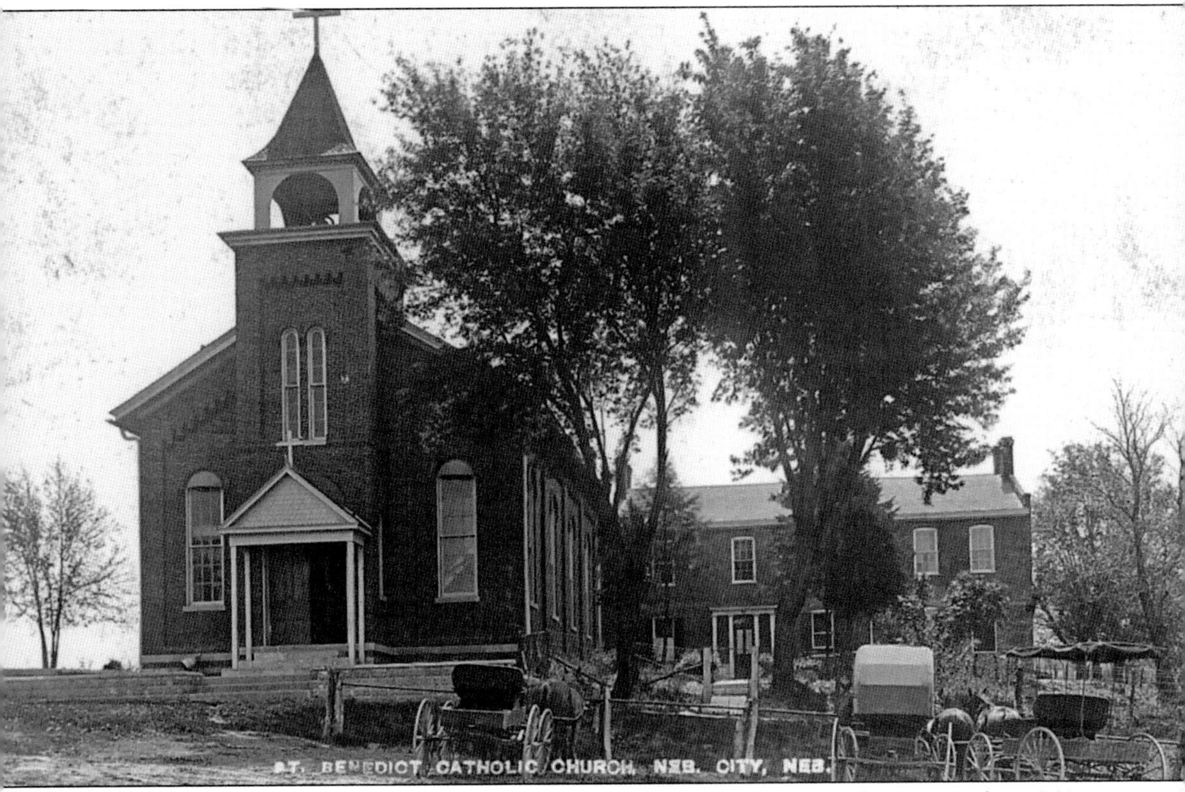

The cornerstone to St. Benedict's Catholic Church at 411 Fifth Rue was laid in September 1860. Completed in 1861, the Romanesque-style structure is the oldest brick church in Nebraska. (Courtesy of Nebraska City Tourism and Commerce.)

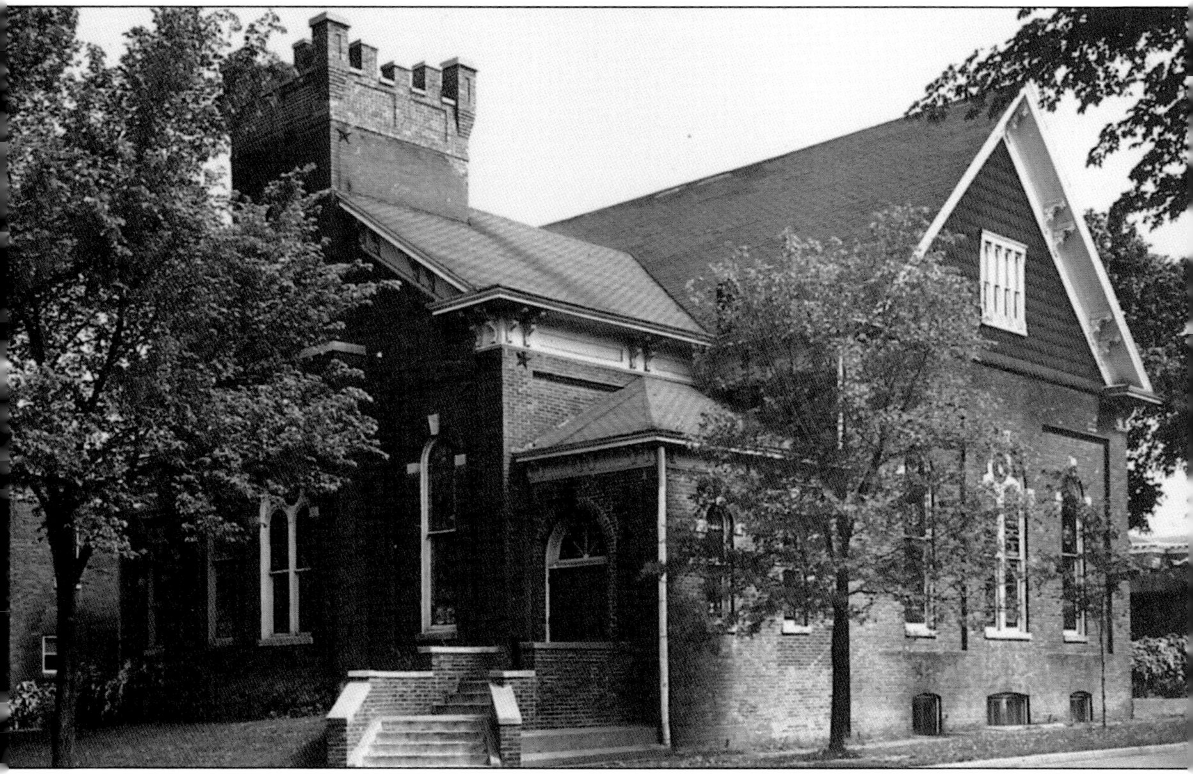

In 1853, the first Methodist service in Nebraska City was preached by Rev. William Gage in one of the abandoned Fort Kearny buildings. In 1855, the Nebraska City Methodist Church was officially established with eight members. Work on a worship hall began in 1856, and the back wall of the current building is part of that first structure. By 1870, there were 14 active church organizations in Nebraska City. Some met in log buildings, a few were brick, and many met in residential homes. (Courtesy of the Nebraska City First United Methodist Church.)

Seven

ORCHARD LIFE

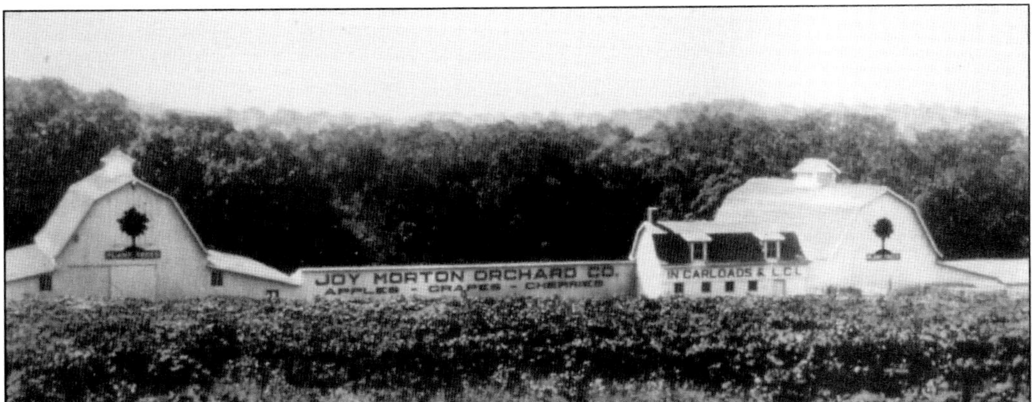

When J. Sterling Morton planted the first apple trees on his property in the 1850s, there is no way he could have foreseen how important orchard life would be to Nebraska City. In the 1920s, Joy Morton and Grove Porter teamed up to create one of the largest commercial apple orchards in the Midwest. By 1934, they had over 300 acres of orchards and vineyards, with more than 17,000 trees. Production topped 100,000 bushels annually, and the Morton Orchard apples were shipped throughout the Midwest in refrigerated trucks and railcars. (Courtesy of the Arbor Day Foundation.)

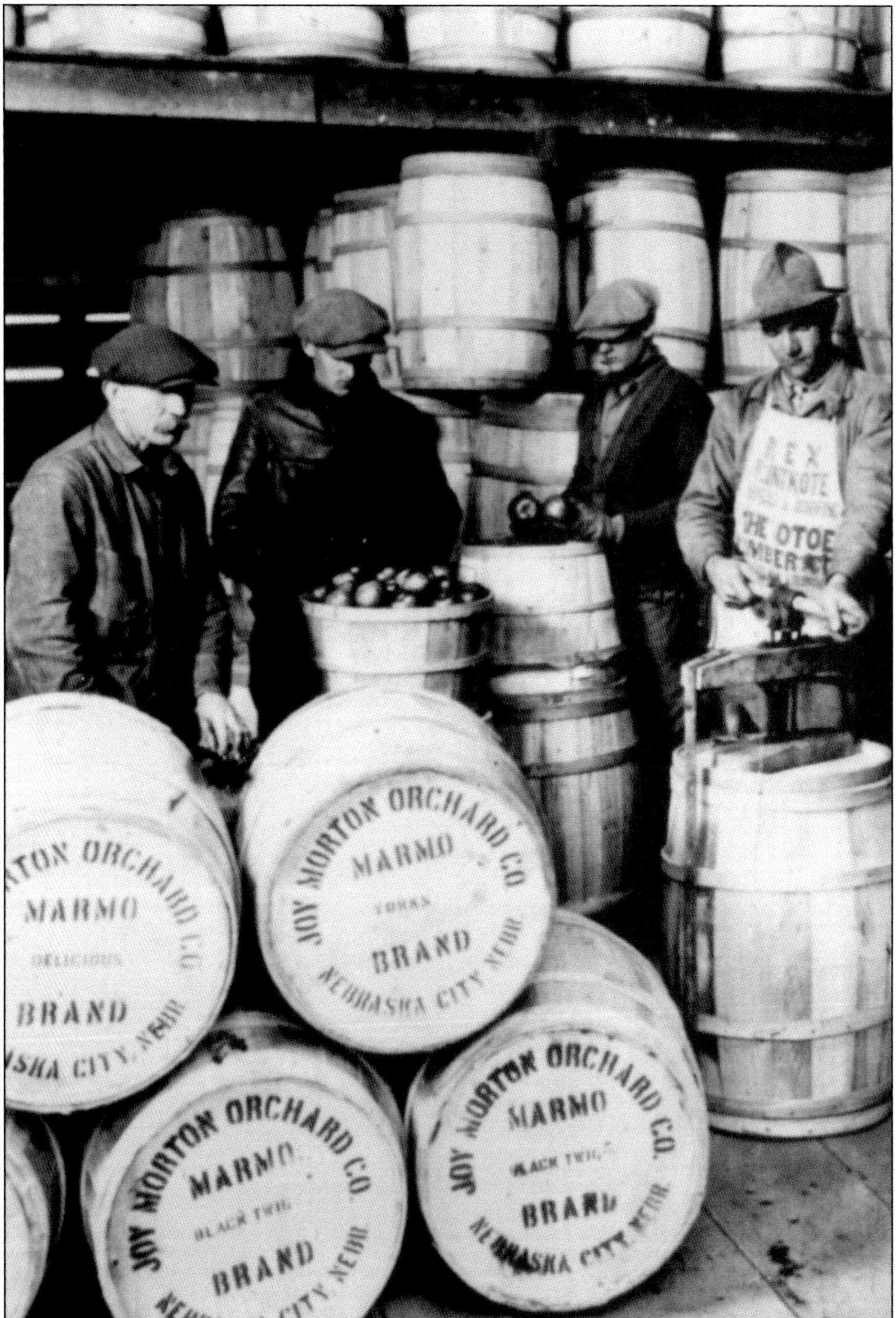

Apples and freshly pressed cider were two standards of the Morton Orchard. Even early on, the orchard was interested in sustainable agriculture. Orchard manager Grove Porter planted trees on terraced land, reducing erosion and saving water. Grove Porter changed the name from Morton Orchard to Porter Orchard after purchasing the property upon Joy Morton's death. Porter sold the property to the Arbor Day Foundation in 1975. (Courtesy of the Arbor Day Foundation.)

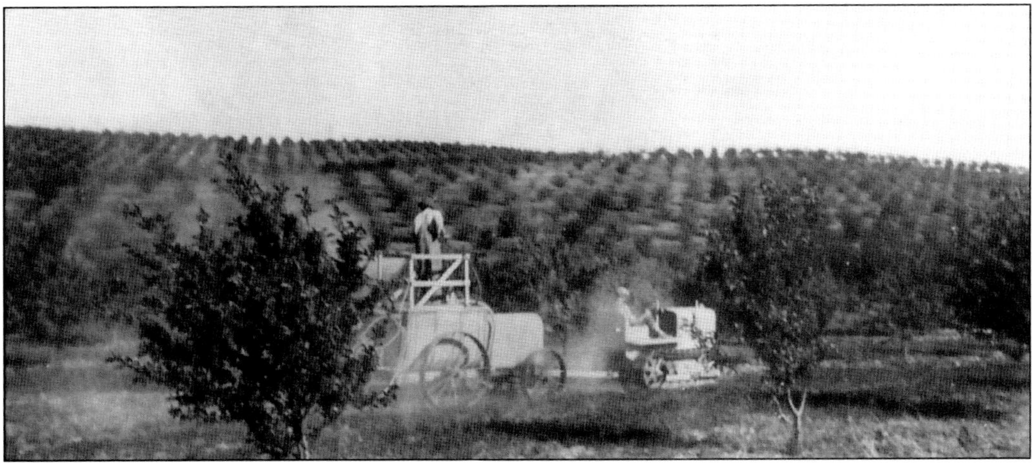

Orchards in the area grew many varieties of apples, including Transparent, Duchess, and Wealthy in the summer, Jonathan, Red Delicious, and Grimes Golden in the fall, and Winesap, Imperial, and Black Twig in the winter. No matter the variety, every tree had to be pruned and sprayed annually. (Courtesy of Kimmel Orchard.)

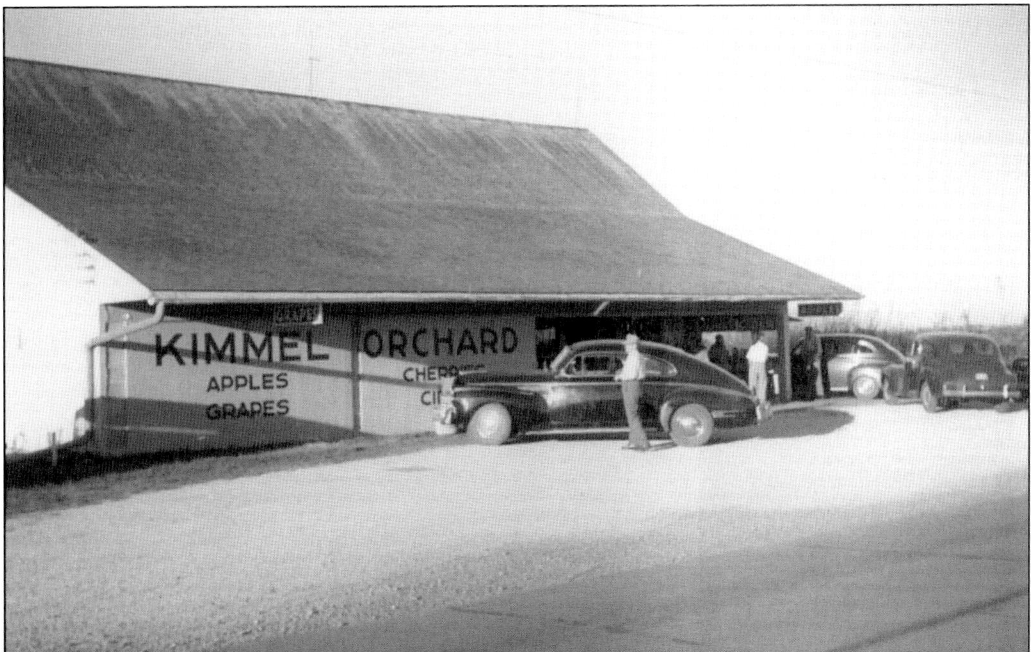

Kimmel Orchard on Highway 75 northwest of Nebraska City opened in 1925 and soon expanded its fruit growing to include cherries and grapes. (Courtesy of Kimmel Orchard.)

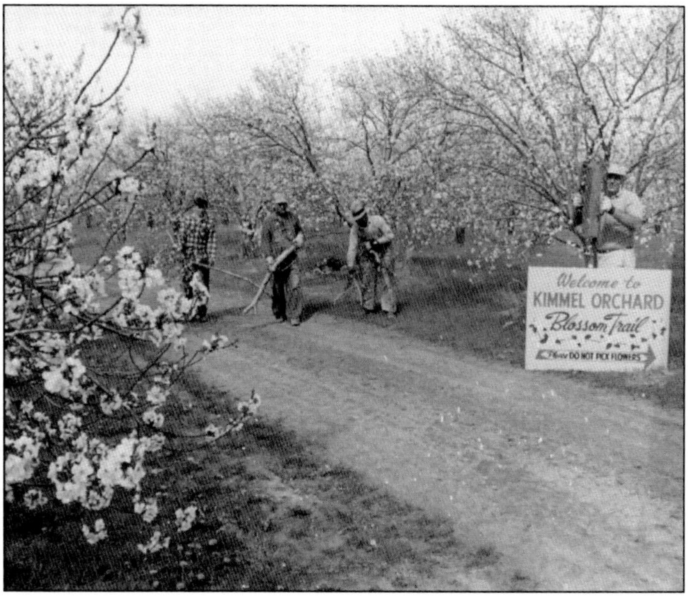

Workers at Kimmel Orchard clear the trail through the orchard in preparation for the annual blossom festival. Kimmel Orchard has documentation showing that starting in the 1930s, a total of 25,000 people would visit Nebraska City annually and travel the blossom trail. An old map lists must-see places such as the Seydlitz Orchard, Raben Orchard, Kimmel Orchard, Porter Orchard (formerly Morton Orchard), Catron Orchard, Homeyer Orchard, and Utterback Orchard. (Courtesy of Kimmel Orchard.)

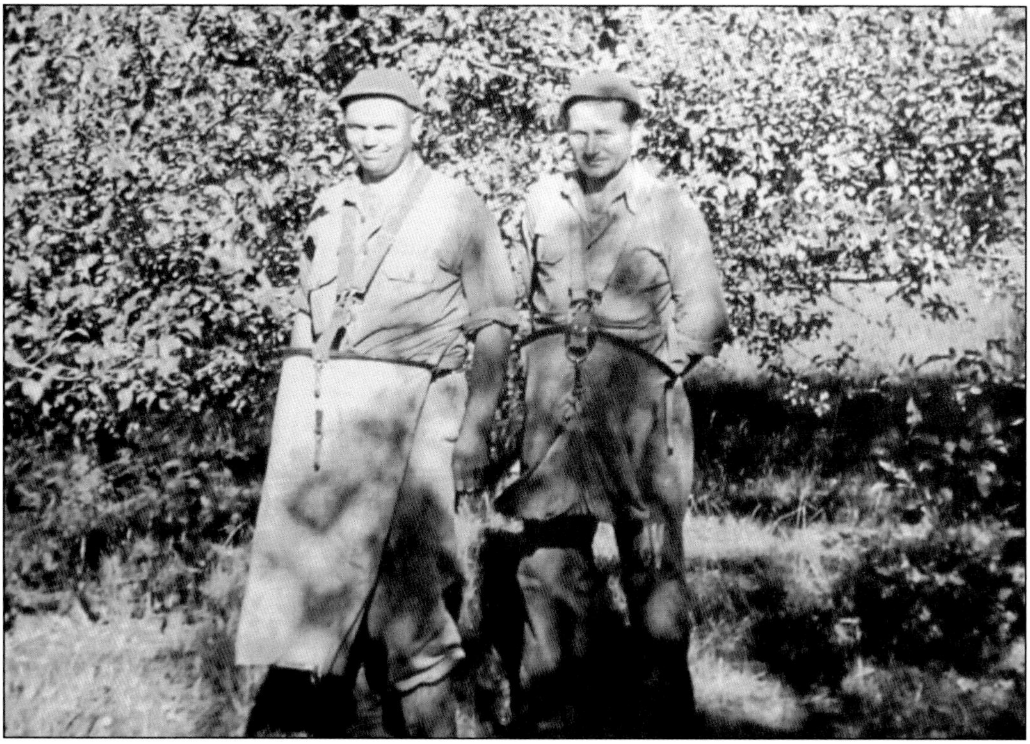

Nebraska City's Kimmel Orchard played a unique part in the nation's World War II history. During the 1940s, a German prisoner-of-war camp was established at Weeping Water, about 30 miles away. Due to the manpower shortage caused by the war, many local orchards were in need of extra help during harvest time. German POWs such as Otto and Fritz, pictured here, were bused to the orchards in the morning for work and then taken back to the camp at night. They were not paid in money but in coupons, which could be traded at the camp for candy, cigarettes, and personal items. (Courtesy of Kimmel Orchard.)

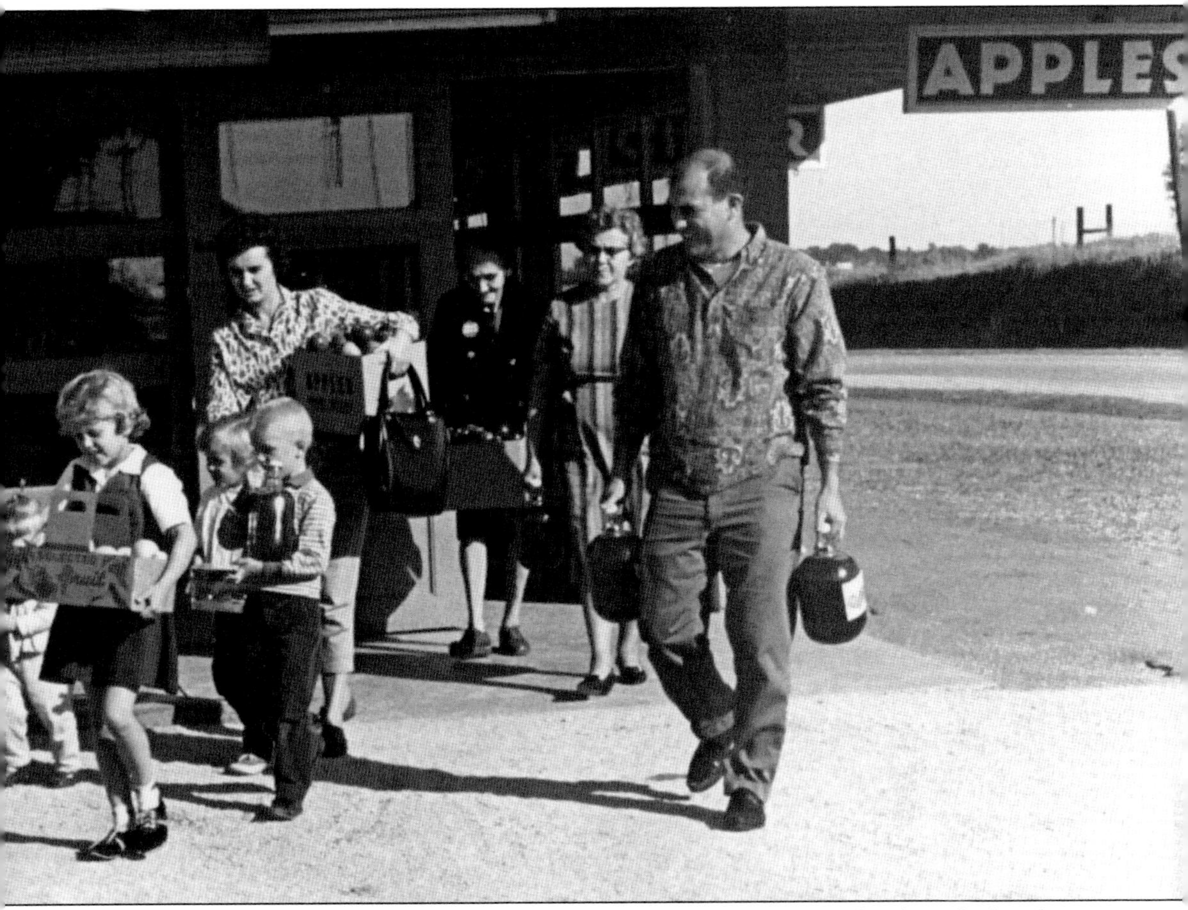

In the early 1900s, families could choose from a dozen Nebraska City orchards to find a place to pick fresh apples, purchase tasty cider, and enjoy the outdoors. That changed on November 11, 1940. A serious weather event called the Armistice Day freeze spread across the Midwest from Sioux City, Nebraska, to the south. After a hot, dry summer, the ground was parched. Two solid days of rain on November 9 and 10 meant the trees could finally drink their fill. But, on the November 11, temperatures in the region plummeted from 60 degrees to zero in a matter of hours. The water in the trees froze, expanded, and ruptured, causing irreversible damage. Orchard managers reported a 75-percent immediate loss of crops. Many smaller orchards never recovered. After the freeze, only four orchards survived as commercial businesses: Morton Orchard, Kimmel Orchard, Catron Orchard, and Union Orchard. (Courtesy of the Kimmel Foundation.)

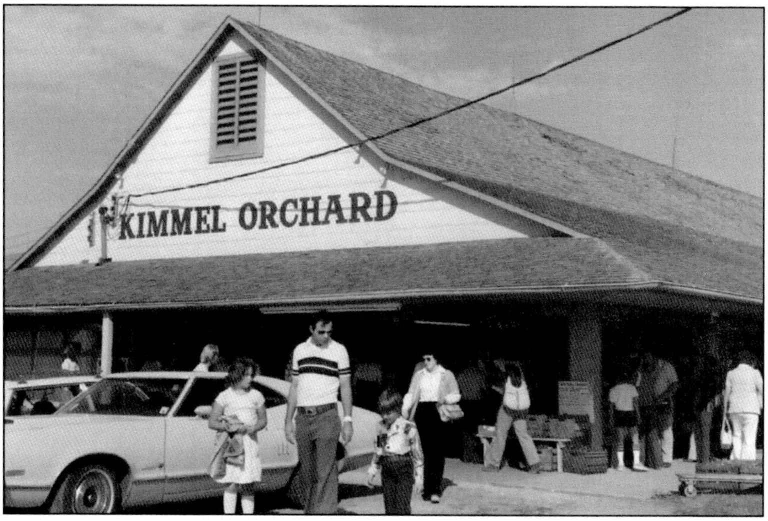

By the 1970s, Kimmel Orchard was making 800 gallons of cider per day during production time. (Courtesy of the Kimmel Foundation.)

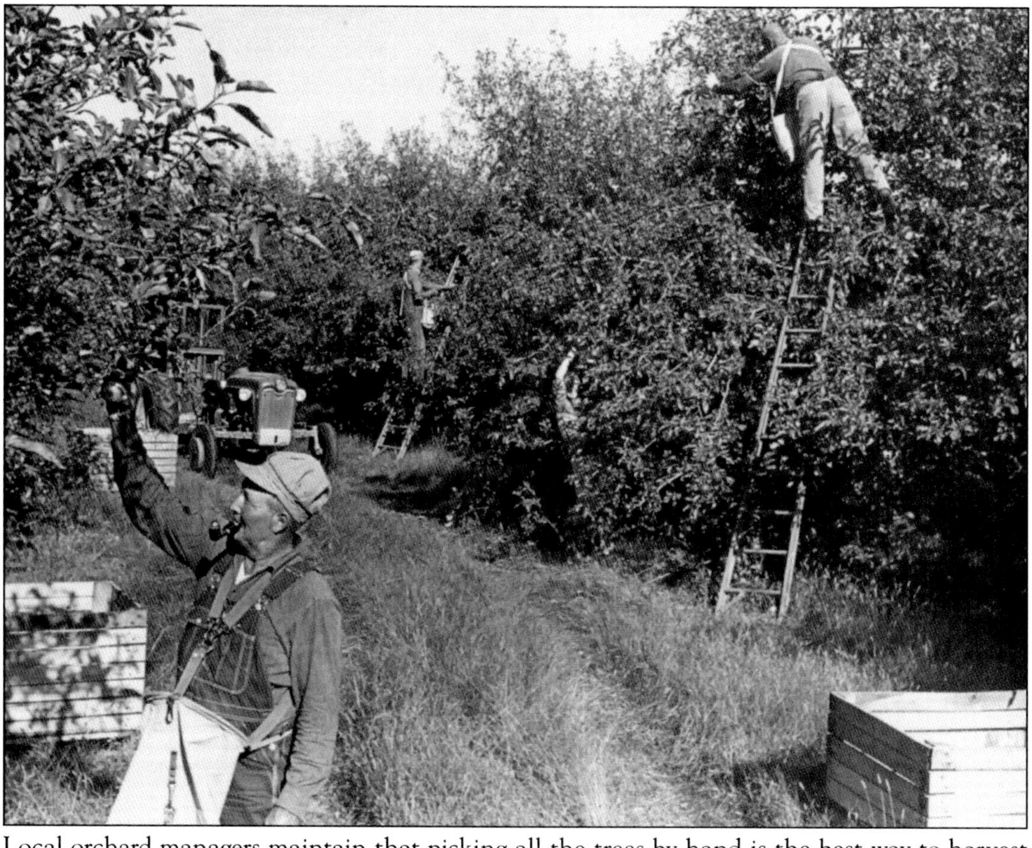

Local orchard managers maintain that picking all the trees by hand is the best way to harvest the apples. Once picked, the apples are washed, sized, graded, and packaged. In addition to apple trees, Kimmel Orchard also specialized in cherry production. In the 1930s, Kimmel Orchard had 250 acres of cherry trees and hired 200 workers daily to pick cherries. (Courtesy of the Kimmel Foundation.)

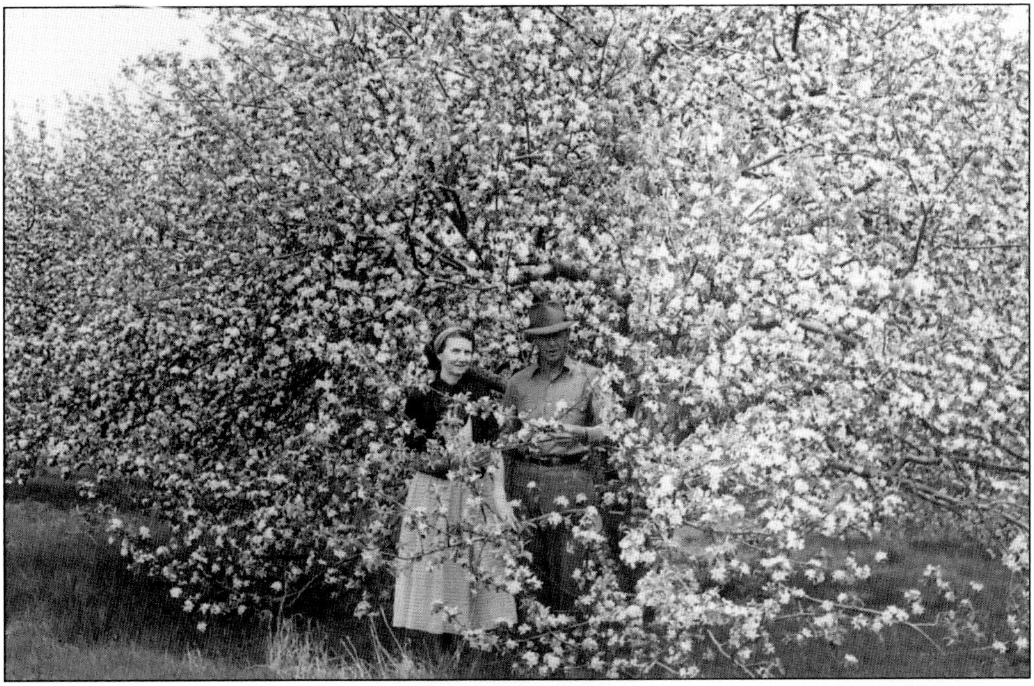

In 1943, Kimmel Orchard was short on manpower to harvest its crops and accepted labor help from German POW camps, several of which were located in Nebraska. One such German soldier was William Oberdieck. Oberdieck developed a strong friendship with Richard and Laurine Kimmel, owners of Kimmel Orchard, pictured above. Oberdieck would write later in life that the Kimmels "tried very hard to show us what life is all about in America." Oberdieck returned to Germany after the war but eventually moved back to America, bringing his family with him. He went to work for the Kimmels and, in 1964, bought the orchard from them. In the photograph at right, Oberdieck is making apple cider. (Above, courtesy of the Kimmel Foundation; at right, Kimmel Orchard.)

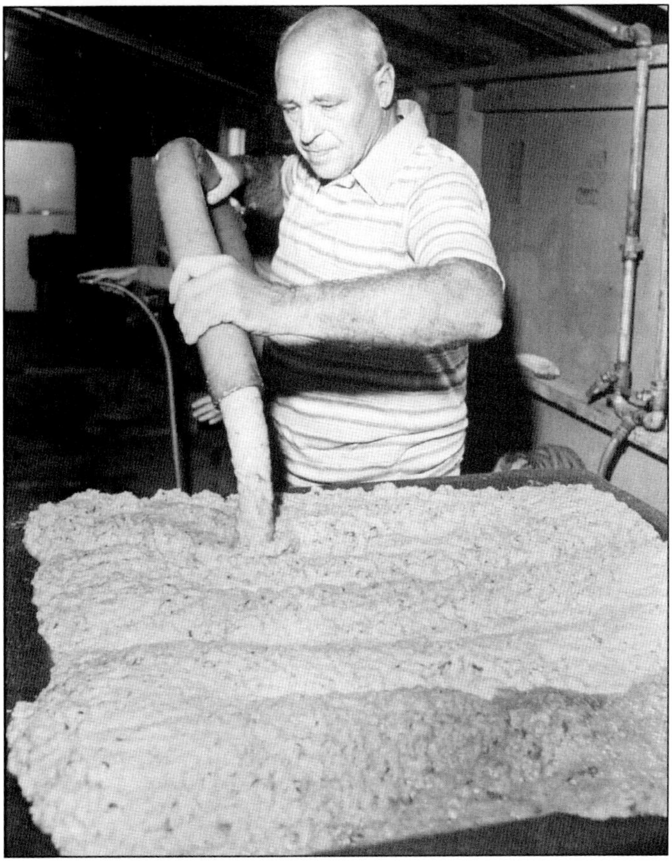

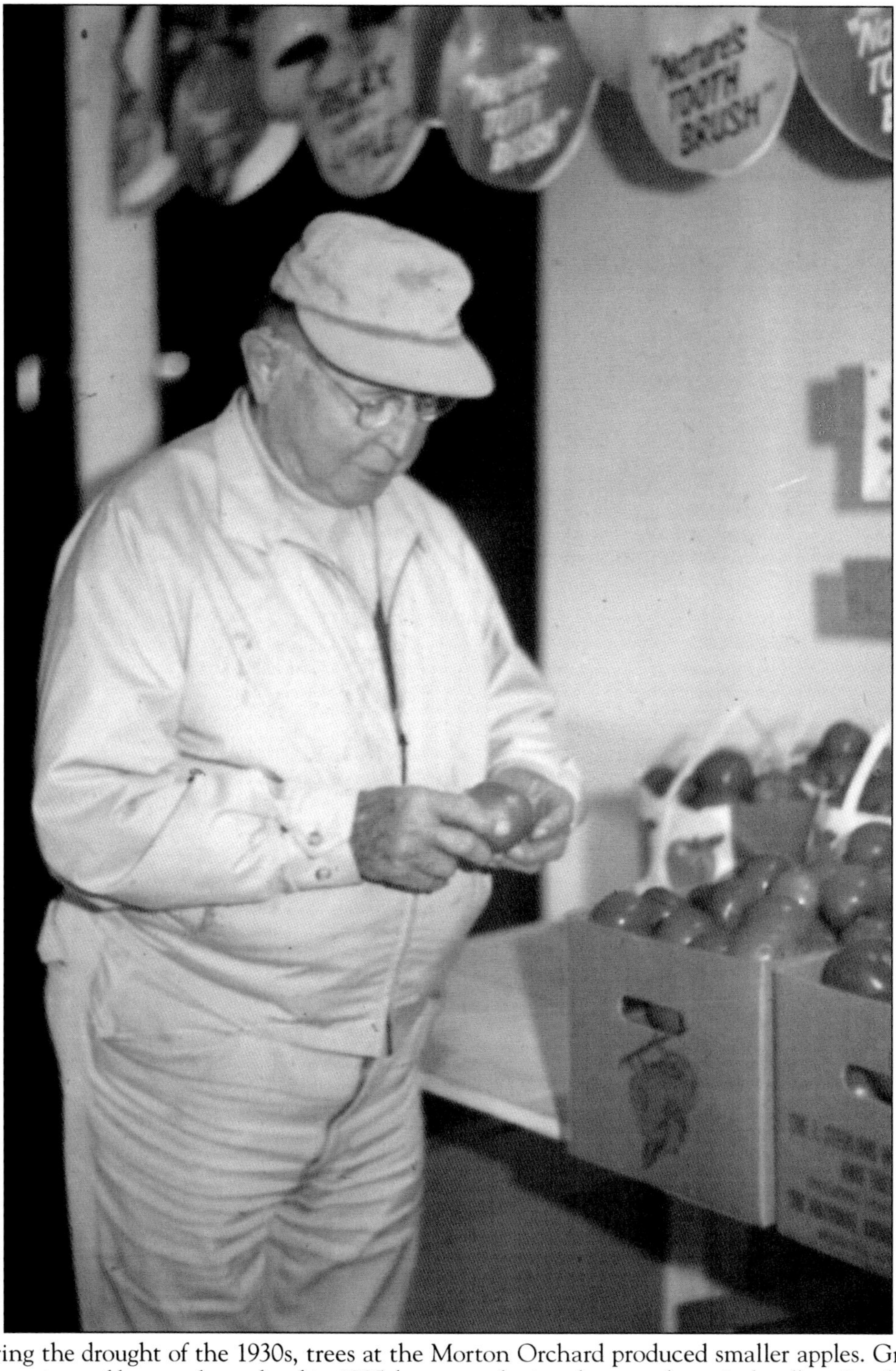

During the drought of the 1930s, trees at the Morton Orchard produced smaller apples. Grove Porter, pictured here at the orchard in 1985, began marketing those apples as "schoolboys" and said they were perfect for a student's lunch. When Porter sold the orchard to the Arbor Day Foundation in 1975, his son Mort took over management. Today, the farm once owned by J. Sterling Morton is known as Arbor Day Farm and Tree Adventure. (Courtesy of the Arbor Day Foundation.)

Eight

FESTIVALS

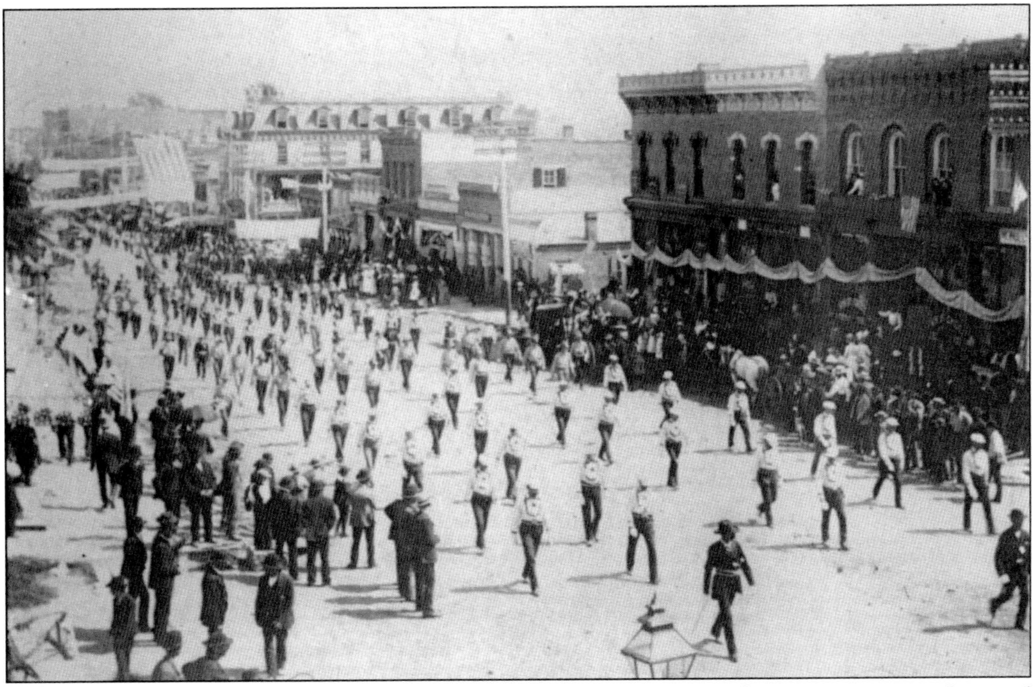

Central Avenue has witnessed hundreds of parades over the years, from patriotic marches and Arbor Day celebrations to stock show parades and the annual AppleJack Festival. (Courtesy of the Arbor Day Foundation.)

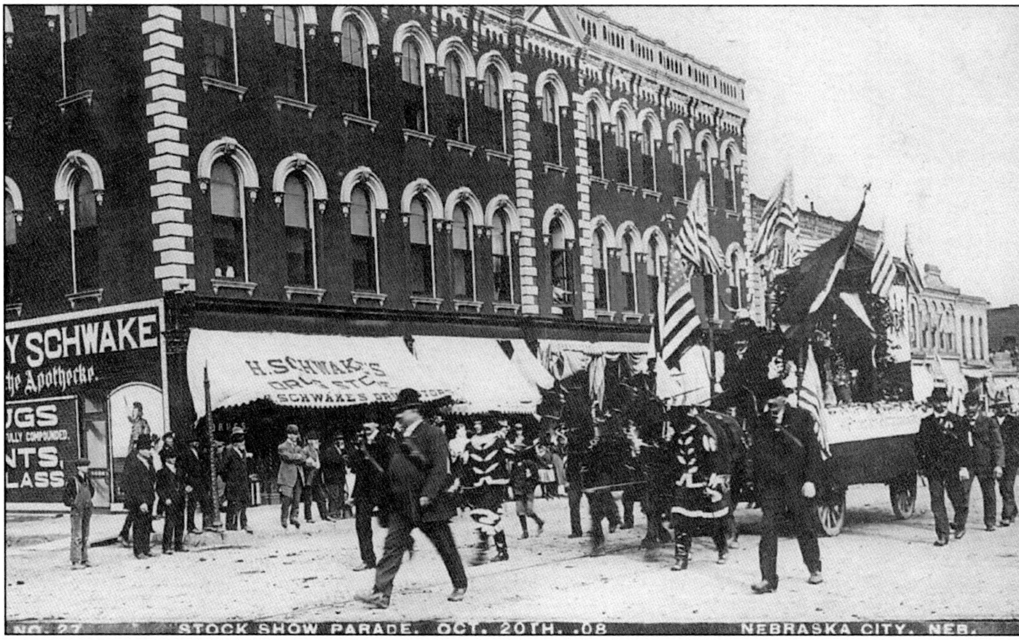

The stock show parade of October 20, 1908, featured patriotic regalia. While today's parades generally run eastward from Sixteenth Street to Sixth Street on Central Avenue, parades used to travel in the opposite direction. (Courtesy of the Arbor Day Foundation.)

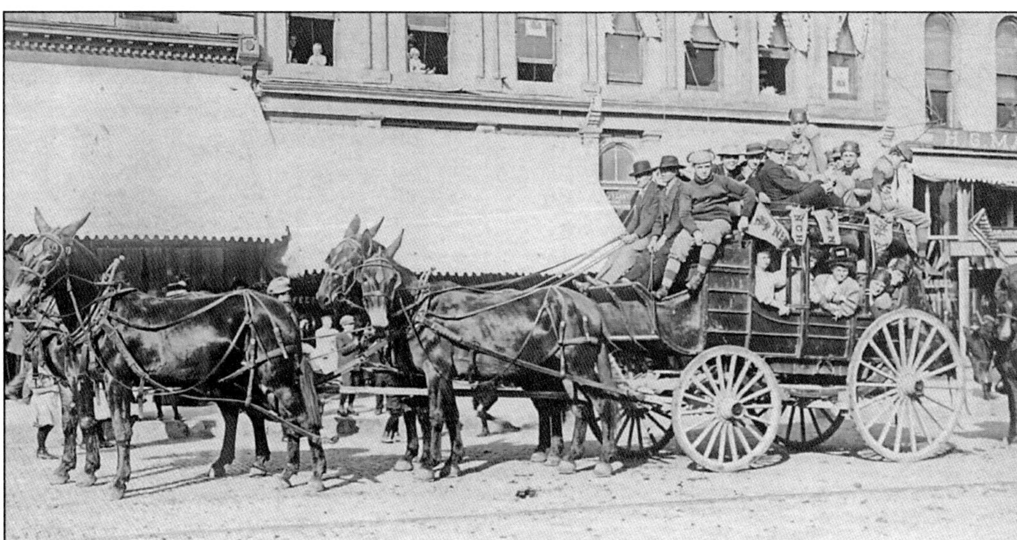

Residents of the upstairs apartments on Central Avenue enjoy a sweeping view of the many parades downtown. Even though the automobile had arrived in Nebraska City seven years prior to this 1908 stock show parade, horses and wagons were still the primary modes of transportation. Stagecoaches, like the one pictured here, were used primarily for show. (Courtesy of the Arbor Day Foundation.)

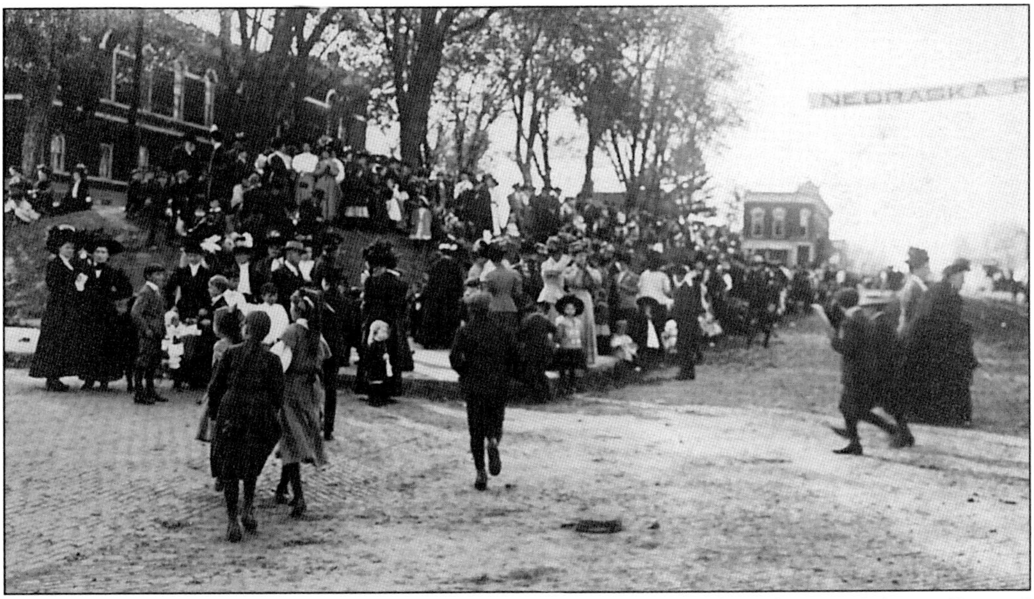

Stock show parades were held in 1908 and 1909. Spectators gathered up and down Central Avenue, including on the Otoe County Courthouse lawn, to watch the parade. (Courtesy of Dorris Sackles.)

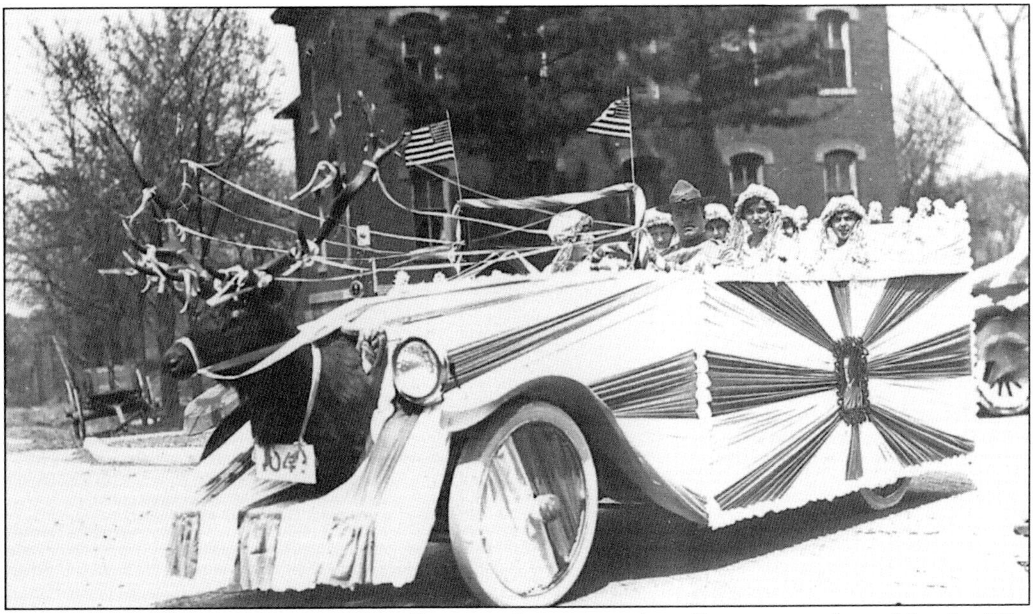

For every parade, participants went all out in decorating their floats, as evidenced by the Elks Club entry. Patriotic themes were popular. (Courtesy of Dorris Sackles.)

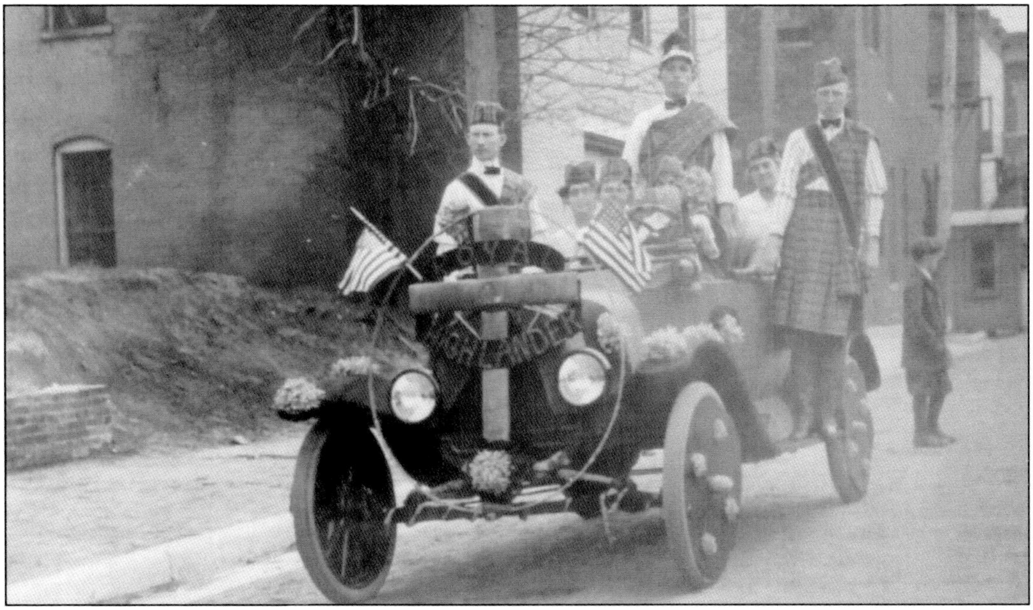

Local businesses and organizations used parades to connect with the public. The 1917 Arbor Day Parade featured both an outfit from the Royal Highlanders (above) and the Kregel Windmill Factory service truck (below). (Above, courtesy of the Nebraska City Historical Society; below, the Kregel Windmill Factory Museum.)

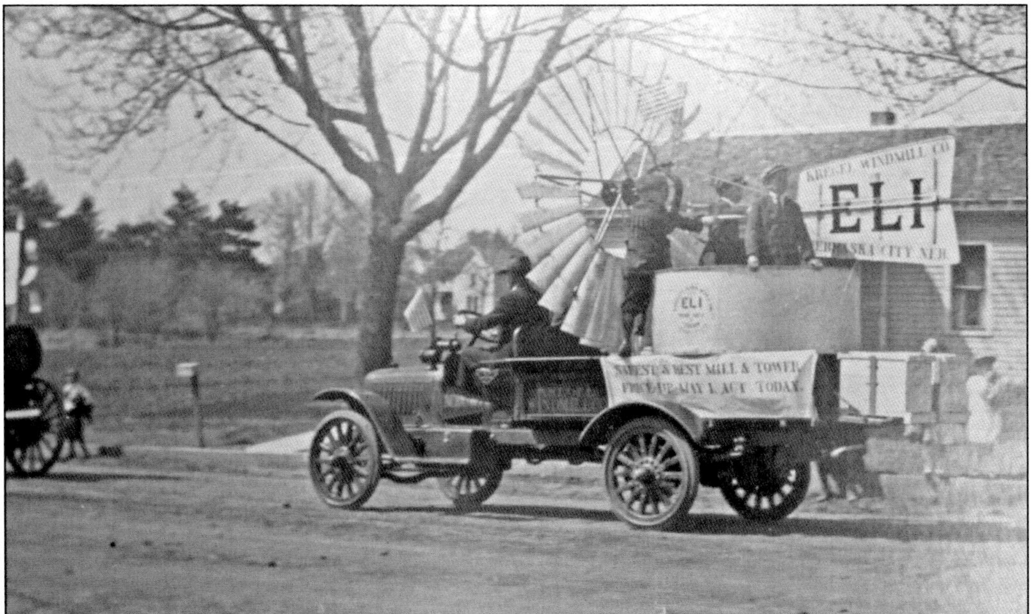

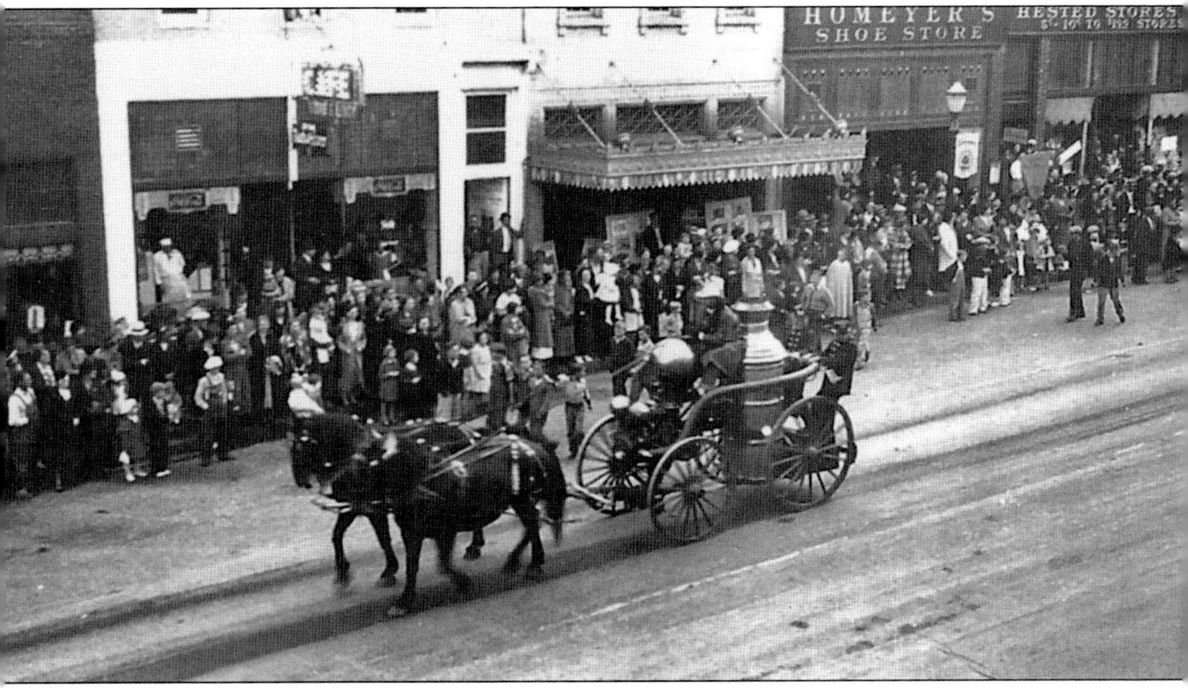

The Nebraska City Volunteer Fire Department's 1884 steam pumper had long been retired by the time this photograph was taken at the Apple Harvest parade on October 9, 1936. It was still a crowd favorite. (Courtesy of the Nebraska City Museum of Firefighting.)

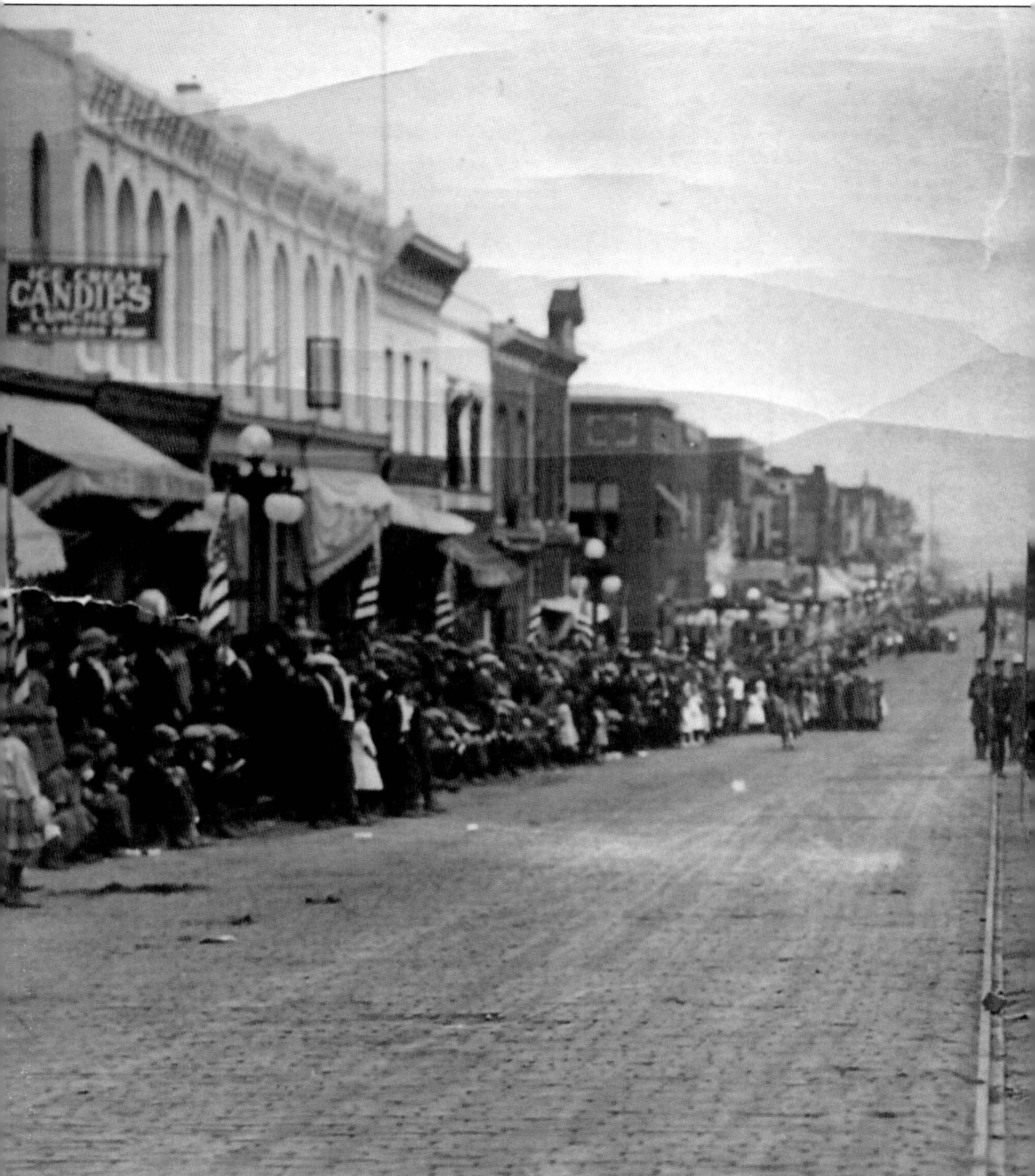

In 1923, Joy Morton transferred the ownership of the Arbor Lodge mansion and the surrounding grounds to the State of Nebraska to be maintained as a museum and park. To commemorate

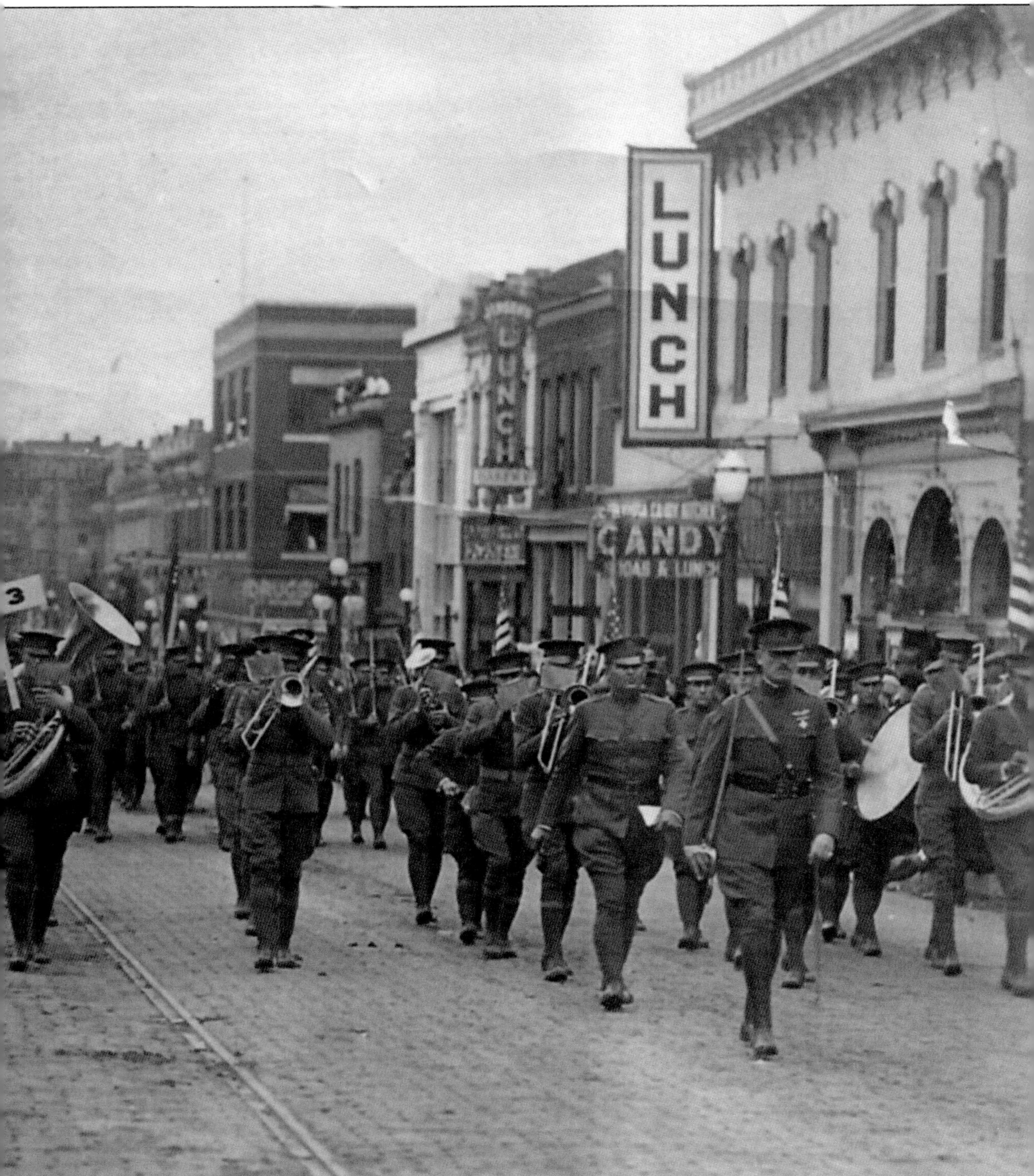

the event, a celebration called Transfer Day was planned, complete with parties, speeches, and a parade. (Courtesy of the Nebraska City Historical Society.)

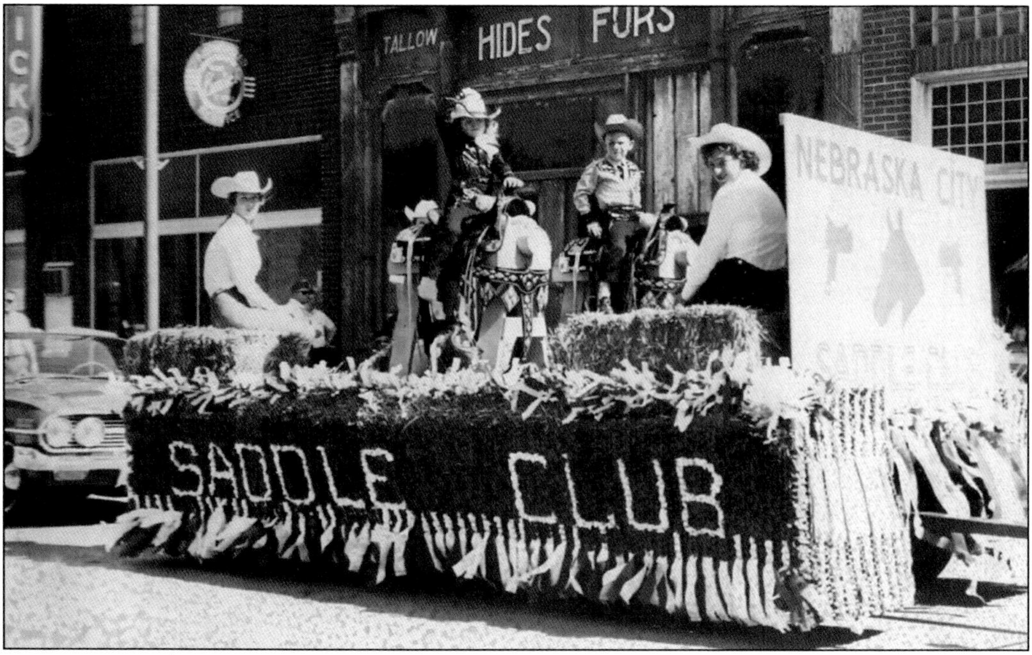

A special parade was held in 1963 to commemorate the 10-year anniversary of the opening of the American Meter Plant. The parade traveled west from Sixth Street and Central Avenue all the way through town to the American Meter Plant. (Courtesy of Nebraska City Tourism and Commerce.)

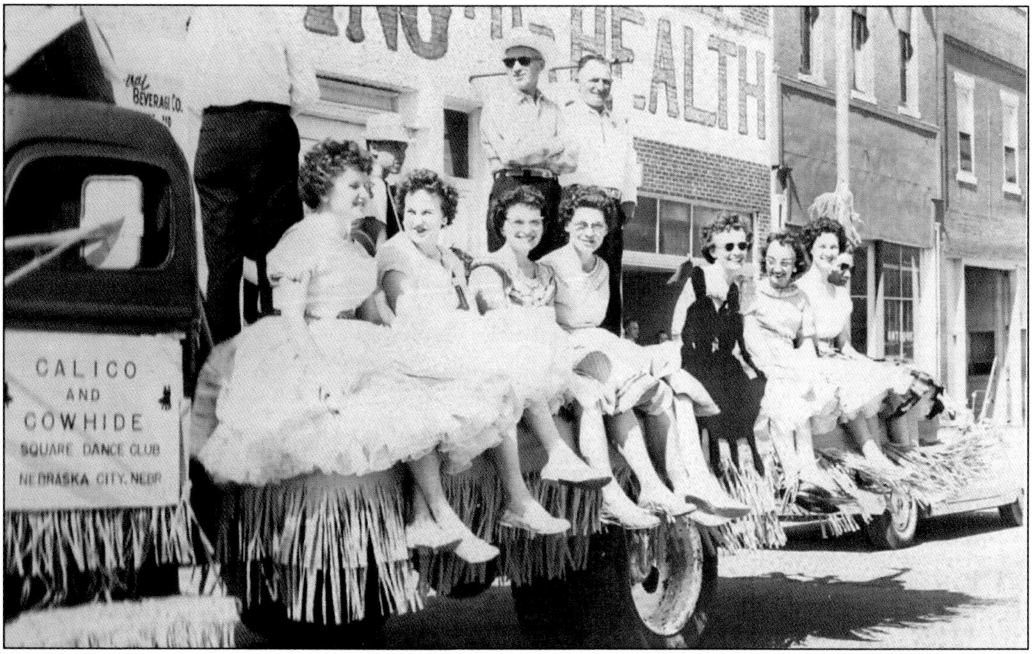

The Nebraska City Calico and Cowhide Square Dance Club was featured in the 1963 American Meter parade. The most popular parade in modern times is the annual AppleJack Festival parade held every September. A highlight of the parade is a marching band competition. (Courtesy of Nebraska City Tourism and Commerce.)

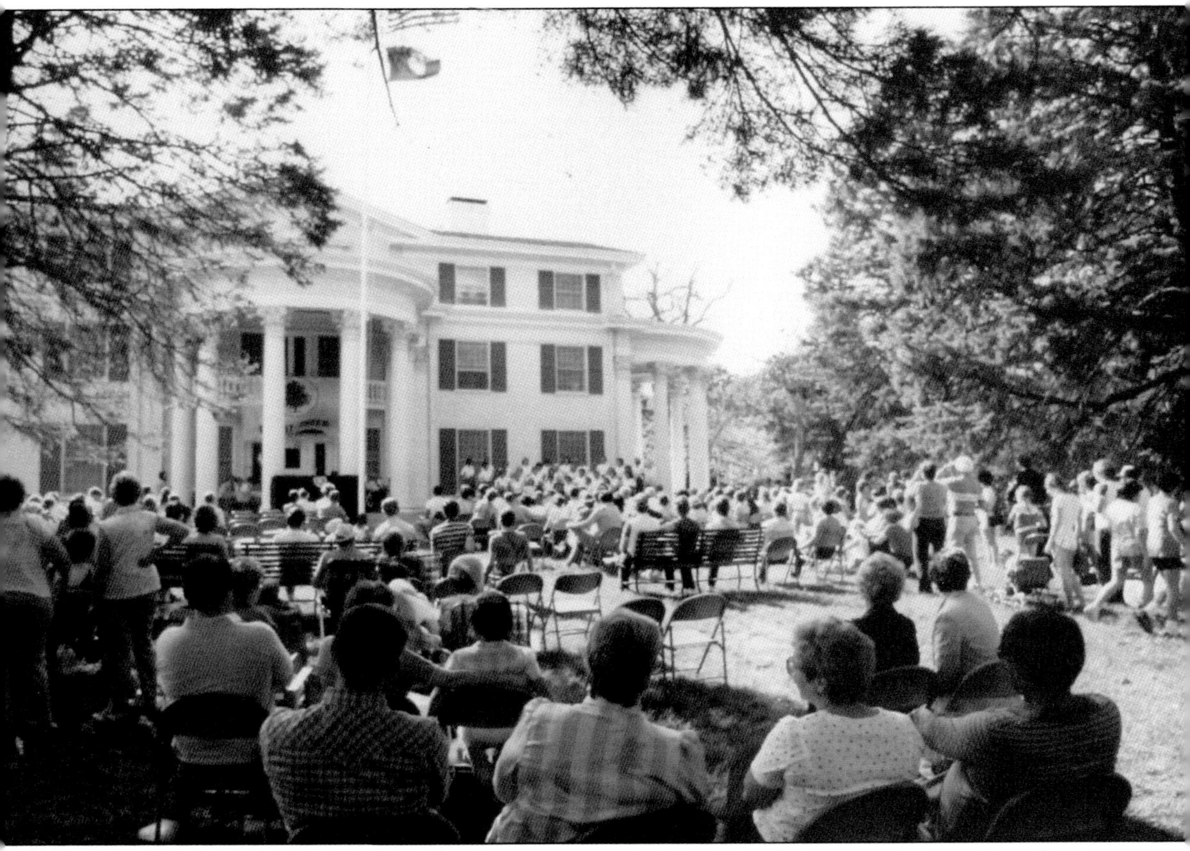

Every spring since 1872, Nebraska City has recognized Arbor Day. It is now celebrated in all 50 states and in many countries throughout the world. (Courtesy of the Arbor Day Foundation.)

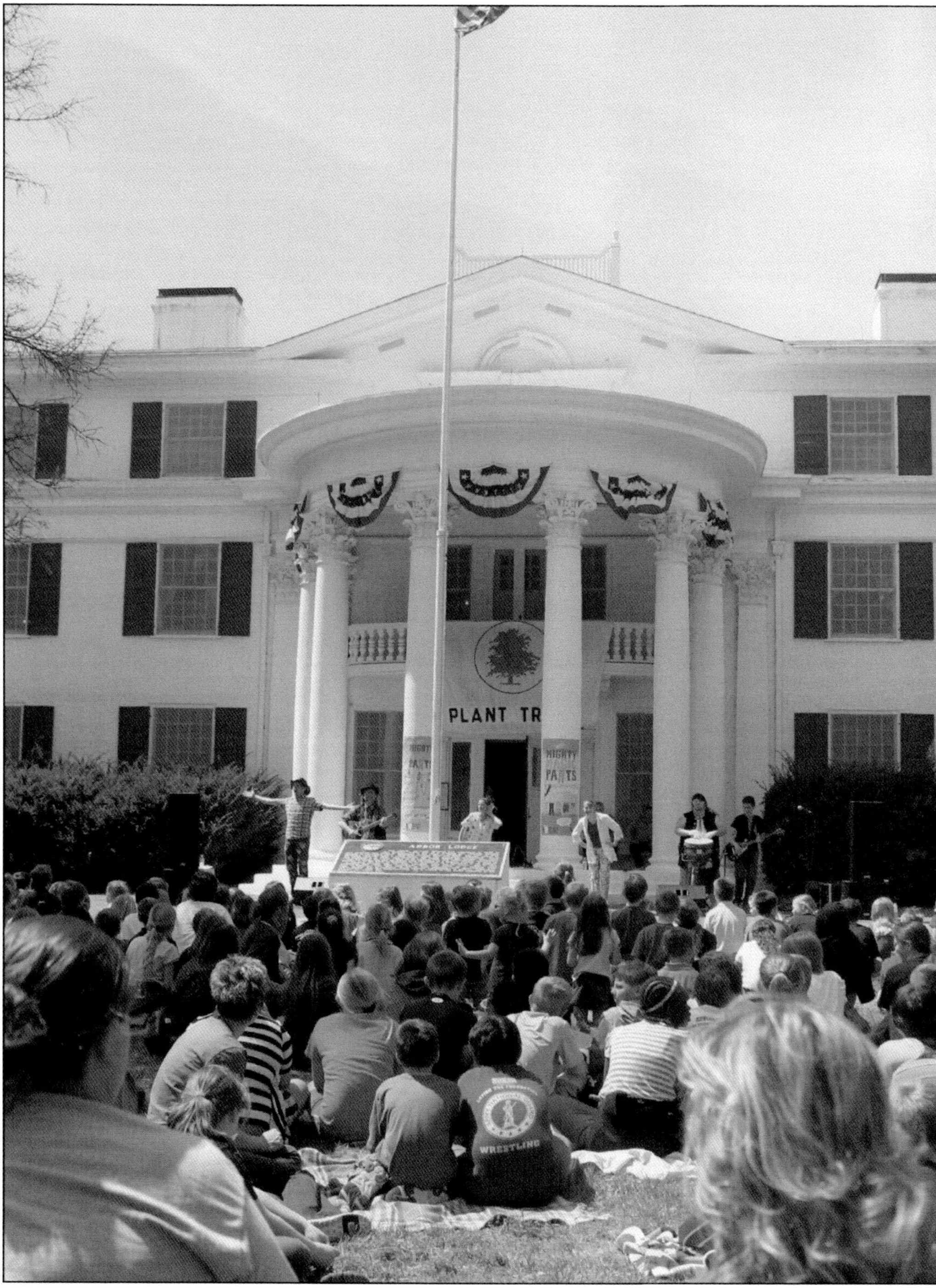

On the last Friday of each April, all the schoolchildren in Nebraska City are welcomed to Arbor Lodge for a special Arbor Day program. They learn about the history of J. Sterling Morton and hear tips on how to care for trees. As they leave to head back to school, every child receives a free tree of his or her own. In that way, every child is connected to Nebraska City's rich historical past as they grow into the future. (Author's collection.)

BIBLIOGRAPHY

A Glimpse of the Past: A Pictorial History of Otoe County. Nebraska City, NE: *Nebraska City News Press*, 1996.

Arbor Lodge, Volumes 1, 2, and *3*. Nebraska City, NE: Arbor Day Centennial Committee.

Bartling, Edward. *John Henry Kagi and the Old Log Cabin Home*. Nebraska City, NE: Nebraska City, 1938.

Nebraska City Centennial. Nebraska City, NE: Women's Division Chamber of Commerce, 1954.

Nebraska City: The Most Beautiful City of Nebraska. Nebraska City, NE: Morton Printing Company, 1906.

Noble, Glenn. *Frontier Steamboat Town*. Lincoln, NE: Midgard Press, 1989.

———. *Historically Eventful Nebraska City*. Nebraska City, NE: Otoe County Historical Society, 1981.

Porter, Joy Morton. *Arbor Day Farm Past & Present, Volumes I and II*. 2003.

Victorian Architecture in Nebraska City. Nebraska City, NE: Otoe County Historical Society, 1979.